CREATIVE (AND CULTURAL) INDUSTRY ENTREPRENEURSHIP IN THE 21ST CENTURY

CONTEMPORARY ISSUES IN ENTREPRENEURSHIP RESEARCH

Series Editor: Volumes 1–6: Gerard McElwee;
Volume 7 onward: Paul Jones

CONTEMPORARY ISSUES IN ENTREPRENEURSHIP RESEARCH   VOLUME 18A

CREATIVE (AND CULTURAL) INDUSTRY ENTREPRENEURSHIP IN THE 21ST CENTURY

EDITED BY

INGE HILL
The Open University, UK

SARA R. S. T. A. ELIAS
University of Victoria, Canada

STEPHEN DOBSON
University of Leeds, UK

and

PAUL JONES
Swansea University, UK

United Kingdom – North America – Japan
India – Malaysia – China

Emerald Publishing Limited
Howard House, Wagon Lane, Bingley BD16 1WA, UK

First edition 2024

British Library Cataloguing in Publication Data
A catalogue record for this book is available from the British Library

ISBN: 978-1-80382-412-3 (Print)
ISBN: 978-1-80382-411-6 (Online)
ISBN: 978-1-80382-413-0 (Epub)

ISSN: 2040-7246 (Series)

Printed and bound by CPI Group (UK) Ltd, Croydon, CR0 4YY

INVESTOR IN PEOPLE

CONTENTS

ABOUT THE AUTHORS

Emmanuel Aboagye-Nimo is a Chartered Construction Manager (MCIOB) and a Senior Lecturer in Construction Management. He is a Fellow of the Higher Education Academy. He has a background in Quantity Surveying and Construction Management. He has researched and consulted on health and safety practices for numerous small and micro construction firms as well as safety groups. He has advocated for the acknowledgement of safety ideologies adopted by small teams on construction projects due to their overlooked and yet invaluable wealth of health and safety experience, which is often tacit. He is an Advocate for equality in the workplace and was the Former Chair for Race, Ethnicity, and Cultural Heritage at Nottingham Trent University. He has worked with a range of academic institutions and construction firms in implementing policies to enhance transparency and fair treatment of employees and also to improve employee well-being.

Doreen Adusei, MBE, FRSA, did a MA in Fashion from the Royal College of Art in London. She worked for Liberty of London, Harvey Nichols, and multinational companies including Courtaulds Textiles as a Designer and Trend Forecaster for many years. She has evolved to become an Educationalist and Creative Business Strategist. Her journey has involved many successful firsts within the UK including developing targeted programmes to win the UK Government's National Skills Challenge Award competition. This led to the establishment of the Fashionworks' programmes, which support employment and sustainable growth within the fashion and manufacturing sectors in London. In the last 20 years, Fashionworks has established an excellent track record and reputation within the wider creative industry for its inclusivity in delivery. In recognition of these high-impact programmes and initiatives, she was awarded an MBE in the Queen's Birthday Honour List in 2006 for services to the Fashion industry.

Fiona Armstrong-Gibbs, PhD, is Programme Leader in Executive Education at Liverpool Business School and Chair of Baltic Creative Community Interest Company based in Liverpool. She combines her practice and research to explore how social enterprises and community-owned business models are a catalyst for responsible business growth, better ecosystems and contribute to sustainable local and regional economies.

Bhawana Bhardwaj, PhD, is Senior Assistant Professor at the School of Commerce and Management Studies, Central University of Himachal Pradesh, India. Her area of specialisation is HRM and OB. She has 17 years of teaching and research experience. She has been meritorious throughout her studies and has merit scholarships throughout her studies. As a Committed Academician and Prolific Writer, she has contributed by raising various social and organisational issues. She has also published two books on *Organizational Effectiveness* and *Women Empowerment*. She has published more than 34 research papers and book chapters in reputed refereed national and international journals. She has participated as well as acted as a resource person in different national and international conferences. She has also attended and organised numerous faculty development programmes along with workshops. As a resource person she has been immensely appreciated by the organisers for her pedagogy and content.

Jan Brown, PhD, is a Senior Lecturer in Marketing and Entrepreneurship at Liverpool Business School, Liverpool John Moores University (LJMU), UK. She obtained a PhD in Service Ecosystems and works collaboratively with a wide range of partners, from both academia and industry, who are willing to challenge boundaries to link theory to practice more creatively. Her current research includes social return on investment, creative ecosystems, and digital networking.

Eduardo P. B. Davel, PhD in Management from the École des Hautes Études Commerciales de Montreal (Canadá). Professor at the School of Management, Federal University of Bahia, Brazil. Leader of the research collective OCA – Organization, Culture, and Art (CNPq). Editor-in-chief of O&S – *Organizations & Society Journal*. He develops research and publishes on cultural entrepreneurship, management education, qualitative methods of research, learning, culture, creativity, art, and aesthetics in and around organisations.

Stephen Dobson, PhD, is Associate Professor in Creativity and Enterprise at the School of Performance and Cultural Industries, University of Leeds. His research interests span several areas relating to cultural and creative industries and entrepreneurship including entrepreneurial identity and creative enterprise, the creative workplace and leadership for fostering innovation and creativity, critical management, cross-disciplinary creativity, cultural and creative industries policy, and digital enterprise. At the wider scale he explores urbanism and especially the appropriation of degraded and abandoned spaces, fringe landscapes, and derelict space as opportunities for creativity, enterprise, and urban regeneration, creative clusters, and creative labs. He is also the Director of International Activities for the School of Performance and Cultural Industries.

Sara R. S. T. A. Elias, PhD, is an Associate Professor at the University of Victoria's Peter B. Gustavson School of Business and a Research Associate of the Center for Psychosocial Organization Studies. Her research interests include creative entrepreneurial processes, entrepreneurial imagining, arts entrepreneurship, aesthetics in organisations and entrepreneurship, entrepreneurship as practice, and qualitative methodologies. These research interests stem from Sara's background in Business, Engineering, and Music as well as from her experience as an Arts Entrepreneur, Music Manager, Performing Artist, and Managing Director of *Associação CICO*, an international centre for promoting the performing arts, headquartered in Portugal. She is Associate Editor of the *Scandinavian Journal of Management* and is a Member of the Editorial Boards of *Art, Culture & Entrepreneurship* and *Organizações & Sociedade*. She has published in *Organization Studies, Organization Theory, Organization, Journal of Management Inquiry, International Journal of Entrepreneurial Behavior & Research, Organizational Research Methods*, among others.

Sandrine Emin, PhD in Management Science, is Senior Lecturer in Management and Entrepreneurship at the University of Angers (France) and Researcher at the laboratory GRANEM (Angevin Research Group in Economics and Management). Member of the Scientific Academy for Innovation and Entrepreneurship where she is the Co-director of Tracks on Cultural Entrepreneurship. Specialist of entrepreneurship, her research areas focus on collective entrepreneurship in economy solidarity and cultural industries – cultural clusters, local scenes – and on accompaniment of artist–entrepreneurs. She notably co-edited a special issue of the *Review of Entrepreneurship/Revue de l'Entrepreneuriat on Cultural and Creative Entrepreneurship* (2018, Vol. 18/1). Co-investigator of several research programs, currently the SCAENA project (Cultural Scenes, Atmospheres and urban transformations), a national program that aims to analyse the complex embeddedness between the cultural and artistic activities, presence of start-ups or creative entrepreneurs, and the socio-urban configuration of a territory.

Hannah Grannemann is an Assistant Professor and the Director of the Arts Administration Program at The University of North Carolina at Greensboro. She has published in the *Journal of International Council on Small Business*, *Cultural Management: Science and Education*, *Arts Professional (UK)*, and *Business Issues in the Arts* (chapter) published by Routledge. Presentations include conferences for the *Association of Arts Administration Educators (AAAE)*, *Association of Theatre in Higher Education (ATHE)*, *Hong Kong Academy for the Performing Arts*, *Society of Arts Entrepreneurship Educators (SAEE)*, the *International Council on Small Business*, and the *Beijing Dance Academy Forum*. She holds a BFA in Theatre from New York University/Tisch School of the Arts and an MFA/MBA in Theatre Management from Yale School of Drama/Yale School of Management. She was Executive Director of Children's Theatre of Charlotte and Managing Director of PlayMakers Repertory Company. She writes about arts audiences on her blog Row X on ArtsJournal.com.

Inge Hill, PhD, FRSA, is a Lecturer in Entrepreneurship at The Open University. Her research investigates micro-exchange processes of SMEs and is rooted in process and practice theories. She investigates creative industry entrepreneurship, strategic business advice, and local economic development in urban and rural contexts and publishes on qualitative methodologies. She is an Associate Fellow with the Research England-funded cross-university National Innovation Centre of Rural Enterprise and co-leads the project's research stream on rural creative enterprises. She has published widely including in *Local Economy*,

Entrepreneurship and Regional Development, and the *International Journal of Entrepreneurial Behaviour and Research*, where she serves on the Editorial Review Board. She acts as Associate Editor for *SN Business and Economics* and regularly reviews AHRC/ESRC funding applications and for many journals including *Cultural Trends* and the *European Journal of Management*. She serves on the *Council of the British Academy of Management* and is the Lead Editor of this edited book.

Jacqueline Jenkins, PhD, is a Senior Lecturer at Nottingham Business School, Nottingham Trent University, UK. Her research is multidisciplinary as it encompasses creative disciplines/creative industries, gender, and entrepreneurship. Her research fits under four main themes: entrepreneurial identity, entrepreneurs in the creative industries, female entrepreneurship, and higher education shaping entrepreneurial outcomes. Her PhD thesis is entitled *Creative Discipline Education Shaping Entrepreneurial Outcomes in the Creative Industries, a Gender Perspective*. The research explored the role that higher education plays in shaping entrepreneurial outcomes in supporting students' preparation for obtaining work in their chosen industry including working self-employed/freelance. She teaches on a variety of courses at both undergraduate and postgraduate levels with particular focus on management, project management, and entrepreneurship. She brings her research into her teaching by understanding the significance of situating academic theories and models into a business context and real-life business case studies.

Paul Jones, PhD, Professor, is Head of School and Professor of Entrepreneurship and Innovation at the School of Management, Swansea University. He is Editor-in-Chief on the *International Journal of Entrepreneurial Behaviour and Research* journal. He is also Associate Editor with the journal *International Journal of Management Education* and a Senior Editor on *Information Technology and People*. He is also Series Editor of the *Contemporary Issues in Entrepreneurship Research* book series published by Emerald Publishing. He is a prolific entrepreneurial researcher and has authored over 100 refereed journal articles in his career to date. In addition, he has co-edited 14 books to date on various contemporary entrepreneurial topics. His research predominantly explores entrepreneurial behaviour and small business management.

Rajeev Kamineni, PhD, started his working career in a bookstore almost three decades ago and then moved onto Area Sales Manager, Director, Executive Director, Chief Officer, Lecturer, and Head of Program positions. He is a multiple award-winning lecturer with lecturing stints in Australia, South Africa, Singapore, Japan, India, and Dubai. Currently Associate Head of accreditation at Adelaide Business School and teaching management for University of Adelaide's students, he is an active Rotarian for many years and is currently the 100th President of Rotary Adelaide. He was actively involved in financing 35 movies and producing 14 movies in the Indian movie industry. With a PhD in movie entrepreneurship and a lifelong passion for cinema, he was also an Organiser and Executive Committee Member of the Chennai International Film Festival (CIFF) and with

Ruth Rentschler published the renowned book *Indian Movie Entrepreneurship: Not Just Song and Dance* (Routledge, 2020). It was judged one of the top movie books of all time.

Ellen Loots, PhD in Applied Economics from Antwerp University, Belgium, is specialised in Arts Management, Cultural Organisations, and Creative Entrepreneurship, and has a special interest in the motivations and behaviours of individuals and organisations in the cultural and creative industries. Social challenges such as justice, community, and sustainability influence many of her choices in research and teaching. She currently works at Erasmus University Rotterdam, the Netherlands.

Simony R. Marins, PhD in Management at the School of Management, Federal University of Bahia, Brazil; Visiting Scholar at the Faculty of Business and Law of University of Portsmouth, UK; Master in Management at the State University of Ceará, Brazil; Bachelor of Tourism at the Fluminense Federal University, Brazil; and Researcher at the collective OCA – Organization, Culture, and Art (CNPq). Researches and publishes on cultural and arts entrepreneurship, tourism, learning, qualitative methods, aesthetics, and organisations.

Maggie Murphy is the Art & Design Librarian at The University of North Carolina at Greensboro, where she works with students, faculty, and curators in the School of Art, interdisciplinary Arts Administration Program, Department of Interior Architecture, and Weatherspoon Art Museum. She is also affiliated faculty in the Department of Religious Studies, teaching a course on fandom and popular culture through the analytic lens of religion. She previously worked as the Visual Resources Curator at Queens College (CUNY). Her research interests include artistic research practice, craft entrepreneurship, creative pedagogy, and contemporary engagement with print culture.

Ernestine Nnam Ning, PhD, is a Senior Lecturer in Entrepreneurship and Small Business Management, at the Faculty of Business and Law, University of Portsmouth Business School, UK. She was previously a Lecturer in Enterprise and Entrepreneurship at Coventry University, UK, a Teaching Assistant at the University of Edinburgh Business School, Scotland, UK, where she earned her PhD in Management (Entrepreneurship and Innovation). Prior to her PhD program, she was a full-time Assistant Lecturer at the University of Buea in Cameroon. Her research and expertise revolve in the broad areas of entrepreneurship, new venture creation and family business, with a special interest in the nature and role of family networks and their effects on the entrepreneurial performance of pluriactive entrepreneurs in Africa. She has authored book chapters and has published articles in leading entrepreneurship journals.

Samuel Osei-Nimo, PhD, is a Senior Lecturer in Business and a Higher Education Academy Fellow. His doctoral studies and previous research projects influenced his interests. He has studied organisational environments using Systems-thinking and Information Systems methodologies. He is interested in power, knowledge, and systems approaches. Utilising his background in business and information systems, he has also explored and successfully investigated the effectiveness of Soft Systems Methodology in assisting with Foucault's poststructuralist approach to addressing problematic situations in Western culture. He uses systemic (holistic) methodologies to identify, classify, and contrast different discourses, practices, and organisational actors in the fashion and creative industries. He is a Course Director and Link Tutor at Birmingham City University's Business, Law, and Social Sciences Research Ethics Committee. He has supervised doctoral research in entrepreneurship, organisational identities, and diversity.

Balkrishan is a PhD scholar at the HPKVBS, School of Commerce and Management Studies, at Central University of Himachal Pradesh, Dharamshala, India. He is three times UGC-NET (University Grant Commission – National Eligibility Test) qualified in the subject of Labour Welfare/Personnel Management/ Industrial Relations/Labour and Social Welfare/Human Resource Management. He holds a Master's of Business Administration postgraduate degree from the Central University of Himachal Pradesh, Dharamshala, India, with a specialisation in the field of Human Resource Management and Organisational Behaviour.

Ulrike Posselt writes a PhD thesis at the University of Gloucestershire, studies Philosophy/Sociology at the Friedrich-Schiller-Universität Jena, and holds Diplomas in Communication Design and Business Administration. She is an Independent Researcher and has been a Visiting Lecturer. Her research focuses on intra-/interpersonal flow experiences in teams. She works as a communications consultant and helps entrepreneurial clients in Europe and North America to realise their business models and develop their organisations to meet their clients' needs. She worked for private and public clients such as Deutsche Bank, AirLiquide, and the states of Hessen and Rhineland-Palatinate. She began her career with formal training as a Typographer and won State and National Awards.

Ruth Rentschler, PhD, OAM (BA Hons Melbourne PhD Monash) is Professor of Arts & Cultural Leadership at the University of South Australia. She has a strong interest in the creative and cultural industries, entrepreneurship, diversity, and inclusion. She serves the community as Chair of the Board of Australian Dance Theatre and No Strings Attached Theatre of Disability. She has published in top journals such as *Journal of Business Ethics*, *British Journal of Management*, *Personnel Review*, and *European Journal of Marketing*, to name a few. With Rajeev Kamineni she published the renowned book *Indian Movie Entrepreneurship: Not Just Song and Dance* (Routledge, 2020). It was judged one of the top movie books of all time.

Jennifer Reis, Assistant Professor of Arts Administration at The University of North Carolina at Greensboro, is a Creative Entrepreneur, Artist, Educator, and Curator with 25 years' experience in Arts Business and Administration. Her earned degrees include a BFA from Columbus College of Art and Design and graduate degrees in Arts Management, Studio Art, and Arts Education from Syracuse University and Morehead State University. She is a Master Facilitator for adult learning initiatives such as the Kauffman Foundation's FastTrac entrepreneurship education program and the AIR Institute's courses in arts-based community and economic revitalisation. Through her consulting company Make Do Creative, she supports foundations invested in developing artist–entrepreneurs and with community and economic development, trade, governmental, and cultural organisations to design, manage, and deliver creative entrepreneurship curriculum.

Nathalie Schieb-Bienfait, PhD in Management Science, is Full Associate Professor and Director of Research in Management and Entrepreneurship at Nantes University. Researcher at the laboratory LEMNA, Associate Editor with the academic Journal *Review of Entrepreneurship* (*Revue de l'Entrepreneuriat*) and Member of the Board of AEI (Academy for Innovation and Entrepreneurship). Specialist of entrepreneurship in cultural and creative industries, accompaniment of artist–entrepreneurs, innovation process, and small business management, she has authored over 80 refereed journal articles in her career to date. Director for several multidisciplinary research programmes on the evaluation of cultural activities value, on the artistic work, and on the entrepreneurial competences. She notably co-edited a special issue of the *Review of Entrepreneurship/ Revue de l'Entrepreneuriat on Cultural and Creative Entrepreneurship* (2018, Vol. 18/1), in the *International Journal of Arts Management* (2018, Vol. 20/1), in the book *Entrepreneurship in Culture and Creatives Industries* (2018, Springer). Her last book is entitled *From the Entrepreneur to Entrepreneuring* (Paris, EMS, 2022; https://www.univ-nantes.fr/nathalie-schieb-bienfait).

Marie Segares, has launched or expanded programs in every full-time job she has held during her career in the non-profit health and education industries. She has earned her AB in Sociology from Barnard College, her MPH in Sociomedical Sciences from Columbia University, her MBA in Entrepreneurship & Innovation and Leadership & Change Management from New York University, and her EdD in Organizational Leadership Studies from Northeastern University. She has taught business, entrepreneurship and social entrepreneurship, human resources, management and organisational behaviour, marketing, health education and public health, and health care management courses at the undergraduate, post-baccalaureate, and graduate levels in face-to-face, online, and hybrid learning environments. She is an Associate Professor and the Founding Director of the MS in Management at St. Francis College. Her areas of research interest include artisan entrepreneurship, creative business, microenterprise, leadership, small business marketing, and gender and diversity in entrepreneurship and organisations.

Dipanker Sharma is Professor at Central University of Himachal Pradesh in the School of Commerce and Management Studies and teaches Human Resource Management and Organisational Behaviour. Specialised in Human Resource

Management, he has total work experience of 17 years. He carries rich industrial exposure and has conducted extensive research. With an illustrious industrial experience for more than a decade as a Corporate Trainer with many renowned MNCs, his contribution to academia becomes unparalleled. He has received several national and international awards for capacity building and patents. He has done short assignments in Asian countries like Hong Kong, Dubai, Bhutan, and Singapore and has taken up many research projects on women empowerment and related issues. His area of research includes Entrepreneurship, Brain Circulation of Human Capital, Leadership, Work-life Balance, Workforce Diversity, and Knowledge Management.

David Sharpe is a Business Consultant specialising in digital and creative industries. Based in Wollongong, Australia, he undertakes strategic research and analysis for government agencies and provides management and operational advice to companies and not-for-profit organisations working across the full range of cultural and creative industries. He is completing a PhD at the University of Wollongong focusing on narrative accounts of creative industries entrepreneurs. He blogs about the process at https://creativebusinessleadership.com/. He has taught at the University of Technology, Sydney and the Australian Film Television and Radio School. His seminar paper on narrative accounts of careers within the cultural and creative industries is available at https://pathwaysbeyondeconomicgrowth.wordpress.com/.

FOREWORD

The cultural and creative activities are perhaps the Cinderella of the industrial policy, business and the entrepreneurship and innovation worlds. However, in the last decade they have not only 'come to the ball' but are also being proposed as the great hope of the future. This should give us caution as well as hope. The hope of course is that the field of the cultural and creative industries is given its appropriate moment in the spotlight and more research is encouraged; however, the concern is that simplistic and erroneous lessons will be proposed. As the contributors to this volume demonstrate, there are a vast wealth of experiences, contexts, processes, and outcomes to absorb, let alone draw lessons from. I particularly welcome the breath of authorial origin, gender, and generation: something that reflects the economy studied. These contributions will repay careful consideration both in terms of their variety and their unique response to (social, cultural, economic, and regulatory) embeddedness.

Sadly, much of the scholarship in this field has been nationally or locally based; the challenges and opportunities of learning through comparison and contrast are so seldom taken. This collection is a welcome exception to that rule. Moreover, it is a reminder that the creative economy is a feature of ALL economies and societies, not just those of the Global North, or of World Cities. This collection is expansive in its selection of context and contrast. We are reminded by UNCTAD in its regular creative economy report updates that the growth rate of the creative economy is greater in the Global South than the Global North.

It is a further welcome aspect of this collection that it takes a more 'open' view of what economies and entrepreneurship is and whom it is 'for'. The expansion of the Creative economy to embrace both, the for- and the not-for profit as well as the formal and informal, and the social and the economic echoes that of the wider understanding of business organisations. To be sure, it is a complex challenge for researchers; but it is also one that is 'resolved' each and every day by practitioners.

In the light of the (hopefully) post-COVID world we have been given a strong reminder of the challenge of sustainability for those working in the creative economy. Sustainability can be seen from two dimensions here, both are picked up in the collection. First, sustainability, as in resilience and the ability of 'go on'. It is notable that many creative businesses are past masters in dealing with crisis and risk. In fact, the degree to which these businesses do not just survive, but thrive, indicates that there are lessons to be learned. Second, sustainability in the environmental sense. We have been too slow to recognise the impacts that cultural and creative activities can have on the environment; we seem to have assumed them to be benign. However, the lessons of struggling to understand the experiences of working in the creative economy have encouraged more relational ideas

of co-dependency and more generally circular and heuristic thinking. We will
certainly need them in the coming years.

Andy Pratt
UNESCO Chair for Global Creative Economy
Professor of Cultural Economy and Director of the
Centre for Culture, and the Creative Industries
City University, University of London

CHAPTER 1

CREATIVE (AND CULTURAL) INDUSTRY ENTREPRENEURSHIP IN THE 21ST CENTURY – STATE OF THE ART

Inge Hill, Sara R. S. T. A. Elias, Stephen Dobson and Paul Jones

ABSTRACT

This chapter examines emerging theoretical approaches and thematic aspects of creative and cultural entrepreneurship and the significant societal and economic contributions of creative firms. It reviews the concepts and definitions essential to examining creative industry entrepreneurship. The authors then provide framing for this exceptional collection of chapters in Volume 1 (of 2) and discuss existing research approaches from surveys and small-scale qualitative studies. Then, the chapter's overview showcases the range of international research included in three sections: conceptual reflections on creative and cultural entrepreneurship, resilience and adaptation of creative and cultural enterprises, and insights into creative subsectors. Finally, the chapter proposes a research agenda for developing the field further, addressing methodological gaps (longitudinal studies and cluster research), emerging thematics (rural creative industries and creative placemaking) and sector studies (game and film industries).

Keywords: Creative industry research agenda; international creative entrepreneurship; resilient creative entrepreneurship; rural creative entrepreneurship; creative entrepreneurial identities; rural creative entrepreneurship; creative placemaking

Creative (and Cultural) Industry Entrepreneurship in the 21st Century
Contemporary Issues in Entrepreneurship Research, Volume 18A, 1–14
Copyright © 2024 by Inge Hill, Sara R. S. T. A. Elias, Stephen Dobson and Paul Jones
Published under exclusive licence by Emerald Publishing Limited
ISSN: 2040-7246/doi:10.1108/S2040-72462023000018A001

Creativity is the industry of tomorrow. (UNESCO, 2021)

We are delighted to bring together the latest thinking and empirical insights from across the world on what creative and cultural industry (CCI) entrepreneurship looks like in the twenty-first century! The call for chapters generated within a month a great interest, attracting over 30 fascinating abstracts, submitted from Ghana to Nigeria, the USA, Australia, Spain, Cameroon, Malaysia, India, the UK, France, Switzerland, Norway, Brazil, Estonia, and Zimbabwe. Thank you to all authors for engaging with the call and the wish to take stock of the past, present, and future of CCI entrepreneurship – we were positively overwhelmed! It was our aim to ensure that selections were as inclusive and diverse as possible in terms of author gender, country of origin, career stage, and disciplinary background across two volumes. We are also delighted to feature a foreword from Andy Pratt, a leading CCI researcher, and currently UNESCO Chair of the Global Creative Economy.

With this book, we take a fresh perspective on creative and cultural businesses, the processes leading to their formation and development as well as their founders. CCIs are abundant in all countries and nations and have been the fastest growing contributors to world economies for the last two decades pre-COVID-19 (UNCTAD, 2018). Knowing more about these entrepreneurial ventures and their development steps and needs is of interest not only because of this economic growth but also due to the many stakeholders looking to improve their socio-economic contribution to the well-being and economic success of global societies (Jones et al., 2018). These stakeholders include not only scholars of entrepreneurship and organisation studies but also active creative entrepreneurs, policymakers and creative industry networks. Most significantly, as a result of the various worldwide lockdowns, different strategies and business models emerged showing the resilience of this sector to external changes. Business strategies changed, new businesses emerged, and new business channels developed.

Whilst CCIs were great economic and societal contributors to economies pre-COVID-19 (Hill, 2021; UNCTAD, 2018), they are not as visible and recognised by the public for their socio-economic contributions to society as other industries such as manufacturing. Reasons for this limited public visibility are manifold: one significant cause is the large number of freelancers and micro-businesses (with 1–9 employees, an EU definition) and the comparatively few high-growth businesses within the industry. This characteristic means that government support has less focus on this sector, which typically does not provide substantial employment. Other reasons include a lack of physical presence: many freelancers work from home; indeed, there are less creative industry entrepreneurs in enterprise parks, villages, and towns, leading to fewer creative business premises. Nonetheless, studies of creative hubs have made visible the particular locations where creative firms cluster (Hill et al., 2021; Pratt, 2021; Pratt et al., 2019; Velez et al., 2022), with recent research also highlighting, for the first time, that rural and urban clusters do not differ greatly in their drivers for agglomeration and co-location of rural creative industries (Velez et al., 2022).

These mounting developments indicate that it is the ideal time for research on creative industry entrepreneurship to seek insights into recent progressions, changes, and successes, to gain a more nuanced understanding of how creative businesses themselves change and develop in various contexts. These contexts include economic, spatial, social, technological, time-related, and institutional settings (Welter, 2011). However, it is important to continue investigating CCI entrepreneurial ventures, as their development steps and needs are of interest to many stakeholders for improving their socio-economic contribution to the well-being of societies and economies, not only entrepreneurship and organisation studies scholars but also practicing creative entrepreneurs, policy-makers and creative industry networks.

The following section clarifies some core concepts and reiterates the most important contributions that CCIs have been making to societies and economies. Before we provide insight into the chapters included in this volume, we discuss some emerging trends prevalent to the field.

1. CULTURAL INDUSTRIES, CREATIVE ECONOMY, CREATIVE AND CULTURAL ENTREPRENEURSHIP – CLARIFYING CONCEPTS

The term 'creative industries' subsumes a wide range of entrepreneurs, from non-profit volunteers running museums, to fashion and IT designers, craft and artisan entrepreneurs, gallery owners, architects, to game creators. There is growing interest in the creative industries from policy-makers and those who start these businesses, as to how these entrepreneurs create, sustain, and market their services and products and how their contexts influence their 'doing business'. The specification of 'CCIs' emerged in the 1990s, as a 'new' term to replace the then commonly used 'cultural industries' due to changes in policy leadership in the UK (Pratt et al., 2019). Scholarly attention to the creative (and cultural) industries has grown in recent years, along with a recognition that they provide fruitful venues for studying, for example, entrepreneurial processes of novelty (co-)creation (Elias et al., 2018).

So then, what does 'cultural industries' denote? According to UNESCO (1982), 'cultural industry' applies to those industries that combine the creation, production, and marketing of content that is by nature cultural and intangible. Content is protected by intellectual property rights and can take the form of goods and services. Cultural industries represent one of the few economic sectors where dynamic future development is expected and referred to as the 'culturalisation' or 'creativisation' of the economy (Pitts, 2015). Although cultural and creative industries are considered to be one and the same in many areas of policy and indeed research, academic scholarship is less clear, and cultural industries are shown as a sub-group of the creative industries. This allocation is due to the fact that, while they share most of the creative industry firm characteristics (creation, system of production, tendency to generate copyright, potential to create wealth), cultural industries have particular social and cultural significance (McElwee, 2022).

Klamer (2011, p. 141) describes the cultural entrepreneur as one 'who is entrepreneurial in the realization of cultural values', and so, rather than being distinguished by a particular approach or even a specific subsector within the broader creative industries, we might consider that the cultural industries and their entrepreneurs do indeed create much more than purely economic value. Cultural value can be defined as our appreciation and acknowledgment of the societal importance of the 'rich complex of meanings, beliefs, practices, symbols, norms, and values prevalent among people in a society' (Schwartz, 2006, p. 138). The cultural entrepreneur, therefore, is a custodian of these intangible values, which may be evident in the art, music, theatre, heritage, tourism development, or artisanal crafts that may typify their mode of production.

The UK defines nine creative subsectors (DCMS, 2016) that fall under 'creative industries'. These are crafts, architecture, visual and performing arts, fashion, advertising and marketing, design, film/TV/radio/video and photography, publishing, museums/galleries and libraries, and IT/software, and computer services (including the games industry). In other countries, education or cultural heritage tourism is included in the CCI industry sector. Over the last 10–20 years, the term 'creative economy' has emerged to capture the connectedness between the creative and cultural industries (Pratt, 2021; UNESCO, 2018). As a term, 'creative economy' captures the element of creativity and novelty that underlies all these subsectors. This sector of the economy is a significant contributor to the national gross domestic product and demonstrates the confluence of the commercial and cultural value of creativity to society.

2. THE CONTRIBUTIONS OF CCI ENTREPRENEURSHIP

What do we know about the value and contribution of CCIs to societies? We start with a discussion of the contributions to the economy, followed by health and well-being, and improvements to community development.

2.1. Economic and Sustainable Development Contributions

Self-employment is common for many of those working in CCIs, not just in the UK. Indicative for many other countries, the UK creative industries have a large number of freelancers often choosing self-employment (32% in 2019; DCMS, 2021). In the music, performance, and visual arts sectors, the rate of fragmentation and micro-businesses without employees rises to 72% (in 2018, UK Office for National Statistics, ONS, 2022). Illustratively, most performance dancers have multiple income streams, such as 'training other professionals and/or the wider public, and sometimes non-arts-related part-time jobs' to survive economically (Hill et al., 2021, p. 629; Roberts & Townsend, 2016).

Pre-COVID-19, the contribution of CCIs to the world economy amounted to 3% of the global GDP and offered about 30 million jobs worldwide (UNESCO, 2021). At that time, the estimate was that CCIs could create 8 million additional jobs by 2030. In Nigeria, for example, the music industry alone was growing annually by 13.4%. Nollywood, the national film industry sector, produced over 2,000 films a year and employed about 1 million people. Similarly, in Australia, over half a million of Australians worked in CCIs, with exports of over a billion dollars. In 2016, India had become, for the first time, the leading film market with 2.2 billion movie tickets sold. In Switzerland, the design industry was a great success, exporting for over nearly 16 billion US dollars (UNCTAD, 2018), whereas in Estonia, the designed goods for interior design and fashion industries were leading subsectors. These numbers are only indicative of the significant economic role CCIs play in just some of the countries represented by the authors of this book's chapters.

The year 2021 was declared the *International Year of Creative Economy for Sustainable Development* at the 74th United Nations (UN) General Assembly. An exciting year of events and publications highlighted particular contributions to the implementation of the UN Sustainable Development Goals (Hill & Rowe, 2021a). Our introductory chapter to Volume 2 will talk more about it.

2.2. Societal Contributions – Health and Well-Being

What else do we know about the value and contribution of CCIs to societies? My (Inge Hill) studies have shown that the health and well-being benefits for audiences and consumers as co-producers of creative outputs are often overlooked and undervalued. Hence, some important insights include these aspects (Meyrick & Barnett, 2021): studies have shown that dance and musical activities can improve mental and physical health, for example, relieving depression and improving flexibility (Murcia et al., 2010; Quin et al., 2007; Stickley et al., 2015). In Hill et al. (2021), my colleagues and I also demonstrated how online dance practice greatly impacted individuals' lives during the 2021 UK lockdown phase.

2.3. Community Development and Placemaking

Similarly, the *community engagement and contribution* of many artists through community work (often unpaid) and education engagement are undervalued. The term 'community artist', which so many artists use for themselves, illuminates how these artists conceptualise their societal engagement and responsibility that often goes unnoticed (Federal Reserve Bank of San Francisco, 2019). In the US, an article collection by public policy-makers, academics, and artists (Federal Reserve Bank of San Francisco, 2019) links the function of community to the engagement of artists, thus illuminating the artists' essential role for regional socio-economic development. While anecdotally acknowledged in Europe, the recognition of this essential contribution by policy-makers and the wider global public is growing only recently.

Linked to community development is the *placemaking role* of CCI entrepreneurship (Courage et al., 2021; Hill et al., 2021). In Volume 2 of this edited book, Jevnaker and Hill, Rae, and Naudin, study selected placemaking activities in rural and urban contexts; they demonstrate the significant social role that economic activities have within the community. 'Placemaking' denotes a temporary materialisation of the social relations and senses of community and belonging in physical locations (Hill et al., 2021). In the UK, the government has called for a re-building of inner cities by local authorities as effective spaces for living and meeting; the same call has been issued in summer 2022 for villages and rural towns.

3. EMERGING TRENDS FOR AND WITH CCI ENTREPRENEURSHIP

We consider the emergent topics that need further research to include the impact of COVID-19 on the CCI sector, rural CCI entrepreneurship, the aesthetics of CCI entrepreneurship, the role of imagination in driving entrepreneurial practices in the CCIs and the impact of recent disruptive socio-economic events for Europe, such as Brexit and the war in Ukraine.

For example, COVID-19-induced lockdown periods severely impacted the creative and cultural sectors, with many CCI entrepreneurs leaving the sector altogether, interrupting their CCI businesses and taking other temporary jobs – developing brand new ventures on- and offline and taking their services online in different ways (Hill et al., 2021). Often overlooked is how the value of the creative and cultural industries stretches far beyond solely its economic contribution to society. Throughout the global pandemic, the need for cultural connection and creative consumption highlighted that CCI entrepreneurs indeed offer a wide range of cultural value for societies. The UK-based Centre for Cultural Value recently published its ongoing work assessing UK CCIs within the pandemic context in its *Culture in Crisis* report (Walmsley et al., 2022). Key findings were threefold: first, although the shift to digital did indeed transform cultural experiences for those already engaged with the sector, these digital offerings have failed to diversify and expand audiences and customer bases. Second, those working in the cultural sector currently experience impact on their capacity; the research points to significant effects of sector 'burnout' and significant gaps in technical and digital skills. Third, many cultural organisations are currently engaged in re-evaluating their purpose and relevance to local communities, especially in light of the 'Black Lives Matter' movement, and the issue of the digital divide highlighted by the pandemic (Walmsley et al., 2022). The collection of research in this volume connects with these calls to action, and beyond, outlining current and future research trends.

Rural creative entrepreneurship is often overlooked in research on 'the' CCIs (Balfour et al., 2018; Bell & Jayne, 2010; Hill et al., 2021). For this reason, among others, the recent Research England-funded National Innovation Centre for Rural Enterprise (NICRE) operates a research strand on this sector that I, Inge Hill, am delighted to co-lead (Hill & Rowe, 2021a and b). The cause of this oversight of CCIs in rural areas lies in that rural research seems to have its own journals and publication outlets and that the validity of mainstream research implicitly is assumed to cover all areas in countries including rural locations (Bell & Jayne, 2010; Velez et al., 2022). Additionally, COVID-19 lockdown phases meant that many urban professionals moved into rural areas.

In the general entrepreneurship literature, there is some differentiation between 'rural businesses' and 'businesses in the rural' (Bosworth & Turner, 2018; Hill & Mole, 2022). 'Rural businesses' have at least some local and regional customers, staff and suppliers, in contrast to those businesses located in rural areas without much of the above that defines a 'rural business' (Bosworth & Turner, 2018). Rural creative industries and their characteristics have been studied less.

4. INSIGHTS INTO THE ENTREPRENEURSHIP STORIES IN THIS VOLUME

We invite you, readers, to join us on a journey of discovery through many countries across the world and hopefully share our excitement about what CCIs can achieve. This first volume allows you to dip into topics of new conceptual insights on CCI entrepreneurship, learn about adaptations to COVID-19 in Africa and the UK, and gain a deeper insight into sectors less studied, such as the Indian movie industry, living arts in Europe, UK ethnic minority fashion entrepreneurs, photographers, and architects.

We have divided the chapters into two volumes. We begin this first volume with a number of *Conceptual reflections on creative and cultural entrepreneurship*, with insights from taking a fresh look at old concepts to exciting extensions with concepts from other disciplines for CCI entrepreneurship. Loots reflects on the fragmentation that pervades the field of entrepreneurship, arising from its interdisciplinary nature. While identifying key ingredients in the 'hodgepodge' of entrepreneurship, the author contributes to our theoretical understanding of entrepreneurial action and the agency–structure relationship within the CCIs. Significantly, this chapter sheds light on fundamental entrepreneurship concepts in the context of CCIs, providing important insights that researchers, teachers, students, and practitioners may use as they contribute to the bright future that lies ahead for CCI entrepreneurship.

In their chapter, Marins and Davel explore the aesthetic dimension of cultural and arts entrepreneurship, building from three perspectives in organisational aesthetics theory: sensible knowing, connection, and judgements. Placing aesthetics at the very core of cultural and arts entrepreneurship, the authors delve deep into the beauty and complexity of what drives innovative processes. The result is an insightful and much-needed exploration that brings back into the fore the body and the senses, as well as the interactions, interconnections, relations, and the tacit, non-verbal and (inter)subjective understandings that fuel entrepreneurial practices and how entrepreneurs make sense of themselves – and their innovations – in relation to the world. The authors conclude with a call for entrepreneurship scholars to embrace difference, otherness and delight as fundamental components of aesthetic entrepreneuring.

Building from the old, now rarely-used verb 'to indite', meaning to compose or give expression, Posselt introduces and takes the first steps to theorise the notion of inditation as the creative, complex process of forming entrepreneurial brainchildren. These entrepreneurial brainchildren refer to 'the new', or the novel, unique offerings that creative entrepreneurs develop, such as artworks and creative products or services. This chapter explores the origins of the term, distinguishing it from related concepts such as creation, ideation, intuition, inspiration, invention, and imagination. It also provides a first-person, auto-ethnographic perspective on inditation, building from the author's experience as a practitioner, creative entrepreneur, and researcher. The author concludes with a roadmap for the future theorisation of inditation as a process- and practice-based approach for creative entrepreneurs to bring their brainchildren into the world.

To investigate how venture creation unfolds in the cultural and creative industries, Sharpe critically investigates the slipperiness of entrepreneurial intention within this context. Reflecting on, and in a way destabilising what we currently know about venture creation as a planned, deliberate, and precise act, the author questions whether extant models of entrepreneurial intention hold true for cultural and creative entrepreneurs. Based on narrative research of 18 entrepreneurs from a range of cultural and creative industries in Australia, Sharpe shows that entrepreneurial intention, as experienced by these entrepreneurs, is an organic, undefined, fluid, spontaneous, and uncertain process. The author concludes with a call for scholars to recognise the slipperiness of entrepreneurial intention in the context of cultural and creative entrepreneurship, which also provides an opportunity to explore concepts and ideas that are currently missing from extant entrepreneurship models and theories.

Resilience and adaptation of creative and cultural enterprises offers insights into examples of resilient behaviours as a reaction to COVID-19 lockdown phases. Grannemann et al. explore themes from a sample of predominantly female-identifying participants, who created an enterprise or added a product line to an existing business. The sample included individuals who did not identify as a 'creative entrepreneur' prior to the pandemic, but did identify as an entrepreneur after a mask-making venture. Informed by entrepreneurship literature, the chapter observes how these nascent entrepreneurs articulate recognisable motivations for social entrepreneurship, show signs of pre-existing entrepreneurial mindsets, and employ business models and marketing tactics of entrepreneurs, largely without any business training. Study implications include increased recognition of latent entrepreneurial readiness, interest of women in social entrepreneurship, and higher levels of business knowledge among women than previously recognised.

Bhardwaj et al.'s chapter explores the role of creative entrepreneurship in supporting and helping self-help groups to function seamlessly during the COVID-19 pandemic. The chapter analyses pandemic and post-pandemic creative entrepreneurship through self-help groups in the Himachal Pradesh region in India. The authors identify that creative entrepreneurship initiatives have significantly changed and supported the livelihood of rural people during the pandemic. The chapter also highlights challenges faced by the self-help groups during the lockdown, as well as illuminates their resilience strategies.

Armstrong-Gibbs and Brown discuss the adaptation strategies of a UK social enterprise during COVID-19 lockdowns. This community-owned property development company was established to regenerate a post-industrial area and support creative industries. In 2022, they are focused on acting as a creative hub offering premises to small- and medium-sized creative businesses. Using an organisational ethnographic approach with data collection during the pandemic, they demonstrate in a unique way how this organisation developed new behaviours to sustain its existence and support its tenants, demonstrating resilience with a future-forward effect. Their findings are organised around six themes (operational compliance and guidance; adapting to suit tenant needs; innovation, opportunity and change; communication from the creative hub; networking and advocacy; maximising the financials).

Insights into creative subsectors sheds light upon subsectors studied less often from an entrepreneurship perspective. Rajeev Kamenini and Ruth Rentschl discuss critically the small number of women entrepreneurs in the Indian movie industry. They introduce the reader to the role of women in the Indian movie industry. Based on 17 interviews with women movie producers, and employing life history analysis, they use the lens of social capital to unpack how movie producers use family ties and networks for career progression. Framed by the three key themes of innovation, risk taking and pro-activeness, family ties and networks, they tell the stories of how movie producers advance their careers, along with the role of gender. The rich illustration with quotes gives unique, contextualised insight into the construction of gendered entrepreneurial careers in this subsector. They suggest, amongst other things, that support should be focused on raising awareness and skills in developing social capital for career construction.

The Schieb-Bienfait and Emin chapter considers policies in CCIs, which are often based on implicit assumptions that work in the cultural and creative sectors is 'good work', with dominant discourses tending to over-celebrate entrepreneurship. The chapter argues that sufficient attention has been paid to the 'real work' in CCIs. The stake is to more effectively address the symptoms observed for a sustainable and inclusive economy in CCIs. Adopting an entrepreneurship-as-practice perspective, the chapter documents professionalisation difficulties in the music sector, with a qualitative study set in a French city and a focus on the marginalisation experienced by young artists. With the identification of their work specificities and the tendencies for the twenty-first century, the chapter identifies the diversity of the tasks, the multiactivity and collective practices, and the need for some innovative organisational forms of support to develop training and skilling (both artistic and entrepreneurial).

Osei-Nimo et al. focus on UK fashion entrepreneurs from black and minority ethnic backgrounds. They discuss these entrepreneurs' positioning in this subsector, applying Foucault's concepts of power and governmentality. The chapter focuses on the essential role of Black, Asian, and Minority Ethnic fashion entrepreneurs and their challenges in promoting young designers from disadvantaged communities. Critically evaluating the discourse on fashion and creative industries over the last two decades, they recommend applying intersectionality consistently to challenge existing support for talent development. Similarly, they suggest all stakeholders to engage in change processes to ensure that talent in ethnic minorities is spotted and supported for the gain of all involved, proposing specialist mentoring as an important tool.

Ning's chapter evaluates how the creative industries contribute to the economic and social development of the country. The author also explores the creative industries in Cameroon, with a specific focus on the artists of popular and folk music and the challenges they face. The chapter offers suggestions for optimising the value of this sector to the benefit of the Cameroon economy.

Finally, Jenkins unpacks the role of creative identity as well as how creative identity intertwines with entrepreneurial identity. Building from the notion that creative people often struggle with also being an entrepreneur, the author critically examines the creative and entrepreneurial identities of creative practitioners and how these enable them to work commercially, creating offerings that possess commercial value whilst also validating their creative and professional identity. The author uses in-depth, semi-structured interviews of 14 creative practitioners in the UK, working as either architects or photographers, to illuminate that creative identity and entrepreneurial identity are varied, contextualised, and complex concepts. By highlighting the quest to operate successfully as a creative practitioner as a driver for entrepreneurial identity, the author paves the way for continued research and discussion on creative practice as well as theory and education in the creative industries.

5. THE WAY FORWARD

5.1. Theoretical Framing and Approaches

As our selection of chapters demonstrates, research can only apply a limited amount of theoretical lenses, and often, these are not made explicit. Sara Elias and myself, are passionate practice-theory researchers. We see the need to conceptualise the verbal, non-verbal, and physical doing of creative entrepreneurship through a process-relational lens to gain more cogent knowledge relevant for practitioners and policy-makers, following the call for more impactful research echoing through all disciplines (Thompson et al., 2020; Welter, 2011). The enactment of 'entrepreneuring' is conceptualised as entrepreneurial practices that evolve when we take a practice-theory lens for investigating the situated performances of creative and cultural entrepreneurs. To do so, we need to consider *how* creative industry practices are resourced and include socio-materiality into the investigation (Hill, 2022; Orlikowski and Scott, 2016). This inclusion entails considering tangible and intangible resources and how ideas for the future materialise from imagination into products and actions (Thompson & Byrne, 2022; Elias et al., 2022).

As explored in Throsby's (2008) Concentric Circles model for the CCIs, those entrepreneurs acting within the core cultural industries (e.g. film, museums, galleries, libraries, and photography) and the wider cultural industries (e.g. heritage services, publishing, television and radio, digital media, video, and computer games) provide the critical connection between the core creative arts and wider related industries. Any theoretical lens needs to consider entrepreneurial activity in the CCIs as part of a wider and interconnected ecosystem, which positions the arts and creative industries as intrinsic to innovation efforts across a much wider range of industries. In this sense, the work of the core creative arts at the beginning of the value chain cannot be disassociated with the products and services developed by those wider industries further down the line. Understanding the role of CCIs in a holistic sense is thus an important way forward, requiring varied topics of research focus and a diversified agenda.

5.2. *Methodological Approaches*

Creative industry research has generally been either qualitative, with relatively small sample sizes, or quantitative, analysing large-scale business survey data, extracting information on creative industries or using a small number of specific surveys, such as the UK Creative Radar Survey (Siepel et al., 2020); few studies employ a mixed-method approach. There is currently a need for further longitudinal studies, using quantitative and/or qualitative methodologies, to identify how creative entrepreneurial practices emerge over time, in different spatial and social contexts (Hill et al., 2021; Pratt, 2021). As a field, we need to step away from overviews of 'creative city' or 'rural creatives' and instead seek to capture the multilevel complexity of CCI entrepreneurship in its diversity and the varying contexts of rural and urban areas. Future research can help develop an understanding of a number of important topics, such as how creative businesses change their income streams and customer groups.

For studying subsectors within the CCIs, a focus on clusters of creative entrepreneurs (Siepel et al., 2020; Velez et al., 2022) will facilitate greater visibility. Relatedly, these clusters can materialise as creative hubs, which are themselves the focus of an emerging research stream (Pratt, 2021; Pratt et al., 2019) in urban and rural contexts (Hill, 2021; Hill et al., 2021; Merrell et al., 2021a). Yet, we still need to understand how the allocation of studio spaces and hub productivity is impacted by existing ownership and management structures. Moreover, we need to foreground the voices of hub users, the resident artisan entrepreneurs (Pratt, 2021) in enterprise hubs, to gain further insights into the living worlds of co-located creative entrepreneurs (Hill, 2021). Hence, creative hub research is one of the core areas for further research (Pratt & Gill, 2019) that will illustrate a vision for the *Future of Work* (OECD, 2019). Particularly, with the rising numbers of enterprise hubs (Merrell et al., 2021b), co-working spaces and other types of shared and temporary work arrangements outside of homes (as a result of COVID-19-induced lockdown phases), this clustering will only increase. These insights will also provide lessons for industries outside of the CCIs (Hill, 2021), as many more sectors increasingly focus on less core employed workers, outsourcing highly specialist functions to freelancers; as the post-COVID-19 months have shown, these freelancers will use some form of co-working spaces. Managers and freelancers alike need to discover how to manage these new ways of working from the positive effects of working from home, in isolation, to synergy effects of co-working spaces, using the same space with other freelancers (Merrell et al., 2021b). Creative professionals have fine-tuned insights such as these over time.

5.3. Subsectors Within the CCI and Their Entrepreneurship

Craft entrepreneurship has recently gained attention (Bell et al., 2018; Hill, 2021; Pret & Conan, 2019; Ratten et al., 2022). Yet, topics such as how daily activities of income generation unfold, following a passion, and garnering community support, need greater investigation in the future. Similarly, community creative entrepreneurship is an overlooked area; some artists self-identify as *community artists*, whose core purpose is supporting local communities through teaching in schools and beyond and making a difference to community life. Yet another subsector in need of further research is gaming and video creation businesses (Wirtz, 2020).

5.4. Impact of Recent Significant External Economic Events

We have so far minimal understanding regarding the effects of the triple impact of Brexit, the COVID-19 pandemic and the Ukrainian war on creative and cultural entrepreneurship in the UK and throughout Europe. The UK has entered a period of significant political instability with the likelihood of a long-lasting economic recession. This development will undoubtedly lead to higher failure rates by small and medium enterprises, along with increased challenges for the CCI business community and their changing markets. These creative firms will need to demonstrate considerable resilience to ensure survival, which researchers need to continue investigating, ideally with longitudinal studies considering the ecosystem in detail (OECD, 2018).

ACKNOWLEDGEMENTS

We are very grateful to the authors and reviewers for the generosity of their time; they were critical in bringing these two volumes to fruition. Moreover, we thank the publisher Emerald for their ongoing support and the opportunity to publish these two volumes.

REFERENCES

Balfour, B., Fortunato, M.-P., & Alter, A. (2018). The creative fire: An interactional framework for rural arts-based development. *Journal of Rural Studies, 63*, 229–239.

Bell, D., & Jayne, M. (2010). The creative countryside: Policy and practice in the UK rural cultural economy. *Journal of Rural Studies, 26*(3), 209–218.

Bosworth, G., & Turner, R. (2018). Interrogating the meaning of a rural business through a rural capitals framework. *Journal of Rural Studies, 60*, 1–10.

Courage, C. (2021). Preface: The radical potential of placemaking. In: C. Courage, T. Borrup, M. R. Jackson, K. Legge, A. Mckeown, L. Platt, & J. Schupbach (Eds.), *The Routledge handbook of placemaking* (pp. 217–223). Routledge.

Department for Culture Media & Sports (DCMS). (2016). *Creative industries economic estimates methodology.* DCMS. Retrieved, December 1, 2022, from https://assets.publishing.service.gov.uk/government/uploads/system/uploads/attachment_data/file/499683/CIEE_Methodology.pdf

Elias, S. R. S. T. A., Chiles, T. H., & Crawford, B. (2022). Entrepreneurial imagining: How a small team of arts entrepreneurs created the world's largest traveling carillon. *Organization Studies, 43*, 203–226.

Elias, S. R. S. T. A., Chiles, T. H., Duncan, C. M., & Vultee, D. M. (2018). The aesthetics of entrepreneurship: How arts entrepreneurs and their customers co-create aesthetic value. *Organization Studies, 39*, 345–372.

Federal Reserve Bank of San Francisco. (2019). Transforming community development through arts and culture. Federal Reserve Bank of San Francisco Community Development Innovation Review 2019-2. Retrieved, August 20, 22, from https://www.frbsf.org/wp-content/uploads/sites/3/transforming-community-development-through-arts-and-culture.pdf

Hill, I. (2021). Spotlight on UK artisan entrepreneurs" situated collaborations: Through the lens of entrepreneurial capitals and their conversion. *International Journal of Entrepreneurial Behavior & Research, 27*(1), 99–121

Hill, I. (2022). Ethnographic methods for capturing the sociomateriality of entrepreneurial practices. In N. Thompson, O. Byrne, B. Teague, & A. Jenkins (Eds.), *Research handbook on entrepreneurship as practice* (pp. 266–280). Research handbooks in business and management series. Edward Elgar Publishing.

Hill, I., Manning, L., & Frost, R. (2021). Rural arts entrepreneurs' placemaking – How 'entrepreneurial placemaking' explains rural creative hub development during COVID-19 lockdowns. *Local Economy, 36*(7–8), 627–649.

Hill, I., & Mole, K. (2022). State of the art review. *Supporting rural businesses*. National Innovation Centre for Rural Enterprise. SOTA Review 4. Newcastle. https://nicre.co.uk/media/1wmhonux/nicre-sota-no-4-july-2022-supporting-rural-businesses.pdf

Hill, I., & Rowe, F. (2021a). *Rural creative industries – An untapped potential for UK economic recovery*. National Innovation Centre for Rural Enterprise. https://nicre.co.uk/blog/2021/may/rural-creative-industries-an-untapped-potential-for-uk-economic-recovery/

Hill, I., & Rowe, F. (2021b). *Bridging enterprise, policy and practice: Creating social and public value*. Working Paper. Institute of small business and enterprise annual conference, Cardiff.

Jones, P., Klapper, R., Ratten, V., & Fayolle, A. (2018). Emerging themes in entrepreneurial behaviours, identities and contexts. *International Journal of Entrepreneurship and Innovation, 19*(4), 233–236.

Klamer, A. (2011). Cultural entrepreneurship. *The Review of Austrian Economics, 24*(2), 141–156.

McElwee, G. (2022). Artisan enterprise in the rural economy: Drystone walling in North Yorkshire. In L. D. Dana, -V. Ramadani, R. Palalic, & A. Samzadeh (Eds.), *Artisan and handicraft entrepreneurs. Past, present and future* (pp.71–88). Springer.

Merrell, I., Fuzi, A., Russell, E., & Bosworth, G. (2021b). How rural co-working hubs can facilitate well-being through the satisfaction of key psychological needs. *Local Economy, 36*(7–8), 606–626.

Merrell, I., Rowe, F., Cowie, P., & Gkartzios, M. (2021a). 'Honey pot' rural enterprise hubs as microclusters: Exploring their role in creativity-led rural development. *Local Economy, 36*(7–8), 589–605.

Meyrick, J., & Barnett, T. (2021). From public good to public value: Arts and culture in a time of crisis. *Cultural Trends, 30*(1), 75–90.

Murcia, C. Q., Kreutz, G., Clift, S., & Bongard, S. (2010). Shall we dance? An exploration of the perceived benefits of dancing on well-being. *Arts & Health: An International Journal of Research, Policy and Practice, 2*(2), 149–163.

OECD. (2018). The value of culture and the creative industries in local development. *Handbook*. https://www.oecd.org/cfe/leed/2018-SACCI-Handbook.pdf

OECD. (2019). The future of work. OECD Employment Outlook 2019. *Highlights*, New York, NY.

Office for National Statistics (ONS). (2022). *Creative, cultural and digital industries. Employment, employees, and turnover in the UK 2017–2021*. https://www.ons.gov.uk/businessindustryandtrade/business/activitysizeandlocation/adhocs/15046creativeculturalanddigitalindustries

Orlikowski, W. J., & Scott, S. V. (2016). Digital work: A research agenda. In B. Czarniawska (Ed.), *A research agenda for management and organisation studies* (pp. 88–95). Cheltenham, UK and Northampton, MA, USA: Edward Elgar Publishing.

Pitts, F. H. (2015). A hidden history: Defining and specifying the role of the creative industries. *Creative Industries Journal, 8*(1), 73–84.

Pratt, A., Virani, T. E., & Gill, R. (2019). Introduction. In: R. Gill, A. Pratt, & T. E., & Virani (Eds.), *Creative hubs in question* (pp. 1–26). Palgrave Macmillan.

Pratt, A. C. (2021). Creative hubs: A critical evaluation. *City, Culture and Society*, *24*, 100384.

Pret, T., & Cogan, A. (2019). Artisan entrepreneurship: A systematic literature review and research agenda. *International Journal of Entrepreneurial Behavior and Research*, *25*(4), 529–614.

Quin, E., Redding, E., & Frazer, L. (2007). *Dance science research report*. Hampshire Dance, Laban, Arts Council England.

Ratten, V., Jones, P., Braga, V., & Parra-López, E. (2022). *Artisan entrepreneurship*. Emerald Publishing.

Roberts, E., & Townsend, L. (2016). The contribution of the creative economy to the resilience of rural communities: Exploring cultural and digital capital. *Sociologia Ruralis*, *56*(2), 197–219.

Schwartz, S. (2006). A theory of cultural value orientations: Explication and applications. *Comparative Sociology*, *5*(2–3), 137–182.

Siepel, J., Camerani, R., Masucci, M., Velez Ospina, J., Casadei, P., & Bloom, M. (2020). Creative industries radar. Mapping the UK's creative clusters and microclusters. Creative Industries Policy & Evidence Centre. NESTA.

Siepel, J., Velez Ospina, J. A., Camerani, R., Bloom, M., Masucci, M., & Casadei, P. (2021). *Creative Radar 2021: The impact of COVID-19 on the UK's creative industries*. Creative Industries Policy and Evidence Centre.

Stickley, T., Paul, K., Crosbie, B., Watson, M., & Souter, G. (2015). Dancing for life: An evaluation of a UK rural dance programme. *International Journal of Health Promotion and Education*, *53*(2), 68–75.

Thompson, N. A., Verduijn, K., & Gartner, W. B. (2020). Entrepreneurship-as-practice: Grounding contemporary theories of practice into entrepreneurship studies. *Entrepreneurship & Regional Development*, *32*, 247–256.

Throsby, D. (2008). The concentric circles model of the cultural industries. *Cultural Trends*, *17*(3), 147–164.

UNCTAD. (2018). Creative economy outlook. Trends in international trade in creative industries 2002–2015. UNCTAD.

UNESCO. (1982). *Cultural industries: A challenge for the future of culture*. UNESCO.

UNESCO. (2018). *Reshaping cultural policies*. Retrieved, November 16, 2022, from https://uis.unesco.org/sites/default/files/documents/reshaping-cultural-policies-2018-en.pdf

UNESCO. (2021). *International year of creative economy for sustainable development*. https://en.unesco.org/commemorations/international-years/creativeeconomy2021

United Nations (UN). (2015). *17 Goals to transform our world*. https://www.un.org/sustainabledevelopment/. United Nations.

United Nations Industrial Development Organisation (UNIDO) (2017). *Agro-food, tourism and creative industries. An integrated cluster approach*. UNIDO.

Velez, J. E., Siepel, J., Hill, I., & Rowe, F. (2022). Mapping and examining the determinants of England's rural creative microclusters. NICRE Research Report. No. 7. National Innovation Centre for Rural Enterprise and Creative Industries Policy & Evidence Centre. https://nicre.co.uk/media/xlnpaeli/nicre-research-report-no-7-with-creative-pec-may-2022-mapping-and-examining-the-determinants-of-england-s-rural-creative-microclusters.pdf

Walmsley, B., Gilmore, A., O'Brien, D., & Torreggiani, A. (2022). *Culture in crisis impacts of Covid-19 on the UK cultural sector and where we go from here*. Centre for Cultural Value, Leeds University. Retrieved, November 17, 2022, from https://www.culturehive.co.uk/CVIresources/culture-in-crisis-impacts-of-covid-19/

Welter, F. (2011). Contextualizing entrepreneurship – Conceptual challenges and ways forward. *Entrepreneurship Theory and Practice*, *35*(1), 165–184.

Wirtz, B. W. (2020). Business models and value creation in the video and gaming market. In B. W. Wirtz (Ed.), *Media management* (pp. 169–182). Springer Texts in Business and Economics.

CONCEPTUAL REFLECTIONS ON CCI ENTREPRENEURSHIP

CHAPTER 2

ENTREPRENEURSHIP RESEARCH IN CULTURAL AND CREATIVE INDUSTRIES: IDENTIFYING KEY INGREDIENTS OF A 'HODGEPODGE'

Ellen Loots

ABSTRACT

The aim of this chapter is to provide a relevant theoretical contribution to the field of entrepreneurship in cultural and creative industries (CCI) and suggestions for a research agenda. Entrepreneurship research is characterised by an apparent fragmentation, even if scholars advocate the development of a 'stronger paradigm' to strengthen the discipline. Rather than making explicit what is specific to entrepreneurship in CCI, or delineating the boundaries of a new community of scholars, in this chapter, the author attempts to identify certain key ingredients of a 'hodgepodge'. The Schumpeterian entrepreneur, the opportunity seeker, and the everyday entrepreneur are introduced as well as an action model in which the reciprocal agency–structure relationship finds a place. It is highlighted how theories such as the Theory of Planned Behaviour, Social Identity Theory, Institutional Theory, Practice Theory, and Paradox Theory (can) inform research on entrepreneurship in CCI.

Keywords: Entrepreneurship; cultural and creative industries; action model; theory; agency; structure; motivation; self-efficacy

Creative (and Cultural) Industry Entrepreneurship in the 21st Century
Contemporary Issues in Entrepreneurship Research, Volume 18A, 17–30
Copyright © 2024 by Ellen Loots
Published under exclusive licence by Emerald Publishing Limited
ISSN: 2040-7246/doi:10.1108/S2040-72462023000018A002

The aim of this chapter is to provide a relevant theoretical contribution to the field of entrepreneurship in CCI and suggestions for a research agenda for entrepreneurship in CCI. While the attempt to formulate a theory of entrepreneurship in the field of cultural activities is far from new (DiMaggio, 1982; Peterson & Berger, 1971) and the parallels between creative and entrepreneurial activities have been highlighted (Barry, 2011; Sexton & Smilor, 1986), the accumulating entrepreneurship research offers opportunities for studying CCI. However, the field of entrepreneurship research is characterised by an apparent fragmentation, even if scholars have long advocated the development of a 'stronger paradigm' to strengthen the discipline (Davidsson et al., 2001). Such fragmentation is the result of the various disciplines of entrepreneurship scholars including psychology, sociology, economics, finance, and strategic management (Gartner et al., 2006). Recently, it was argued that: 'Without a common conceptual core, the ongoing call for increased contextualisation threatens to accelerate the fragmentation of the field and to encumber the progression of knowledge about entrepreneurship' (McMullen et al., 2021, p. 1198).

Rather than making explicit what is specific to entrepreneurship in CCI or delineating the boundaries of a new community of scholars, in this chapter, I attempt to identify certain key ingredients of the 'hodgepodge' (Shane & Venkataraman, 2000) of entrepreneurship research that can advance the (theoretical) understanding of CCI activities. By doing so, I hope to enlighten researchers, educators, students, and practitioners about the promising future of entrepreneurship in CCI.

1. THREE TYPES OF ENTREPRENEURS

At least three archetypical entrepreneurs have been distinguished in the literature: the Schumpeterian entrepreneur, the opportunity seeker, and the everyday entrepreneur. All are associated with something new: from radical innovations, through novel opportunities, to the establishment of new companies.

1.1. Radical Innovators

According to Joseph Schumpeter, entrepreneurs are unique change agents who are responsible for innovation. In his *theory of economic development*, entrepreneurs carry out new combinations in different ways, for example, by introducing new goods or production methods, opening up new markets, or reorganising an industry (Schumpeter, 1934).

Creativity – a key input in CCI – is considered to be a, if not *the* source of innovation (Amabile, 1996). Artists are sometimes seen as innovators and entrepreneurs who disrupt markets with their new, creative products (Ellmeier, 2003). However, the radical changes in product type, processes, and entire value chains that Schumpeter's theory refers to are observable within CCI as well. A pioneering article by Peterson and Berger (1971), sociologists with an interest in the phenomenon of entrepreneurship, documents entrepreneurial innovation at the industry level. The authors explain how in the turbulent environment of music production in the 1960s, a new role emerged, which disrupted the traditional value chain. The move towards a more sustainable fashion industry accompanied by the circular fashion and textile movement, or the growing interest in community engagement and participatory models in museums, may serve as contemporary examples of innovations that depend on the entrepreneurial activity of newcomers or incumbent companies to introduce radical change.

1.2. Opportunity Seekers

Entrepreneurship can be associated with novel opportunities. Indeed, 'opportunity' is the keyword in one of the most cited papers in entrepreneurship research. According to Shane and Venkataraman (2000, p. 218), entrepreneurship relates to the opportunities to create future goods and services that can be 'discovered, evaluated, and exploited'. A stream of literature has illustrated this approach, for example, by distinguishing between the processes of discovering and exploiting opportunities and relating each to business success. An important insight is that individuals make different estimations of the potential success of an opportunity. For example, new and experienced entrepreneurs value opportunities differently (Baron & Ensley, 2006). This resonates with the comparison between the 'business' opportunities that young geniuses (such as Picasso) and old masters (Cézanne) typically identify in the arts, as shown by Galenson (2011).

The definition of entrepreneurship in CCI used by Chang et al. (2021) articulates entrepreneurial discovery in line with Shane and Venkataraman (2000):

> Cultural entrepreneurs are therefore not necessarily artists, but those who discover opportunities by observing and creating connections between the subjective meanings of the cultural production and the intersubjectivity developed across consumer networks, groups, and markets.

1.3. The Self-employed as Founders of New Businesses

Entrepreneurship may also refer to the mere act of starting a new business. Welter et al. (2017, p. 314) coin the notion of 'everyday entrepreneurship' as an alternative to entrepreneurship that 'valorizes economic outcomes of wealth accumulation and job creation as the supreme and often the only goal'. In CCI, making a living out of someone's creativity is a potentially attractive career path. Individuals who are self-employed establish a 'new' business. Scholars engaged in critical labour studies have discussed the risks, precariousness, inequalities, and injustices (e.g. Banks, 2017; de Peuter, 2011) that arise from the current organisation of CCI including its strong focus on freelancing and 'gigging'. Cultural economists identify creative individuals' preference for this type of work as the cause of low incomes (e.g. Throsby, 2007). In this context, many studies suggest the need for a more appropriate entrepreneurial education. These studies seek to identify the knowledge, skills, and attitudes that are needed to increase the chances of success of entrants to CCI and the survival rates of micro-businesses.

These three entrepreneurial types are depicted at the centre of Fig. 1. Next, the precursors of such entrepreneurship are explored, followed by structure, in a CCI context.

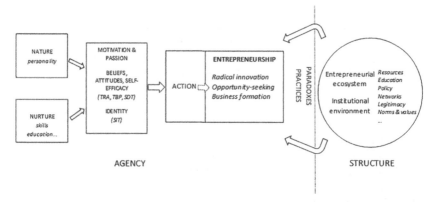

Fig. 1. A Theoretical Foundation Model for Entrepreneurship Research (in CCIs).

2. NATURE, NURTURE

The nature versus nurture debate in the entrepreneurship realm, which is grounded in psychology, involves the question whether someone's preferences and behaviour are the results of either inherited or acquired influences. Entrepreneurial behaviour has been explained by properties of individuals such as personality, knowledge, attitudes, motivation, and preferences (see, e.g., Frese & Gielnik, 2014). The baseline in various theoretical angles is that individuals possess specific features to a greater or lesser extent, which lead to preferences and attitudes that form the basis for *action* in the realm of entrepreneurship. There is no entrepreneurship without action, but what leads to (appropriate) action (and if this is the result of nature or nurture) is still unclear.

2.1. Action and Its Antecedents

Several scholars theorise that action is at the heart of entrepreneurship. Without action, features such as personality, motivation, education, and knowledge will not affect any phase in the entrepreneurial process – be it identifying opportunities, acquiring resources, survival, or growth.

2.1.1. Motivation and Passion

First, in the *action characteristics model*, Frese and Gielnik (2014) argue that different action characteristics lead to different outcomes in different phases of the entrepreneurship process. The more specific the construct, the more likely it will influence entrepreneurial outcomes. For example, motivation is more specific compared with someone's personality. In the model, cognitive and social preconditions such as education and family examples (nurture) and personality traits such as the need for achievement and risk-taking (nature) co-exist and are positioned at an equal distance from entrepreneurial outcomes. This means that nature and nurture characteristics jointly feed into the passion and motivational antecedents that lead to the actions (searching for opportunities, planning, processing feedback, and seeking resources) required for entrepreneurship (Frese & Gielnik, 2014).

2.1.2. Attitudes, Beliefs, and Self-efficacy

A second theory that acknowledges the important role of action comes from social psychology. Fishbein and Ajzen (1975) theorise action in their *Theory of Reasoned Action* (TRA). This theory posits that behavioural intentions are the immediate antecedents to behaviour and a function of someone's beliefs that a particular behaviour will lead to a particular outcome. These beliefs, in turn, underlie someone's attitude towards performing the behaviour as well as the person's subjective norms related to doing this. TRA postulates that other variables can influence someone's behaviour as long as they affect either someone's attitude or subjective norms. In other words, innate traits, as well as external influences such as education, could affect someone's behavioural intentions and behaviour as long as they affect a person's attitude or norms. In a much-cited follow-up article, Ajzen (1985) extends the theory by including 'perceived behavioural control' as an exogenous variable with a direct and indirect effect on behaviour. The *Theory of Planned Behavior* identifies 'perceived behavioural control' as a construct that captures (the magnitude of) someone's beliefs of owning the resources and opportunities for performing a specific behaviour. The interest of entrepreneurship scholars in Ajzen's (1985) theory can be traced back to the articulation of this belief – the confidence that someone has in their opportunities – as an important precursor to entrepreneurial behaviour. It strongly resonates with a very prominent notion in entrepreneurship research, namely self-efficacy (Bandura, 1977).

2.1.3. Social Identity

Third, *Social Identity Theory* assesses a person's identity as an important predictor of behavioural choices and actions (Tajfel & Turner, 1979). Someone's social identity increases their sensitivity and receptivity to certain cues for behaviour. On the other hand, individuals tend to display behaviours and actions consistent with their identity. Underlying someone's identity are their social interactions and identification with particular social groups. Membership in specific social categories serves as a frame of reference for self-evaluation and establishing self-worth (Turner et al., 1987). Two identity studies related to entrepreneurship are worth noting. First, Cardon et al. (2009) distinguish three entrepreneurial identities that stir the passion for starting a venture: an *inventor role identity* sets in motion a passion for activities such as exploring opportunities, a *founder role identity* underlies a passion for activities such as exploiting opportunities, and a *developer role identity* epitomises a passion for activities related to growing a business. Second, Fauchart and Gruber (2011) distinguish between *Darwinians* who possess a social identity type suited to becoming a successful founder of a company in regular competitive market systems, *communitarians* who view their companies as social objects, and *missionaries* who see their companies as political objects.

Taken together, someone's motivation and self-belief – and the identity that someone most strongly identifies with – are important precursors to the entrepreneurial activity of any sort: founding, running, or growing a business. As such, the question with which this section started (nature or nurture) has over the years been refined by entrepreneurship scholars, inviting researchers to consider action and the various aspects that lead to action.

2.2. Nature and Nurture in CCI

The nature/nurture debate has been less explicit in a CCI context. There is considerable support within society for the view that artists are born with a vocation or calling, an innate talent. There is also the understanding that artists create out of a passion, regardless of market demand. Self-efficacy and passion have been identified as prominent precursors to entrepreneurial activity in CCI (Bhansing et al., 2018; Cardon & Kirk, 2015; Shaw et al., 2021). At the same time, abundant literature articulates how challenging it is to merge artistic and entrepreneurial aspects within a single person, career, organisation, education programme, or policy (Bhansing et al., 2012; Bilton et al., 2020; Eikhof & Haunschild, 2006; Schediwy et al., 2018).

Studies have started to explore the psychological traits and deep motives of individuals wishing to start or pursue an artistic career (Hofmann et al., 2021), and how these differ among creatives and across groups (Caniëls et al., 2014). The *Theory of Planned Behavior* (Ajzen, 1985) has served as a frame of reference (Chen et al., 2017) as well as the motivational *Self Determination Theory* developed by Ryan and Deci (2000) (Cnossen et al., 2019). In addition, the skills and capabilities that young artists need after graduating are explored in arts entrepreneurship education research. The notion of 'identity' has been applied to emerging musicians: bohemian and entrepreneurial career identities are conceptualised and related to career development choices (Schediwy et al., 2018).

Already in their pioneering work on identity, Fauchart and Gruber (2011) advance the view that the identity types of the 'communitarians' and 'missionaries' could be recognised in entrepreneurship in CCI. Hence, communitarians tend to rely on personal capabilities, deploy 'highly individualized and artisanal production methods (products often considered works of art)' (p. 947), and oppose using intellectual property rights protection as that runs counter to their values of sharing and community. Missionaries wish to address society as their audience, make use of new social (consumption) practices, and deploy new or socially responsible production methods (Fauchart & Gruber, 2011). So far, evidence of the micro-foundations of creative work is too limited and scattered to enable drawing general conclusions. In other words, there are plenty of avenues for future research.

3. AGENCY, STRUCTURE

In the above, the entrepreneur is seen as an innovator, opportunity seeker, or business owner, whose agency was highly likely to depend on their social identity, action, and specific features such as self-efficacy, passion, and creativity. However, what has been largely ignored until now is the role of the environment in which an entrepreneur operates. A great deal has been written about the relationship between agency and structure. In social theories, structures are considered to be constituted by 'rules' (Giddens, 1979) or 'schemas' such as 'conventions, recipes, scenarios, principles of action, and habits of speech and gesture' (Sewell, 1992, p. 8). Structures shape people's practices and imply agency, which arises from an actor's knowledge of schemas and control of resources. Sewell's (1992, p. 20) observation that 'a capacity for agency – for desiring, for forming intentions, and for acting creatively – is inherent in all humans' is the perfect bridge to entrepreneurship. Indeed, the mere desire to set up an enterprise is a clear manifestation of agency.

3.1. The Impact of the Environment on Entrepreneurship

Entrepreneurship and entrepreneurs can experience constraints as well as enablers that originate in their environment. These may include the availability or lack of resources, regulation, supportive governments, and societal norms related to entrepreneurship. Jointly and separately, constraints and enablers affect the rate and size of new venture creation, the nature of the entrepreneurial agency of individuals and groups as well as the entrepreneurial climate of an area. Approaches such as that of the entrepreneurial ecosystem and institutional theory provide useful lenses to look more closely at the structural features of the environment for entrepreneurship.

3.1.1. The Entrepreneurial Ecosystem

An *entrepreneurial ecosystem* (EE) has been conceived of as the entirety of 'benefits and resources produced by a cohesive, typically regional, community of entrepreneurs and their supporters that help new high-growth ventures form, survive, and expand' (Spigel & Harrison, 2018, p. 152). The strength and functionality of EE are a result of the continuous 'development and flow of entrepreneurial resources such as human and financial capital, entrepreneurial know-how, market knowledge, and cultural attitudes' (Spigel & Harrison, 2018, p. 152). This notion, which has long been embraced by policy-makers, has in recent years been approached by scholarship with increasing conceptual rigour, with the wish to make its theoretical underpinnings more explicit (Wurth et al., 2021).

Similar to *Cluster Theories* (Porter, 2000) and (*Entrepreneurial*) *Regional innovation systems arguments* (Cooke, 2001), the developing EE theory relies on a neo-Schumpeterian view of regional innovative capacity and a neo-Marshallian view of the advantages of clustering. It embraces the processes that drive clusters and regional innovation systems: economies of scale, economies of scope, and knowledge spill overs. Concretely, EE studies scrutinise the localised economic and social contexts and the role in those contexts of various elements – the stickiness of workers and knowledge, cognitive proximity and networks, education, policy, and the availability of other resources – in stimulating the entrepreneurship process over time (Mack & Mayer, 2016).

3.1.2. Institutional Theory

The influential *institutional theory* also explains how structure affects agency. It is preoccupied with the regulatory, social, and cultural influences (Scott, 1987) that have an impact on the legitimacy and survival of organisations (Bruton et al., 2010). Rather than downplaying social forces as motives of action, institutional theorists emphasise the roles of contextual structures and processes (rules, norms, beliefs) that are taken for granted (institutionalised) and affect organisational behaviour, with entrepreneurship as a case in point (Bruton et al., 2010). Numerous case studies have elicited how entrepreneurial organisations need to behave in accordance with the explicit and implicit norms and values in their environment and understand what is appropriate and important to gain the legitimacy necessary to deploy their activities (Bruton et al., 2010; Powell & DiMaggio, 1991; Suchman, 1995). The social environment encourages particular strategies and behaviours that will lead to the legitimacy of (new) companies (Aldrich & Fiol, 1994), which confers on them the right to exist and develop.

Neither institutional approaches nor ecosystem approaches are ignorant of the reciprocal relationship between agency and structure. As an example, the concept of *institutional entrepreneurship* refers to the efforts of individual actors or groups that establish or change their institutional context by infusing new norms and values into social structures (Powell & DiMaggio, 1991). Also, the ecosystem perspective focuses on the agency-structure interaction by acknowledging the socially embedded nature of the entrepreneurship process as well as the involvement of various actors, resources, and capabilities (Spigel & Harrison, 2018).

3.2. Agency and Structure in CCI

The reciprocal agency-structure relationship has regularly been considered in research on CCI, mainly in terms of the theoretical perspective of the externalities and feedback dynamics that result from *geographic clustering* and *Marshallian external economies* in urban contexts (e.g. Chapain et al., 2010; Potts, Hartley et al., 2008a). On the other hand, the location decisions of many creative workers (employed, self-employed, and business owners) are theorised as being informed by the quality of a place in terms of its economic advantages, social aspects, and aesthetic and cultural properties (Florida, 2005; Scott, 2006). The lenses of clustering practices and agglomeration economies have been applied to study the motives of creative workers that make use of coworking spaces as appealing working environments (Wijngaarden, 2019). Studies combine a micro/agency perspective and a macro/structure perspective to examine how the interplay between individual properties and the qualities of an environment (structural features) affects localised entrepreneurship. Specifically, for the development of a workforce capable of maintaining or lifting an EE-specific knowledge base, individuals need to acquire skills, but equally a 'cultural normalization' of career goals and work habits among considerable numbers of workers must take place. Whereas the application of the EE framework to CCI has been limited, for example, in a case study of Porto (Loots et al., 2021), the institutional perspective on CCI has had broader applications (Lindkvist & Hjorth, 2015; Lounsbury & Glynn, 2019). The enforcement of intellectual property rights and the consequences for investment in innovations is a manifestation of institutional entrepreneurship that is relevant to CCI as well as the case of governments that affect the operations of museums and other cultural organisations by requiring business planning (Bruton et al., 2010; Oakes et al., 1998).

4. PROMISING APPROACHES: PARADOXES, PRACTICES

As suggested, there is a need for more research in the various aspects of agency regarding entrepreneurship in CCI, for example, through a (social) psychology lens with a focus on motives, self-perceptions, and identities. Also, studies of how the interplay between agency and structure affects entrepreneurship in a place, possibly by combining institutional, clustering, and ecosystem perspectives, are welcomed. Whereas the above focus on entrepreneurs (micro) and their environment (macro), there are plenty of opportunities to study the 'meso-level' of entrepreneurship. *Paradoxes* and *practices* in entrepreneurship and CCI go beyond the individual level but are still more controllable features compared with the structural characteristics of an environment.

4.1. Paradoxes

CCI is characterised by a challenging relationship between arts and commerce (Caves, 2000). There are theories that explain how the cultural value of creative production is connected to the realisation of economic value (Potts, Cunningham et al., 2008). One example is the **core-*periphery spill-over model*** (Throsby, 2008), which suggests that labour and capital investments in the core arts (e.g. visual and performing arts and literature) eventually spill over to the more commercial outputs of sectors such as design, advertising, and film. However, pertinent in entrepreneurship are the issues of how creative companies experience a tension between creativity and money, and how they commonly deal with conflicting interests.

Paradox theory assumes that organisations could be confronted with paradoxes. Paradoxical in the operations of companies in CCI is, first, that 'their capacity to generate profits and sustain their business operations depends on the willingness and ability of the employees to be constantly creative and generate novel solutions' (Rozentale & van Baalen, 2021). Second, being able to continuously engage in such creative efforts depends on the resources and the efficiency of the company (Lampel et al., 2000). According to this theory, entrepreneurs who face paradoxes must adopt a 'both/and' mindset and be prepared to recognise and deal with the duality of two or more poles in their operations (Rozentale & van Baalen, 2021). Integration is a strategy by which conflicting goals can be addressed simultaneously. A design agency, for example, could rely on 'in-house resourcing' for offering design solutions: creative and production activities are then both executed internally. As such, the paradox perspective focuses on individual level characteristics as key to overcoming paradoxes, including mindsets and leadership styles (Smith et al., 2012), yet also on company-level features, such as decision-making, business models, and strategies (Rozentale & van Baalen, 2021).

Understanding how to deal with paradoxes is not exclusive to entrepreneurial companies nor does the capability of managing paradoxes guarantee successful entrepreneurship. However, being able to integrate practices that allow a company to 'thrive on paradoxal synergies' (Rozentale & van Baalen, 2021) could challenge companies to develop innovative business models, which may eventually be adopted by other companies within an industry. In this manner, paradoxes have the potential to affect individual entrepreneurs as well as the context in which they operate from the moment critical numbers of entrepreneurs start to adopt new ways in which businesses operate.

4.2. Practices

Practice theory is positioned somewhat in the middle between agentic and structural views of the world. In contrast to the views of entrepreneurship as mere individual cognition and behaviour embedded within institutions or social structures, the practice approach in entrepreneurship research advances the view that all entrepreneurial phenomena are 'taking place within, and are aspects or components of, the nexus of practices' (Thompson et al., 2020). Practices include networking practices, resourcing practices, decision-making practices, strategising practices, hiring practices, selling practices, and so forth. Such practices are organised around a shared practical understanding of how things are supposed to be. In line with Giddens (1984), Thompson et al. (2020) state that practices are phenomena that 'link up to form wider complexes and constellations'. Theories of practice put forward an ontological position in which social phenomena such as organisations, strategy, power, science, meaning, as well as entrepreneurship, are the formative components within a nexus of practices (Hui et al., 2017).

Within their value chains, CCI entail a multitude of practices such as selection, intermediation, and certifying practices (Caves, 2000; Loots, 2019; Wijnberg, 2004), various coworking, co-creation, and collaborative practices as well as practices of production and funding, distribution and selling, and buying and consumption (Bourdieu, 1993). A few examples from within the entrepreneurship realm are the practice of career development through mobilising and converting various forms of capital (financial, social, cultural) in the Do-It-Yourself music scene (Scott, 2012), and the practice of company growth through first getting acquainted with the conventions and later spotting competitive advantages in CCI such as fashion and design (Loots & van Bennekom, 2022). In their case study of how a choreographer redefined the social practice of dance, Bizjak et al. (2017) elicit how practice is constituted by dimensions such as space, embodiment, and aesthetics and lays at the roots of crucial artistic as well as entrepreneurial decisions.

5. AN AGENDA FOR ENTREPRENEURSHIP RESEARCH IN CCI

In this chapter, I reviewed entrepreneurship in CCI through a theoretical lens. Research on entrepreneurship in CCI must take stock of the type of entrepreneurship under scrutiny: ground-breaking innovations by Schumpeterian entrepreneurs that disrupt existing systems, novel opportunities that allow for entrepreneurial initiatives to emerge, or the phenomenon of new business formation by many creative individuals trying to make a living out of their passion.

While different manifestations of entrepreneurship lead to different scholarly approaches, reinforced by the heterogeneity of the disciplines with an interest in the matter, one common ground is *action*. It is crucial that entrepreneurship research in CCI relies on (social) psychology literature to investigate to what extent motivation and passion, self-efficacy, and the identification with specific archetypes (social identities) are precursors to entrepreneurial action. There is no agency without structure, though. Future studies can rely on institutional and ecosystem theories that seek to explain the reciprocal relationship between various aspects within the entrepreneurial environment and entrepreneurial activity at the individual as well as overarching levels. Much scope remains for really *theorising* paradoxes and practices in entrepreneurship and CCI research rather than simply describing them. Paradoxes and practices provide angles to tackle unresolved dualities such as those between nature and nurture, and agency and structure. For example, there is scope for research on how paradoxes pave the way for business model innovation in CCI, and how entrepreneurial artists affect the social practice of an art genre.

This chapter has ignored *capital theories* (Becker, 2009; Bourdieu, 2018) or the *ambidexterity literature* in which the two-fold agenda of strategically combining exploration and exploitation takes centre stage (Gibson & Birkinshaw, 2004). *Effectuation theory* and *bricolage theory* are other examples of theories that consider strategic action at the company level as a major precursor to many activities, including entrepreneurship. The *entrepreneurial orientation* construct, which recognises the importance of creativity and innovation at the strategic firm level, has not been discussed (Lumpkin & Dess, 1996). However, the suggested avenues for future research, with the recommendation to incorporate practices and paradoxes in studies, open doors for thorough examinations of entrepreneurship in CCI and beyond.

ACKNOWLEDGEMENT

The author acknowledges Instituut Gak for financial support.

REFERENCES

Aldrich, H. E., & Fiol, C. M. (1994). Fools rush in? The institutional context of industry creation. *The Academy of Management Review*, *19*(4), 645–670.

Ajzen, I. (1985). *From intentions to actions: A theory of planned behavior.* Springer Berlin Heidelberg.

Amabile, T. M. (1996). *Creativity in context: Update to the social psychology of creativity*. Westview Press.

Bandura, A. (1977). Self-efficacy: Toward a unifying theory of behavioral change. *Psychological Review*, *84*(2), 191.

Banks, M. (2017). *Creative justice: Cultural industries, work and inequality: Cultural industries, work and inequality*. Rowman & Littlefield Publishers.

Baron, R. A., & Ensley, M. D. (2006). Opportunity recognition as the detection of meaningful patterns: Evidence from comparisons of novice and experienced entrepreneurs. *Management Science, 52*(9), 1331–1344.

Barry, D. (2011). Art and entrepreneurship, apart and together. In M. Scherdin & I. Zander (Eds.), *Art entrepreneurship* (pp. 154–168). Cheltenham, UK and Northampton, MA: Edward Elgar Publishing.

Becker, G. S. (2009). *Human capital: A theoretical and empirical analysis, with special reference to education.* University of Chicago Press.

Bhansing, P. V., Hitters, E., & Wijngaarden, Y. (2018). Passion inspires: Motivations of creative entrepreneurs in creative business centres in the Netherlands. *The Journal of Entrepreneurship, 27*(1), 1–24.

Bhansing, P. V., Leenders, M. A., & Wijnberg, N. M. (2012). Performance effects of cognitive heterogeneity in dual leadership structures in the arts: The role of selection system orientations. *European Management Journal, 30*(6), 523–534.

Bilton, C., Eikhof, D. R., & Gilmore, C. (2020). Balancing act: Motivation and creative work in the lived experience of writers and musicians. *International Journal of Cultural Policy, 27*(6), 738–752.

Bizjak, D., Calcagno, M., & Sicca, L. M. (2017). Going back to the roots of entrepreneurship. *Academia Revista Latinoamericana de Administración, 30*(2), 173–191.

Bourdieu, P. (1993). *The field of cultural production: Essays on art and literature.* Columbia University Press.

Bourdieu, P. (2018). *The forms of capital.* Routledge.

Bruton, G. D., Ahlstrom, D., & Li, H. (2010). Institutional theory and entrepreneurship: Where are we now and where do we need to move in the future? *Entrepreneurship Theory and Practice, 34*(3), 421–440.

Caniëls, M. C., De Stobbeleir, K., & De Clippeleer, I. (2014). The antecedents of creativity revisited: A process perspective. *Creativity and Innovation Management, 23*(2), 96–110.

Cardon, M. S. & Kirk, C. P. (2015). Entrepreneurial passion as mediator of the self-efficacy to persistence relationship. *Entrepreneurship Theory and Practice, 39*(5), 1027–1050.

Cardon, M. S., Wincent, J., Singh, J., & Drnovsek, M. (2009). The nature and experience of entrepreneurial passion. *Academy of Management Review, 34*(3), 511–532.

Caves, R. E. (2000). *CreativeFl industries: Contracts between art and commerce* (Issue 20). Harvard University Press.

Chang, Y.-Y., Potts, J., & Shih, H.-Y. (2021). The market for meaning: A new entrepreneurial approach to creative industries dynamics. *Journal of Cultural Economics, 45*(3), 491–511.

Chapain, C., Cooke, P., De Propris, L., MacNeill, S., & Mateos-Garcia, J. (2010). *Creative clusters and innovation: Putting creativity on the map.* NESTA.

Chen, M.-H., Chang, Y.-Y., Wang, H.-Y., & Chen, M.-H. (2017). Understanding creative entrepreneurs' intention to quit: The role of entrepreneurial motivation, creativity, and opportunity. *Entrepreneurship Research Journal, 7*(3), 1–15.

Cnossen, B., Loots, E., & van Witteloostuijn, A. (2019). Individual motivation among entrepreneurs in the creative and cultural industries: A self-determination perspective. *Creativity and Innovation Management, 28*(3), 389–402.

Cooke, P. (2001). Regional innovation systems, clusters, and the knowledge economy. *Industrial and Corporate Change, 10*(4), 945–974.

Davidsson, P., Low, M. B., & Wright, M. (2001). Editor's introduction: Low and MacMillan ten years on: Achievements and future directions for entrepreneurship research. *Entrepreneurship Theory and Practice, 25*(4), 5–15.

de Peuter, G. (2011). Creative economy and labor precarity: A contested convergence. *Journal of Communication Inquiry, 35*(4), 417–425.

DiMaggio, P. (1982). Cultural entrepreneurship in nineteenth-century Boston: The creation of an organizational base for high culture in America. *Media, Culture & Society, 4*(1), 33–50.

Eikhof, D. R., & Haunschild, A. (2006). Lifestyle meets market: Bohemian entrepreneurs in creative industries. *Creativity and Innovation Management, 15*(3), 234–241.

Ellmeier, A. (2003). Cultural entrepreneurialism: On the changing relationship between the arts, culture and employment. *International Journal of Cultural Policy, 9*(1), 3–16.

Fauchart, E., & Gruber, M. (2011). Darwinians, communitarians, and missionaries: The role of founder identity in entrepreneurship. *Academy of Management Journal, 54*(5), 935–957.

Fishbein, M., & Ajzen, I. (1975). Belief, attitude, intention, and behavior: An introduction to theory and research, Reading, MA: Addison-Wesley.

Florida, R. (2005). *Cities and the creative class*. Routledge.

Frese, M., & Gielnik, M. M. (2014). The psychology of entrepreneurship. *Annual Review of Organizational Psychology and Organizational Behavior, 1*(1), 413–438.

Galenson, D. W. (2011). Old masters and young geniuses. In *Old masters and young geniuses*. Princeton, NJ: Princeton University Press.

Gartner, W. B., Davidsson, P., & Zahra, S. A. (2006). Are you talking to me? The nature of community in entrepreneurship scholarship. *Entrepreneurship Theory and Practice, 30*(3), 321–331.

Gibson, C. B., & Birkinshaw, J. (2004). The antecedents, consequences, and mediating role of organizational ambidexterity. *Academy of Management Journal, 47*(2), 209–226.

Giddens, A. (1979). *Central problems in social theory: Action, structure, and contradiction in social analysis* (Vol. 241). University of California Press.

Giddens, A. (1984). *The constitution of society: Outline of the theory of structuration*. Polity Press.

Hofmann, R., Coate, B., Chuah, S., & Arenius, P. (2021). What makes an artrepreneur? An exploratory study of artrepreneurial passion, personality and artistry. *Journal of Cultural Economics, 45*, 557–576.

Hui, A., Schatzki, T., & Shove, E. (2017). *The nexus of practices: Connections, constellations, practitioners*. Routledge.

Lampel, J., Lant, T., & Shamsie, J. (2000). Balancing act: Learning from organizing practices in cultural industries. *Organization Science, 11*(3), 263–269.

Lindkvist, L., & Hjorth, D. (2015). Organizing cultural projects through legitimising as cultural entrepreneurship. *International Journal of Managing Projects in Business, 8*(4), 696–714.

Loots, E. (2019). Strings attached to arts funding: Panel assessments of theater organizations through the lens of agency theory. *The Journal of Arts Management, Law, and Society, 49*(4), 274–290.

Loots, E., Neiva, M., Carvalho, L., & Lavanga, M. (2021). The entrepreneurial ecosystem of cultural and creative industries in Porto: A sub-ecosystem approach. *Growth and Change, 52*(2), 641–662.

Loots, E., & van Bennekom, S. (2022). Entrepreneurial firm growth in creative industries: Fitting in… and standing out! *Creative Industries Journal*. doi:10.1080/17510694.2022.2025710

Lounsbury, M., & Glynn, M. A. (2019). *Cultural entrepreneurship: A new agenda for the study of entrepreneurial processes and possibilities*. Cambridge University Press.

Lumpkin, G. T., & Dess, G. G. (1996). Clarifying the entrepreneurial orientation construct and linking it to performance. *Academy of Management Review, 21*(1), 135–172.

Mack, E., & Mayer, H. (2016). The evolutionary dynamics of entrepreneurial ecosystems. *Urban Studies, 53*(10), 2118–2133.

McMullen, J. S., Brownell, K. M., & Adams, J. (2021). What makes an entrepreneurship study entrepreneurial? Toward a unified theory of entrepreneurial agency. *Entrepreneurship Theory and Practice, 45*(5), 1197–1238.

Oakes, L. S., Townley, B., & Cooper, D. J. (1998). Business planning as pedagogy: Language and control in a changing institutional field. *Administrative Science Quarterly, 43*(2), 257–292.

Peterson, R. A., & Berger, D. G. (1971). Entrepreneurship in organizations: Evidence from the popular music industry. *Administrative Science Quarterly, 16*(1), 97–106.

Porter, M. E. (2000). Location, competition, and economic development: Local clusters in a global economy. *Economic Development Quarterly, 14*(1), 15–34.

Potts, J., Cunningham, S., Hartley, J., & Ormerod, P. (2008). Social network markets: A new definition of the creative industries. *Journal of Cultural Economics, 32*(3), 167–185.

Potts, J., Hartley, J., Banks, J., Burgess, J., Cobcroft, R., Cunningham, S., & Montgomery, L. (2008). Consumer co-creation and situated creativity. *Industry & Innovation, 15*(5), 459–474.

Powell, W. W., & DiMaggio, P. J. (Eds.). (1991). *The new institutionalism in organizational analysis* (1st ed.). University of Chicago Press.

Rozentale, I., & van Baalen, P. J. (2021). Crafting business models for conflicting goals: Lessons from creative service firms. *Long Range Planning, 54*(4), 102092.

Ryan, R. M., & Deci, E. L. (2000). Self-determination theory and the facilitation of intrinsic motivation, social development, and well-being. *American Psychologist, 55*(1), 68–78.

Schediwy, L., Bhansing, P. V., & Loots, E. (2018). Young musicians' career identities: Do bohemian and entrepreneurial career identities compete or cohere? *Creative Industries Journal, 11*(2), 174–196.

Schumpeter, J. (1934). *The theory of economic development: An inquiry into profits, capital, credit, interest, and the business cycle.* Transaction Publishers.

Scott, M. (2006). Entrepreneurship, innovation and industrial development: Geography and the creative field revisited. *Small Business Economics, 26*(1), 1–24.

Scott, M. (2012). Cultural entrepreneurs, cultural entrepreneurship: Music producers mobilising and converting Bourdieu's alternative capitals. *Poetics, 40*(3), 237–255.

Scott, W. R. (1987). The adolescence of institutional theory. *Administrative Science Quarterly*, 493–511.

Sewell, W. H., Jr. (1992). A theory of structure: Duality, agency, and transformation. *American Journal of Sociology, 98*(1), 1–29.

Sexton, D. L., & Smilor, R. W. (1986). The art and science of entrepreneurship. University of Illinois at Urbana-Champaign's Academy for Entrepreneurial Leadership Historical Research Reference in Entrepreneurship. https://ssrn.com/abstract=1496717

Shane, S., & Venkataraman, S. (2000). The promise of entrepreneurship as a field of research. *Academy of Management Review, 25*(1), 217–226.

Shaw, A., Kapnek, M., & Morelli, N. A. (2021). Measuring creative self-efficacy: An item response theory analysis of the creative self-efficacy (CSE) scale. *Frontiers in Psychology, 12*, 2577.

Smith, W. K., Besharov, M. L., Wessels, A. K., & Chertok, M. (2012). A paradoxical leadership model for social entrepreneurs: Challenges, leadership skills, and pedagogical tools for managing social and commercial demands. *Academy of Management Learning & Education, 11*(3), 463–478.

Spigel, B., & Harrison, R. (2018). Toward a process theory of entrepreneurial ecosystems. *Strategic Entrepreneurship Journal, 12*(1), 151–168.

Suchman, M. C. (1995). Managing legitimacy: Strategic and institutional approaches. *Academy of Management Review, 20*(3), 571–610.

Tajfel, H., & Turner, C. (1979). An integrative theory of intergroup conflict. In W. G. Austin & S. Worchel (Eds.), *The social psychology of intergroup relations* (pp. 33–47). Brooks/Cole.

Thompson, N. A., Verduijn, K., & Gartner, W. B. (2020). Entrepreneurship-as-practice: Grounding contemporary theories of practice into entrepreneurship studies. *Entrepreneurship & Regional Development, 32*(3–4), 247–256.

Throsby, D. (2007). Preferred work patterns of creative artists. *Journal of Economics and Finance, 31*(3), 395–402.

Throsby, D. (2008). The concentric circles model of the cultural industries. *Cultural Trends, 17*(3), 147–164.

Turner, J. C., Hogg, M. A., Oakes, P. J., Reicher, S. D., & Wetherell, M. S. (1987). *Rediscovering the social group: A self-categorization theory.* Basil Blackwell.

Welter, F., Baker, T., Audretsch, D. B., & Gartner, W. B. (2017). Everyday entrepreneurship – A call for entrepreneurship research to embrace entrepreneurial diversity. *Entrepreneurship Theory and Practice, 41*(3), 311–321.

Wijnberg, N. M. (2004). Innovation and organization: Value and competition in selection systems. *Organization Studies, 25*(8), 1413–1433.

Wijngaarden, Y. (2019). *Spaces of co-working: Situating innovation in the creative industries.* Erasmus University.

Wurth, B., Stam, E., & Spigel, B. (2021). Toward an entrepreneurial ecosystem research program. *Entrepreneurship Theory and Practice, 46*(3), 1042258721998948.

CHAPTER 3

CULTURAL AND ARTS ENTREPRENEURSHIP: THE IMPORTANCE OF BEING AESTHETIC

Simony R. Marins and Eduardo P. B. Davel

ABSTRACT

The very soul of cultural and arts entrepreneurship (CAE) is aesthetic. However, what is the importance of being aesthetic in CAE? An understanding of aesthetics substantially improves both our comprehension of CAE and our capacity to theorise about entrepreneurship and creative industries. Furthermore, when seeking to understand CAE, the authors expand their knowledge about aesthetics, an ordinary but complex and neglected kind of knowledge. The authors mobilise three perspectives in organisational aesthetics theory (sensible knowing, connection, and judgements) to develop and propose initial ways to connect aesthetics to CAE. These perspectives help to explore and explain the vital importance of aesthetics in CAE and its innovation process. Aesthetics is a source of innovation in CAE, and the authors propose to perceive entrepreneurial innovations as aesthetic learning, persuasion, and flow.

Keywords: Cultural entrepreneurship; arts entrepreneurship; aesthetics; innovation; aesthetic entrepreneuring; organisational aesthetics theory

Creative (and Cultural) Industry Entrepreneurship in the 21st Century
Contemporary Issues in Entrepreneurship Research, Volume 18A, 31–43
Copyright © 2024 by Simony R. Marins and Eduardo P. B. Davel
Published under exclusive licence by Emerald Publishing Limited
ISSN: 2040-7246/doi:10.1108/S2040-72462023000018A003

1. INTRODUCTION

In this chapter, we argue that aesthetics is important in improving how we theorise CAE and its innovation. Specifically, aesthetic knowledge (Strati, 1999) leads us to better understand how entrepreneurs embody judgements in the creation of goods or experiences such as the beautiful harmonies in songs that allow our sensibilities to flow. Also, aesthetics can enlighten how, as an audience, we influence these creations based on shared delight. Moreover, aesthetics can help to explore how these aesthetic creations and expressions are related to the construction, diffusion, and change of ideas, translating value and promoting innovations in new ways of living.

Aesthetics is especially what shapes the cultural and artistic fields (Becker, 1951; Laan & Kuipers, 2016), nourishing CAE in multiple and varied ways (Scherdin & Zander, 2011). As subsets of the creative industries (Jones et al., 2015), the cultural and arts industries rely on entrepreneurship that produces perceptions, feelings, and emotions. Indeed, aesthetics allows the creation of goods with significant symbolic value, producing cultural novelty and change, that is, genuine aesthetic advances in culture (Cunningham & Potts, 2015; Hirsch, 1972; Khaire, 2015; Klamer, 2011). Referring directly to aesthetic evocations (Beckman, 2015; Elias et al., 2018; Klamer, 2011; Lindkvist & Hjorth, 2015) in relation to art and culture, CAE integrates critical discussions concerning the different attributes of aesthetic and economic issues (Essig, 2017; Hausmann & Heinze, 2016; Marins & Davel, 2020). Therefore, for aesthetically oriented ventures, aesthetics plays a critical role (Bryan & Harrys, 2015): it is the origin, process, outcome, and energy of entrepreneurship.

However, what is aesthetics? We will follow what organisational aesthetics teaches us to simplify the beauty of aesthetics complexity (see Strati, 2019; Taylor & Hansen, 2005). Aesthetics is knowledge, the perceptions of our body in relation to the world – people, spaces, and materials – through the sensory experiences (sight, hearing, touch, smell, and taste), which contribute to the constitution of perceptions, taste, and connections, for example, through aesthetic categories (Strati, 1999; Taylor & Hansen, 2005). In other words, it is how entrepreneurs feel and perceive the world by transforming or translating these feelings into creations; for instance, music that you will like or not since this appreciation also depends on your aesthetic background or capital. Aesthetics is also increased through analyses regarding aesthetic capitalism, the experience economy, and the aestheticisation of society, in which the importance of the nexus of art, aesthetics, and entrepreneurship is expanded (Holm & Beyes, 2021; Reckwitz, 2017a). A better understanding of aesthetics opens up possibilities to understand the pain and delight of CAE, exploring its micro, meso, and macro aspects, that is, how aesthetics involves or enlaces culture and arts mainly in the contemporary creative economy. It may reveal both the aesthetic side of entrepreneurial life (see Gagliardi, 2006) and entrepreneurship as aesthetics, improving our conceptualisation of entrepreneurship (see Elias et al., 2018).

It is intriguing how few efforts have been made to increase aesthetic knowledge in CAE (e.g. Elias et al., 2018; Holm & Beyes, 2021; Marins & Davel, 2020). In general, some business approaches in CAE (e.g. marketing) flirt with the aesthetic issues without exploring its concept, for instance, when studies talk about the mystery of arts or the importance of the audience's tastes (e.g. Frankelius, 2011), which are aesthetic issues. Furthermore, the differences of innovation processes in CAE remain less explored than innovation in traditional sectors (Frankelius, 2011). The 'non-traditional' innovations should be taken seriously (Frankelius, 2011). Next, we (a) connect current CAE studies to three preliminary aesthetic perspectives and (b) discuss how aesthetics is a source of innovation. In doing so, we stimulate scholars to explore the different and valuable watercolour possibilities of aesthetics in CAE.

2. AESTHETICS IN CAE: AESTHETIC PERSPECTIVES TO AESTHETIC ENTREPRENEURING

2.1. Aesthetics as Sensible Knowing

Aesthetics is a type of dynamic knowledge acquired through senses, feelings, and perceptions (corporeality/embodiment) based on situated and tacit knowledge (Gagliardi, 2006; Strati, 2007) which is embodied in experience and practice in the world – body, space, and materiality (Gherardi, 2019; Strati, 1999, 2019). Thus, aesthetic knowledge is sensible knowing because it is based on practice. This means that, for example, music entrepreneurs learn on the job through experience. While enjoying the pleasure of making us dance, they are learning and knowing how to make us dance without immediately rationalising it. That is why learning and knowing are simultaneously interrelated in practice (Gherardi, 2019). As a knowledge, aesthetics can be scientifically studied, also improving methodological issues (Strati, 1999). Also, sensible knowing is the basis for the development of how arts and culture manifest themselves in practice (Strati, 2007, 2019).

To expand the CAE research, we suggest aesthetics as sensible knowing because, as we see in CAE, it sustains key entrepreneurial processes such as value co-creation, innovation, and entrepreneurship education. The co-creation of aesthetic value, for example, has been found through collaborative processes of imagining, contemplating, and building a consensus between artists and their consumers (Elias et al., 2018). In this case, sensible knowing occurs when the artist and consumer use the sapient body to interact and translate consumer desires and artistic skills into creation. This shows knowing in intersubjective processes and corporeal and micro interrelationships between people and the world.

Sensible knowing is used by cultural entrepreneurs to generate cultural innovations, for example, by improving music cultures through constant everyday negotiations during life (Marins & Davel, 2019). Cultural entrepreneurs' sensible knowing tacitly detects what is hard to perceive if they use only explicit knowledge. This is done through feelings and sensations that show, for example, what an audience likes (Marins & Davel, 2019). That is why sensible knowing becomes a competence practiced by popular entrepreneurs, who, stimulated through the culture, desire, and need to create art, also challenge the lack of specific CAE education (e.g. Marins & Davel, 2019). The different information that sensible knowing captures also creates variability to innovate. For example, by conducting an intellectual analysis of aesthetic issues (Taylor & Hansen, 2005) in dance practice, sensible knowing makes aesthetics an opportunity for the field, showing that a different set of dance practices is a prelude to a different kind of knowledge, for example, discipline and safety, shaping the way that we think and experience and the establishment of organisations and actions, reflecting in entrepreneurship (Bizjak et al., 2017). Sensible knowing also unravels criteria of originality to create and identify innovation (Santoro, 2006). As sensible knowing opens up new entrepreneurial avenues, it reveals the power of micro-analysis to conceive innovation differently.

As a form of knowledge, sensible knowing is recognised as improving CAE education. Considering subjective factors that are critical in aesthetics, such as authenticity, intuition, and beauty, as an aesthetic value exchange, one study suggests an aesthetic paradigm for ventures through the creation of an aesthetic framework in education (Bryan & Harris, 2015). This means considering the subjective needs of art students in aesthetic-inclusive curricula. Aesthetics as knowledge is especially suggested in *Creating Cultural Capital: Cultural Entrepreneurship in Theory, Pedagogy and Practice* (Kuhlke et al., 2015) by several authors, who argue, for example, for an aesthetic value-based system as strategic within educational curricula by offering more 'than learning about', but also 'learning to be' (see Levick-Parkin). Thus, aesthetic knowledge can help to understand and avoid cultural and aesthetic manipulation mechanisms when dealing with a cultural branding society (Poprawski, 2015). The focus of studies on aesthetic education strengthens the argument for aesthetics as a necessary competence for entrepreneurs. That is why similarities and differences between art and non-art entrepreneurs and the implications these distinctions have in the classroom have also been studied, and it has been argued that aesthetics is critical when distinguishing the two (Hart & Beckman, 2021). This highlights the difference between the aesthetic and non-aesthetic knowledge domains and the importance of improving aesthetic knowledge in CAE.

2.2. Aesthetics as Connection

In organisational aesthetics, aesthetics is situated in relational ontologies (Gherardi, 2019; Strati, 1999, 2019), presenting ideas such as empathy (Strati, 1999), belonging to social groups (Taylor & Hansen, 2005), attachment (Gherardi, 2019), and connection in action (Strati, 2019). Thus, aesthetics reveals a singular kind of relationship connecting bodies, objects, and the world. In other words, these relationships involve empathic interactions, belonging, and bonding with people, objects, and the world through the expressiveness of the body (Gagliardi, 1999). Also, it illustrates how historical, situated, and cultural factors intersubjectively (Gherardi, 2019; Strati, 2007) occur in cultural changes; therefore, how entrepreneurial creations result from explicit or implicit interactions mediated, for example, by taste. Aesthetics as a connection in CAE presents this idea.

Since knowledge occurs during interactions, aesthetics is knowledge-in-connection, creating aesthetic networks between people, ideas, and things, which, as a result, generates conditions for innovations. We highlight the co-creation of value as connections with people, and the co-creation of ideas through imaginative processes, showing how these connections reveal the political and the non-verbal character of aesthetics in legitimations.

Co-creating aesthetic value in relations between artists and consumers to create paintings shifts attention from an individualistic perspective to a shared perspective in entrepreneurship, in which 'neither the entrepreneur nor the customer has the final say' (Elias et al., 2018, p. 1). The shared perspective that defines aesthetic value as intersubjective is also implicit in imagination processes (Elias et al., 2018). Imagination generates an internal bodily connection between ideas in relation to external connections with the world. Unifying in the mind different artistic references through empathy, a new authentic style occurs as a kind of cross-fertilisation (Mitra, 2020). More explicitly, an aesthetic collective and creative process shows the ambiguity in creative projects in which a nexus of work or brokerage occurs to integrate ideas; for instance, it emerges from ideas of strategic actors that extract advantage from positions and relational experts that connect others to foster innovation in CAE (Lingo & O'Mahony, 2010). It also highlights how aesthetics as connections presents a political understanding, in which arts entrepreneurship is fundamentally aesthetic, necessarily situated, and invariably political (Holm & Beyes, 2021). The political aspect is special when meetings between different cultures generate value, nourishing different new creations (Frankelius, 2011). In other words, implicit and explicit aesthetic connections illustrate a flow of (different) sensations in innovations.

Aesthetics as connection values verbal and non-verbal negotiations. For example, in a tacit cultural routine based not only on words but also on affection and a sense of belonging, the creation of music, organisational forms, and innovations have been developed, embedding relations or networks within communities, amplified during the organisational career, in relations with a wider audience (Marins & Davel, 2019). These kinds of support crucially show another fundamental aspect of CAE: the legitimacy process. Aesthetic experience is a key issue to the achievement of CAE through the legitimacy of ideas and projects, where this legitimation concerns the creation of value (Khaire, 2015; Lindkvist & Hjorth, 2015).

Aesthetics as a connection treats the idea of aesthetic knowledge as a relational nexus that creates and supports organisations and their innovations, showing political dimensions and legitimation processes related to the creation of value. Indeed, people (e.g. artists and consumers), artefacts (e.g. technologies), insights (e.g. intuition and imagination), places, and experiences are interactive sources of sensemaking and 'aesthetic making'. Cultural and arts entrepreneurs are provoked to innovate in a flow of insights that stimulates spillovers throughout society (e.g. Cunningham & Potts, 2015), that is, forms of intersubjective connections and networks. These 'articulator-entrepreneurs generate new perceptions of what is acceptable and valuable', influencing broader cultural norms (Khaire, 2015, p. 212). Connection and acceptance became interrelated processes in which acceptance is a way to express judgements socially, being built between creators and the audience in negotiation processes that co-create value as judgements and legitimations. Aesthetics as a connection is like music: it unifies creators and the audience, flowing through the appreciation of what these groups have in common (or not).

2.3. Aesthetics as Criteria for Judgements

In organisational and sociological aesthetic theory, judgement is a set of criteria for differentiation or classification expressed by aesthetic categories (e.g. beauty; see Strati, 1999), taste (Bourdieu, 1984; Strati, 1999) and verbal and non-verbal communications (Strati, 1999). Aesthetic judgements are not part of a specific moment or activity in entrepreneurship. They are inseparable from every moment of entrepreneurship processes, practices, and outcomes. Aesthetic judgements consubstantiate entrepreneurship in terms of rational (e.g. what is better for entrepreneurship?) and aesthetic criteria (e.g. what is the most pleasant or beautiful entrepreneurship?). The aesthetic criteria for aesthetic judgements are also supported by intersubjective negotiation, ethics, and moral grounds (Gherardi, 2019). For example, a song may be considered beautiful because it triggers emotions while being morally acceptable. Entrepreneurs deal with this knowledge throughout the entrepreneurial process. Another important aspect of judgements is that they can create predominant aesthetic categories through reification processes, forging an organisational representation (Strati, 1999). Here is a practical example: imagine an audience that likes the songs of a specific band. Possibly, this audience will also like the band. So, that entrepreneurship will be, for example, lovely for a group. Therefore, judgements and their reification are related to what entrepreneurship recognises as a value in both the legitimation and authenticity processes, in which types of audiences capture entrepreneurship aesthetics (whether they are organically or commercially created).

Aesthetics as criteria for judgements appears in the current CAE research through the clear use of aesthetics and other categories and classifications such as both verbal and non-verbal communication, sustaining value creation, and innovation processes. Aesthetic categories and ethical and efficiency judgements, for example, in aesthetic forms (e.g. 'graceful', 'root' to mean authenticity, and 'beautiful' to mean correct functioning), have been used as popular parameters to create a popular cultural entrepreneurship (Marins & Davel, 2019). Taste, expressed as 'like', shows a verbal way to express correct directions in shared imaginary construction processes, persuading, and co-creating meaning in consensus-building processes (see Elias et al., 2018). 'Love' is also a verbal way to empathise taste in different understandings of persuasion (see Elias et al., 2018). Fundamentally, these examples show how aesthetics in CAE is explicitly or implicitly translated or transformed into value through innovation and co-creation processes.

Non-verbal aspects also mean degrees of appreciation (or value) and so of acceptance or legitimation. The non-verbal aspect of aesthetics is key because cultural entrepreneurship studies (e.g. Khaire, 2015; Lindkvist & Hjorth, 2015; Lounsbury & Glynn, 2019) place strength in verbal narratives to build legitimation. Aesthetics expresses intersubjective relevance through non-verbal communications such as gestures and expressions that are fundamentally significant in CAE (Marins & Davel, 2019). Artworks touch us through different ways.

Another example of aesthetics as judgement is the aesthetic mobility within the arts field in the classic division between 'low' and 'high' culture (Pedroni & Volante, 2014). For CAE, this means the value and aesthetic position in a market, that is, how the work is classified and practiced. These classificatory divisions are the result of groups of judgement that define the value of what is low or high, even though this type of division has changed in arts (Maanen, 2009). Judgements are revealed as value criteria, so aesthetics is revealed as value-building or as the value *per se*. Aesthetic judgements are also behind the social process that has transformed individual art into collective art, a process that not only produces a new art classification but also a new cultural and aesthetic category, influencing entrepreneurship (Santoro, 2006). The classificatory power of value is related to culture, taste, preferences, and identity to create innovations (Rentschler, 2007). Aesthetic judgements are interconnected with value, status, and innovation.

The importance of aesthetic judgement springs to the body when entrepreneurs present value and classify innovation as unexpected (e.g. Meisiek & Haefliger, 2011). Since the meaning of novelty in entrepreneurship is related to the aesthetic and ethical sentiments it evokes, the meaning of innovation is translated through value or legitimation processes of novelty throughout society (Meisiek & Haefliger, 2011). As success depends on audiences perceiving works as novelties, the value that CAE creates depends on how far its work rephrases and shifts views, not excluding the monetary relationship, but in a meaning-based one rather than needs-based one (Meisiek & Haefliger, 2011).

Therefore, innovation and value in CAE are about aesthetic judgement and that is also why scholars favour educational improvements that deal with aesthetic value exchange as a critical factor in the success of artistic ventures (Bryan & Harrys, 2015). The need for a flexible individualisation of taste can improve cultural education by strategically dealing with change, in which aesthetics has a critical power to deal with aesthetically informed cultural branding that shapes cultural identities, standards of aesthetic values, etc. (Poprawski, 2015). It is about the improvement of education through the strategic use of aesthetic knowledge and the power of making judgements. Increasing the capacity to judge boosts the quality of legitimations, their value, and the power of innovation.

3. AESTHETICS AS A SOURCE OF INNOVATION FOR CAE

The previous analysis allows us to describe how aesthetics is a source of innovation for CAE. The three aesthetic perspectives indicate ways that entrepreneurs deal with innovations through aesthetic knowing, connections, and judgements. First, aesthetics generates knowledge that acts tacitly while capturing feelings, emotions, tastes, reactions, and non-verbal expressiveness which is hard to perceive. This gives entrepreneurs an advantage in perceiving both what is familiar and what is different or new in terms of reactions in that field, which allows for the processual creation of variability. CAE studies talk about levels of originality or change (Frankelius, 2011; Khaire, 2015; White, 2019). This knowledge will be applied in creations (music, performance, actions) even in unconscious ways because these creations are about relations of pleasure between entrepreneurs and audiences.

Second, this knowing nourishes the connection with the audience through micro relations, aesthetic negotiations that create and sustain artworks and groups of tastes in these variabilities. Thus, taste variability also becomes an aesthetic resource. CAE talks about the role and type of audience, usually related to forms of legitimacy and the process of value creation (Frankelius, 2011; Lindkvist & Hjorth, 2015). Aesthetics promotes what is expressed, increasing opportunities for legitimations in forms of judgement (or value), reifications, and the creation of groups of tastes (or markets). That is the aesthetic variability in audience reception. Variability is crucial to innovations and entrepreneurship (Gartner, 2015; Islam et al., 2016).

Third, aesthetics also increases intuition processes about future tastes, that is, the possibility to not only understand but also feel what will have value and what will be supported by the audience (including stakeholders, etc.). Therefore, aesthetics creates conditions to indicate good or beautiful directions to help entrepreneurship concerning what is aesthetically new, engendering surprise, unexpected appreciations, and thus innovations. These beautiful surprises are the result of aesthetic complexity.

Therefore, aesthetics as a source of innovation for CAE, influencing different entrepreneurial processes, needs to be improved. For example, this micro power of aesthetics can play a particular role at the beginning of entrepreneurship, when the resources to have market information, for example, can be limited. Throughout entrepreneurship, aesthetics can show how innovations and authenticity are mediated.

3.1. CAE Innovations

Furthermore, aesthetics as a source of innovation is clear in CAE because of the special way in which these fields treat innovations. When scholars make efforts to classify innovation, they use understandings from the entrepreneurial world such as the terms 'connected', 'social', and 'open' innovation (e.g. Holm & Beyes, 2021; Mitra, 2020). This brings us closer to aesthetics, but still in a cold way. Nevertheless, the variability and diversity of innovation in the cultural and arts fields already start with the use of 'innovation' as a term. This is not as popular a term as more sociological, critical, aesthetic, and artistic concepts such as 'diversity', or 'conformity' and 'conventions', in which the reference is the lack of 'innovation' (Castañer & Campos, 2002). Even trying to differentiate incremental from disruptive innovation requires different reflections because of the aesthetics of this innovation. For example, in CAE, innovation highlights the strength of 'conventions', aesthetic standards or rules collectively dictate in art (Becker, 1974). Thus, the articulation between being and not being innovative matters. Below we present other innovative ideas aligned with cultural, artistic, and aesthetic understandings to illuminate reflections.

Cultural innovation can be conceived as changes in cultural meanings. Meaning generation, for example, occurs outside organisational boundaries but is usually provided by cultural organisations (Castañer, 2014). Management fields are working on this idea to create value through cultural meanings since cultural innovations make different statements about identities while offering new experiences, interpretations, and interactions associated with the innovation (Ravasi et al., 2012). This helps to create differentiation in organisations and to build new markets since it creates new patterns of demand (Ravasi et al., 2012). Seen as 'new ideologies' infused in products (Holt & Cameron, 2010 cited in Ravasi et al., 2012), cultural innovations differ from managerial innovations (Castañer, 2014). In the creative industries, cultural innovations have been analysed as innovations between novel invention and cultural familiarity, producing simultaneous feelings of intimacy and discovery, not having any clear new functionality (Islam et al., 2016). In CAE where creations embody different cultural meanings, helping to establish, transform and promote a cultural field of popular music (Marins & Davel, 2019).

Artistic innovation refers to changes in the arts. In artistic terms, 'non-conformity', divergences of repertoires or innovativeness (Dimaggio & Stenberg, 1985, p. 111) create new modes of thought and expression (Bourdieu, 1996), that is, the introduction to the field (or market) of something new (Castañer, 2014). Examples include the changes in visual arts between modern art (e.g. impressionism) and contemporary art (e.g. pop art). Through sociological lenses, artistic innovations can occur when artists discover 'a deviation from convention which heightened tension and created emotional response by virtue of its rarity', constantly creating, for example, 'small innovations' 'or deviations' (Becker, 1974, p. 773). That is what happens when a song creates a surprise emotion due to some technique, which will no longer be a surprise since it will be recurring, then becoming a convention in a certain genre or musical field. This is why innovation is field-dependent (Dimaggio & Stenberg, 1985). Yet, in an institutionalist conceptualisation, according to Bourdieu (1996), this kind of innovation depends on structural gaps in a field, being part of innovations in the field and partially depending on external forces. Artistic innovations can radically emerge from existing art conventions, whether locally or globally (Castañer & Campos, 2002). In organisational studies, artistic innovations are seen as the 'trajectory deployed over time by an artist's work', considering their style and aesthetics (Montanari et al., 2016, p.798). It can exhibit 'different degrees of novelty, depending on different referent conventions' – of the cultural field, a particular sub-field, or what an artist imposes on their work (Montanari et al., 2016, p.798). In CAE, artistic innovations present a new kind of art experience (Frankelius, 2011).

Aesthetic innovation involves changes in aesthetic codes, bodily experiences, and perceptions. In organisational and management fields, aesthetic innovation is seen as a central organisational process (Eisenman, 2013), creating additional value (Dalpiaz et al., 2016). When applied to products, aesthetic innovations can be perceived as radically different (Alcaide-Marzal & Tortajada-Esparza, 2007). As such, aesthetic innovations do not interfere with the new functionality or use of the product and increase the perceived value, satisfying taste, social image, and the preference for novelty (Alcaide-Marzal & Tortajada-Esparza, 2007). However, some concepts need to be improved given the advance of aesthetics in organisational studies. For example, seen as a subjective value, aesthetic innovations have been analysed as dependent on the eye of the beholder, taking place when a change is perceived by consumers, giving value to innovation by the means related to the novelty (Schweizer, 2002 in Alcaide-Marzal & Tortajada-Esparza, 2007). Aesthetics has been studied as intersubjective, presenting relational contributions between creators and their audience, which also highlights aesthetics as not only a result but also a process. Nevertheless, aesthetic innovation engenders new effects and experiences. It is the condition of the aesthetic work to mobilise the senses, which is *sine qua non* in the arts (Reckwitz, 2017b).

As we have seen, cultural and artistic innovations are related to aesthetic innovations, presenting aesthetic understandings: cultural innovations shape and are shaped by aesthetics; artistic innovations play with aesthetic aspects. However, little is known about these innovations and aesthetics is a complex field of study as it is largely unexplored in entrepreneurial and CAE research. Recent ideas in CAE can also help us to improve these types of 'aesthetic innovations', such as the innovation as process and practice understandings, which are aligned with the entrepreneurship as a process (Lindkvist & Hjorth, 2015) and practice perspectives (Marins & Davel, 2019). This creates opportunities to recognise the contextual, situated, and temporal aspects of innovation rather than seeing innovation as a simple and pure outcome (Frankelius, 2011; Meisiek & Haefliger, 2011). Plus, these 'aesthetic innovations' can improve the 'aesthetic side' of innovation, thus improving entrepreneurship.

4. DISCUSSION AND CONCLUSION

Aesthetics is crucial for CAE and its singular innovation processes. The three important aspects of aesthetic knowledge (sensible knowing, connection, and judgement) illustrated how CAE studies can be initially related to aesthetics. However, they are also relevant in illustrating entrepreneurial processes. Not only being about 'action or interaction' but 'something else altogether', entrepreneurship is about difference (Gartner, 2015, p. xxii). However, answering how and why the difference is created is a challenge (Gartner, 2015). Bringing the difference is a premise of aesthetics since aesthetics is a difference of feelings: manifesting its paradoxes, conflicts, fusions, interconnections, and specific interpretations (Strati, 1999). Specially, innovation is revealed through aesthetic understandings, in which the perception of the new or different is, first of all, aesthetic. Lying within the aesthetic processes of learning, interacting, and judging, entrepreneurship allows distinctive, sublime and valued creations, representations, reifications, legitimations, and different degrees or types of unexpected experiences or innovations. Thus, this intersubjective understanding of entrepreneurial innovation, the co-translation of difference, deserves special attention.

To guide further research, we approach innovation as substantially aesthetics since aesthetics highlights the embodied, judgemental, taste-driving, political, imbricated, fluid, blurred, symbolic, situated, ordinary, and reifying aspects of innovation. The previous concepts of innovation need to be improved. We suggest three understandings of innovation as aesthetics to contribute to CAE and entrepreneurship: (a) innovation as aesthetic learning, (b) innovation as aesthetic persuasion, and (c) innovation as aesthetic flow. Innovation as aesthetic learning emphasises the aesthetic process of learning to improve what are called soft skills, which are, in CAE, hard skills. Based on a kind of invitational rhetoric not related to domination and control but to openness and equality (Elias et al., 2018), innovation as aesthetic persuasion highlights how this process attractively embodies connections of judgements, being a connected *innovation-in-seduction*. Innovation as aesthetic flow focuses on how innovation moves through various taste connections, where innovation is created, supported, promoted, and disseminated to nourish new aesthetic processes. Therefore, we suggest innovation as aesthetic practice through processual lenses to improve CAE. This entrepreneurship becomes an aesthetic-making process, that is, a sensible, intersubjectively practiced process that plays with judgemental possibilities from the aesthetic perspective.

Adopting CAE and its innovation as aesthetics means challenging the traditionally individualistic entrepreneurship approach to embrace otherness in analyses and methods (see Steyaert, 2007; Taylor & Hansen, 2005). As aesthetics increases the possibility for inter/transdisciplinarity among entrepreneurial fields within arts and humanities, CAE has become a different and beautiful bridge to improve entrepreneurship. As this 'experience' can bring delight and pain, we offer suggestions for delightful aesthetic entrepreneuring.

ACKNOWLEDGEMENTS

We gratefully acknowledge the financial support of the Brazilian *Coordenação de Aperfeiçoamento de Pessoal de Nível Superior* (*CAPES*) and the Brazilian *Conselho Nacional de Desenvolvimento Científico e Tecnológico* (*CNPq*) as well as our reviewers and editors for their contributions.

REFERENCES

Alcaide-Marzal, J., & Tortajada-Esparza, E. (2007). Innovation assessment in traditional industries. A proposal of aesthetic innovation indicators. *Scientometrics*, *72*(1), 33–57. https://doi.org/10.1007/s11192-007-1708-x

Becker, H. (1974). Art as collective action. *American Sociological Review*, *39*(6), 767–776. https://doi.org/10.2307/2094151

Becker, H. (1951). The professional dance musician and his audience. *American Journal of Sociology*, *57*(2), 136–144. https://doi.org/10.1086/220913

Beckman, G. D. (2015). Entrepreneuring the aesthetic: Arts entrepreneurship and reconciliation. In T. Baker & F. Welter (Eds.), *The Routledge companion to entrepreneurship* (pp. 296–308). Routledge.

Bizjak, D., Calcagno, M., & Sicca, L. M. (2017). Going back to the roots of entrepreneurship: Empirical evidence from the practice of dance. *Academia Revista Latinoamericana de Administracion*, *30*(2), 173–191. https://doi.org/10.1108/ARLA-09-2015-0265

Bourdieu, P. (1996). *The rules of art, genesis and structure of the literary field*. Stanford University Press.

Bryan, T., & Harris, D. (2015). The aesthetic value exchange: A potential framework for the arts entre-
    preneurship classroom. *Journal of Arts Entrepreneurship Education, 1*(1), 25–54. https://doi.
    org/10.46776/jaee.v1.29
Castañer, X. (2014). Cultural innovation by cultural organizations. In V. A. Ginsburgh & D. Throsby
    (Eds.), *Handbook of the economics of art and culture*, (pp. 263–276). Elsevier.
Castañer, X., & Campos, L. (2002). The determinants of artistic innovation: Bringing in the role of organ-
    izations. *Journal of Cultural Economics, 26*(1), 29–52. https://doi.org/10.1023/A:1013386413465
Cunningham, S., & Potts, J. (2015). Creative industries and the wider economy. In C. Jones, M.
    Lorenzen, & J. Sapsed (Eds.), *The Oxford handbook of creative industries* (pp. 387–404). Oxford
    University Press.
Dalpiaz, E., Rindova, V., & Ravasi, D. (2016). Combining logics to transform organizational agency:
    Blending industry and art at Alessi. *Administrative Science Quarterly, 61*(3), 347–392. https://
    doi.org/10.1177/0001839216636103
Dimaggio, P., & Stenberg, K. (1985). Why do some theatres innovate more than others? An empirical
    analysis. *Poetics, 14*(1–2), 107–122. https://doi.org/10.1016/0304-422X(85)90007-5
Eisenman, M. (2013). Understanding aesthetic innovation in the context of technological evolution.
    Academy of Management Review, 38(3), 332–351. https://doi.org/10.5465/amr.2011.0262
Elias, S. R. S. T. A., Chiles, T. H., Duncan, C. M., & Vultee, D. M. (2018). The aesthetics of entrepre-
    neurship: How arts entrepreneurs and their customers co-create aesthetic value. *Organization
    Studies, 39*(2–3), 345–372. https://doi.org/10.1177/0170840617717548
Essig, L. (2017). Same or different? The "cultural entrepreneurship" and "arts entrepreneurship" con-
    structs in European and US higher education. *Cultural Trends, 26*(2), 125–137. https://doi.org/
    10.1080/09548963.2017.1323842
Frankelius, P. (2011). Innovation processes: Experience drawn from the creation of Dalhalla. In M.
    Scherdin & I. Zander (Eds.), *Art entrepreneurship* (pp. 98–141). Edward Elgar.
Gagliardi, P. (2006). Exploring the aesthetic side of organizational life. In S. Clegg, C. Hardy, & W.
    Nord (Eds.), *Handbook of organizational studies* (pp. 565–580). Sage.
Gartner, W. B. (2015). Foreword. In T. Baker & F. Welter (Eds.), *The Routledge companion to entrepre-
    neurship* (pp. xxi–xxiii). Routledge.
Gherardi, S. (2019). *How to conduct a practice-based study: Problems and methods.* Edward Elgar.
Hart, J. D., & Beckman, G. D. (2021). Aesthetics, medium, and method: An introduction to the differ-
    ences and similarities between arts and non-arts entrepreneurs. *Entrepreneurship Education and
    Pedagogy, 6*(1), 1–15. https://doi.org/10.1177/25151274211045696
Hausmann, A., & Heinze, A. (2016). Entrepreneurship in the cultural and creative industries: Insights
    from an emergent field. *Artivate: A Journal of Entrepreneurship in the Arts, 5*(2), 7–22. https://
    doi.org/10.1353/artv.2016.0005
Hirsch, P. M. (1972). Processing fads and fashions: An organization-set analysis of cultural industry
    systems. *American Journal of Sociology, 77*(4), 639–659.
Holm, D. V., & Beyes, T. (2021). How art becomes organization: Reimagining aesthetics, sites and
    politics of entrepreneurship. *Organization Studies, 43*(2), 227–245. https://doi.org/10.1177/
    0170840621998571
Islam, G., Endrissat, N., & Noppeney, C. (2016). Beyond 'the Eye' of the beholder: Scent innova-
    tion through analogical reconfiguration. *Organization Studies, 37*(6), 769–795. https://doi.
    org/10.1177/0170840615622064
Jones, C., Lorenzen, M., & Sapsed, J. Introduction. In C. Jones, M. Lorenzen, & J. Sapsed (Eds.), *The
    Oxford handbook of creative industries* (pp. 3–32). Oxford: Oxford University Press.
Khaire, M. (2015). Entrepreneurship in creative industries and cultural change: Art, fashion and
    modernity in India. In C. Jones, M. Lorenzen, & J. Sapsed (Eds.), *The Oxford handbook of crea-
    tive industries* (pp. 200–218). Oxford University Press.
Klamer, A. (2011). Cultural entrepreneurship. *Review of Austrian Economics, 24*(2), 141–156. https://
    doi.org/10.1007/s11138-011-0144-6
Kuhlke, O., Kooyman, R., & Schramme, A. (2015). *Creating cultural capital: Cultural entrepreneurship
    in theory, pedagogy and practice.* Pioneering Minds Worldwide.
van der Laan, E., & Kuipers, G. (2016). How aesthetic logics shape a cultural field: Differentiation and
    consolidation in the transnational field of fashion image, 1982–2011. *Poetics, 56*, 64–84. https://
    doi.org/10.1016/j.poetic.2016.01.001

Lindkvist, L., & Hjorth, D. (2015). Organizing cultural projects through legitimising as cultural entre-preneurship. *International Journal of Managing Projects in Business, 8*(4), 696–714. https://doi.org/10.1108/IJMPB-07-2015-0064

Lingo, E. L., & O'Mahony, S. (2010). Nexus work: Brokerage on creative projects. *Administrative Science Quarterly, 55*(1), 47–81. https://doi.org/10.2189/asqu.2010.55.1.47

Lounsbury, M., & Glynn, M. A. (2019). *Cultural entrepreneurship: A new agenda for the study of entre-preneurial processes and possibilities*. Cambridge University Press.

van Maanen, H. (2009). *How to study art worlds: On the societal functioning of aesthetic values*. Amsterdam University Press.

Marins, S. R., & Davel, E. P. B. (2019). Empreendedorismo como prática: Empreendedorismo cultural na pratica festiva do Pagode Baiano. *Revista Teoria e Prática em Administração, 9*(2), 14–34. https://doi.org/10.21714/2238-104X2019v9i2-43231

Marins, S. R., & Davel, E. P. B. (2020). Empreendedorismo cultural e artístico: Veredas da pesquisa acadêmica. *Revista Pensamento Contemporâneo em Administração, 14*(4), 115–140.https://doi.org/10.12712/rpca.v14i4.46268

Meisiek, S., & Haefliger, S. (2011). Inviting the Unexpected: Entrepreneurship and the arts. In M. Scherdin & I. Zander (Eds.), *Art entrepreneurship* (pp. 78–97). Edward Elgar.

Mitra, J. (2020). On regarding the value of aesthetics for entrepreneurship. In P. Formica & J. Edmondson (Eds.), *Innovation and the arts: The value of humanities studies for business* (pp. 73–90). Emerald Publishing Limited. https://doi.org/10.1108/978-1-78973-885-820201004

Montanari, F., Scapolan, A., & Gianecchini, M. (2016). 'Absolutely free'? The role of relational work in sustaining artistic innovation. *Organization Studies, 37*(6), 797–821. https://doi.org/10.1177/0170840616647419

Pedroni, M., & Volonté, P. (2014). Art seen from outside: Non-artistic legitimation within the field of fashion design. *Poetics, 43*(1), 102–119. https://doi.org/10.1016/j.poetic.2014.01.007

Poprawski, M. (2015). Cultural education organizations and flexible individualization of taste. *Journal of Organizational Change Management, 28*(2), 165–176. https://doi.org/10.1108/JOCM-01-2015-0018

Ravasi, D., Rindova, V., & Dalpiaz, E. (2012). The cultural side of value creation. *Strategic Organization, 10*(3), 231–239. https://doi.org/10.1108/JOCM-01-2015-0018

Reckwitz, A. (2017a). How to senses organize the social. In M. Jonas & L. Beate (Eds.), *Praxeological political analysis* (pp. 56–66). Routledge.

Reckwitz, A. (2017b). *The invention of creativity: Modern society and the culture of the new*. Polity.

Rentschler, R. (2007). Painting equality: Female artists as cultural entrepreneurial marketers. *Equal Opportunities International, 26*(7), 665–677. https://doi.org/10.1108/02610150710822302

Santoro, M. (2006). The Tenco effect. Suicide, San Remo, and the social construction of the can-zone d'autore. *Journal of Modern Italian Studies, 11*(3), 342–366. https://doi.org/10.1080/13545710600806862

Scherdin, M., & Zander, I. (2011). Emerging themes and new research openings. In M. Scherdin & I. Zander (Eds.), *Art entrepreneurship* (pp. 169–186). Edward Elgar Publishing.

Steyaert, C. (2007). "Entrepreneuring" as a conceptual attractor? A review of process theories in 20 years of entrepreneurship studies. *Entrepreneurship and Regional Development, 19*(6), 453–477. https://doi.org/10.1080/08985620701671759

Strati, A. (1999). *Organization and aesthetics*. Sage Publications.

Strati, A. (2007). Sensible knowledge and practice-based learning. *Management Learning, 38*(1), 61–77. https://doi.org/10.1177/1350507607073023

Strati, A. (2019). *Organizational theory and aesthetic philosophies*. Routledge.

Taylor, S. S., & Hansen, H. (2005). Finding form: Looking at the field of organizational aesthetics. *Journal of Management Studies, 42*(6), 1211–1231. https://doi.org/10.1111/j.1467-6486.2005.00539.x

White, J. (2019). A theory of arts entrepreneurship as organizational attack. *Artivate: A Journal of Enterprise in the Arts, 8*(2), 47–60. https://doi.org/10.1353/artv.2019.0002

CHAPTER 4

ON ENTREPRENEURIAL BRAINCHILDREN: THE CONCEPT OF INDITATION – TOWARDS A THEORY

Ulrike Posselt

ABSTRACT

This chapter introduces the concept of 'inditation' to the creative industries. The concept builds on an old verb 'to indite' and the noun 'inditing', meaning 'to make up' and 'to compose'. This chapter attempts to obtain the concept into the actual use of language. The term's meaning gets adjusted in the sense of a conceptual redesign. Furthermore, this chapter introduces the concept of 'inditation' as a process of composing 'the new' by creative entrepreneurs. They indite entrepreneurial brainchildren, 'the new', as unique outcomes such as artwork, product prototypes, or services. The chapter asks what it means to indite and contributes three autoethnographic examples. It also suggests that inditation could evolve a process-oriented framework for bringing 'the new' into the world and outlines further research towards constructing a theory of inditation.

Keywords: Inditation; indite; inditing; entrepreneurial brainchildren; autoethnography; creative industries; creative entrepreneurs

1. INTRODUCTION

Inditation works as a means to an end because it is directed to an outcome. The outcome of the process is aimed at balancing the needs of the creative entrepreneur and the needs of the potential customer or client.

Creative (and Cultural) Industry Entrepreneurship in the 21st Century
Contemporary Issues in Entrepreneurship Research, Volume 18A, 45–57
Copyright © 2024 by Ulrike Posselt
Published under exclusive licence by Emerald Publishing Limited
ISSN: 2040-7246/doi:10.1108/S2040-72462023000018A004

This chapter is aimed at creative entrepreneurs, clients and stakeholders, policy-makers, and grant providers. Creative entrepreneurs could reflect on their inditation processes. Clients and customers of creative entrepreneurs could enhance their understanding of creative, innovative processes, decision-making and issues related to inditation. Policy-makers and grant providers could comprehend the contribution of creative entrepreneurs and improve their knowledge of inditation to understand their mindset better and identify appropriate projects.

The first theory-oriented part of this chapter focuses on conceptualising terms, starting with a description of the terms. It provides examples of former use, followed by the recontextualisation of 'inditing' and the conceptualisation of 'inditation' by distinguishing the term from related concepts such as creation, ideation, intuition, inspiration, invention, and imagination. The practice-oriented second part provides examples relevant to the creative industries. The chapter also contributes an autoethnography; a qualitative research method from a first-person perspective, with examples of inditation by a practitioner, creative entrepreneur, and researcher. This part contributes three examples of inditation: unique results (such as artwork), product prototypes, and services. The last part outlines a roadmap for further research to establish or reject the concept further in constructing a theory of inditation.

In summary, this chapter invites the research community to constitute a framework to construct a theory of inditation within the field of creative entrepreneurship. It conceptualises inditation as an outline for a process- and practice-oriented methodology of bringing 'the new' into the world by creative entrepreneurs.

2. WHAT DOES IT MEAN 'TO INDITE', WHAT IS 'INDITING', AND WHAT IS 'INDITATION'?

The verb 'to indite' appears in van Manen's paper (van Manen & van Manen, 2021), concentrating on 'inditing' texts:

> The example can make the singular experienceable and thus knowable as an *indite* method of phenomenological writing. While the methods of the epoché and the reduction are engaged in an attempt to gain insights into the originary meaning of a phenomenon, it is the indite methods, the vocative aspects of writing, that assist in bringing phenomenological insights to textual understanding. The online Oxford English Dictionary defines the term 'indite' in this way: 'to put into words, compose (a poem, tale, speech, etc.); to give a literary or rhetorical form to (words, an address); to express or describe in a literary composition'. We use indite here to focus on the semiotic or writing practices that present the linguistic, methodological dimension to phenomenological thinking, inquiring, and writing. (pp. 1078, emphasis in original)

Merriam-Webster (n.d.) contributes:

> Indite looks like a misspelling of its homophone indict, meaning 'to charge with a crime', and that's no mere coincidence. Although the two verbs are distinct in current use, they are in fact related etymologically. Indite is the older of the two; it has been in the English language since the 1300s. Indict, which came about as an alteration of indite, appeared in the 16th century. Ultimately, both terms come from Latin indicere, meaning 'to make known formally' or 'to proclaim', which in turn comes from in- plus dīcere, meaning 'to talk, speak, or say'.

[…]

History and Etymology for indite

Middle English enditen, from Anglo-French enditer to write, compose, from Vulgar Latin *indictare, frequentative of Latin indicere to make known formally, proclaim, from in- + dicere to say

The term is rarely, though powerfully, used: Purcell (1685) and Handel (1727) composed, 'My heart is inditing'. Both compositions were coronation anthems for British Kings. The chorus sings a psalm: 'My heart is inditing a good matter: I speak of the things which I have made touching the king: my tongue *is* the pen of a ready writer' (*Bible King James Version Standard*, 2011, Psalm 45:1, emphasis in original). Poe used the term in his Marginalia in *Graham's Magazine*, March 1846:

Some Frenchman – possibly Montaigne – says: 'People talk about thinking, but for my part I never think except when I sit down to write'. It is this never thinking, unless when we sit down to write, which is the cause of so much indifferent composition. But perhaps there is something more involved in the Frenchman's observation than meets the eye. It is certain that the mere act of inditing tends, in a great degree, to the logicalisation of thought. Whenever, on account of its vagueness, I am dissatisfied with a conception of the brain, I resort forthwith to the pen, for the purpose of obtaining, through its aid, the necessary form, consequence, and precision. (Poe, 1846a)

To logicalise means to understand a logic behind something or to build a logical explanation, for example, in texts. This means focusing and clarifying thinking. I consent with van Manen's interpretation of the term – and attempt to 'reanimate' the term to obtain it into the actual use of language, combined with a conceptual adjustment in the sense of a conceptual redesign. Poe (1846) began his essay 'Philosophy of Composition' by quoting Charles Dickens; 'are you aware that Godwin wrote his "Caleb Williams" backwards?' and '[n]othing is more clear than that every plot, worth the name, must be elaborated to its *dénouement* before any thing be attempted with the pen' (Poe, 1846; emphasis in original). 'Dénouement' means an intention directed to the solution, outcome or output of a story, and he described his work on a poem in the essay. Poe continued, '[t]here is a radical error, I think, in the usual mode of constructing a story', and he 'prefer[red] commencing with the consideration of an *effect*' (Poe, 1846; emphasis in original). Poe controlled the writing process:

It is my design to render it manifest that no one point in its composition is referrible either to accident or intuition — that the work proceeded, step by step, to its completion with the precision and rigid consequence of a mathematical problem. (Poe, 1846)

Poe indited a poem. He composed by using a method that he described in the essay. Inditation is based on the experience of the inditer, the person who indites. It is a process that experts use, an inner search of options and playing with options to decide whether an option might work to bring 'the new' into the world. A form of 'the new' could be words, though not necessarily. For example, Poe indited texts, and Kant indited his Critique of Pure Reason for about 10 years before writing it on paper. Handel indited music, and Michelangelo indited paintings, drawings, and sculptures such as the sculpture of David.

Inditing might happen in a controlled manner, as with Poe. However, it may be that he had an idea before composing the text. The idea is crucial in inditation.

It could emerge in a seemingly immersed way as Philosopher Wittgenstein (1998, p. 24e) wrote: 'I really do think with my pen, for my head often knows nothing of what my hand is writing'. He described: 'Sometimes one sees ideas, as an astronomer sees stars in the far distance. (Or at least it seems so.)' (Wittgenstein, 1998, p. 66c), and '[t]he idea working its way towards the light' (Wittgenstein, 1998, p. 54c). There is fuzziness and vagueness in ideas. They might emerge as something that is seen or gets identified and even caught, captured, and formed. It means to choose and to decide on options. Inditation includes writing texts as an author, formulating music into notes as a composer, writing down a formula as a mathematician, or designing a service or a material product. Experts use the process and build on their experience and knowledge. Inditation is an inner search of options, inquiring about options and playing with options to decide whether an option might work. It is influenced by the expertise of the inditer as the outcome will be influenced by the person's experience and knowledge. The outcomes are perceivable by others through a medium, for example, a page with letters that form words. Frutiger (Fox, 2015), one of the most relevant contemporary-type designers, indited typefaces and signs. He said:

> If you remember the shape of your spoon at lunch, it has to be the wrong shape. The spoon and the letter are tools; one to take food from the bowl, the other to take information off the page .... When it is a good design, the reader has to feel comfortable because the letter is both banal and beautiful. (Campsie, 2015)

An inditer uses a tool (e.g. letter, spoon, number, pen, brush, and software) and a medium (e.g. paper, canvas, marble, and hardware) and forms an outcome. The inditer creates and designs something from almost nothing and sells it. Sells what? Hot air? A miracle? No. The creative entrepreneur indites the outcome of an inditation process. Creative entrepreneurs indite something they aim to sell later to make a living, such as Frutiger, and work in various sectors. The result could take various forms, for example, a book or a movie. The physically manifested outcome is not inditation anymore because the brainchild was manifested in physical, material gestalt, shape, and form. There might even be a tendency to skip a traditional, physical medium and sell digitally as software. The hard- and software are the body and carrier of the brainchild. The inditation process creates and shapes the identity of the brainchild, be it a corporate or brand identity. The concept of inditation might serve as a framework for constructing a theory of inditation. It might be a process of bringing 'the new' into the world. This might be at the heart of the creative industries, possibly, reaching beyond.

2.1. Distinguishing Inditation From Other Concepts

How can we distinguish inditation from other concepts such as creation, ideation, intuition, inspiration, invention, and imagination?

Creation means the act of bringing something into existence such as creatures and plants. The term creation has anaffiliation with God creating the universe, earth, creatures, and plants. Creation relates to the teleological argument in philosophy that the universe is like a machine having an intelligent designer: God. Inditation does not include the making of living creatures, whether humans, animals, or plants. It is a process to bring 'the new' – an artifact – into the world such as unique artwork, prototypes and services, using creativity to indite an outcome. This is aimed to be sold to meet the needs of the creative entrepreneur and the customer or client. These needs might be in a balance of fairness. However, the inditer decides to see him- or herself connected to a higher order that might have a name.

Ideation is a creative process to generate ideas and aims more towards the number of ideas. Ideation is included in inditation because ideation could be integrated at any stage in the inditation process where alternatives, variations or add-ons are searched. Inditation enhances the quality of a concept in the imagination; it plays, transforms, and optimises it over time.

Intuition is a tricky concept. First, in German philosophy, it seems to mean observing something, as in the German term 'Anschauung' translated into intuition by Kant's and Husserl's translators. Second, intuition means inner knowledge. For example, in a drawing: a painter might intuit the golden ratio without measuring. Third, it means to have a sudden inner insight, for example, in the shower or middle of the night. Intuition could be the dawn of an inditation process.

Inspiration – possibly even trickier than intuition – is an impulse from the outside that could start an inditation process. Someone might have said something, or you were inspired by words or music or the concept behind them. A concept could be convincingly 'true' and solid, which we might call a sound concept.

Invention means that an indited concept is 'born'. It came into existence and could be something 'new' that had never existed before. While the inventing process might be close, in inditation, the creative entrepreneur also 'plays' with ideas and includes the vision, mission, and business model. An invention is an outcome. It might become an innovation but not necessarily. Innovation is set up for earning money. An invention might never accumulate money but eventually burns much time and money. Inditation would include the mental invention process, where a material outcome becomes more apparent, like in a funnel. The outcome with the 'price tag' of an inditation process could be an invention or become an innovation, perhaps disruptive (Christensen, 1997; Christensen & Euchner, 2020). The evaluation of the outcome is an interpretation and not part of an inditation process.

Inditation uses the *imagination*. Sartre (2004) described the imagination and the imaginary:

> We may therefore conclude that imagination is not an empirical power added to consciousness, but is the whole of consciousness as it realises its freedom; every concrete and real situation of consciousness in the world is pregnant with the imaginary in so far as it is always presented as a surpassing of the real. (p. 186)

Inditation is a process in the entrepreneurial imagination (Elias et al., 2022) to clarify thinking. A creative entrepreneur indites a concept in the imaginary to sell the outcome of the process. Inditation is a mental process and method used by creative entrepreneurs where the output could be an innovation. It is the process of the birth of a unique outcome such as artwork, a prototype, service, or product. These are a means to an end as they include the creative entrepreneur's aim to sell successfully. A creative entrepreneur might aim for innovation and perhaps even disruptive, scalable innovation and a sustainable business model, integrating the vision, mission, and even parts of the strategy into the concept. The focus of this chapter is on creative entrepreneurs who indite by themselves.

3. WHAT DOES IT MEAN THAT CREATIVE ENTREPRENEURS INDITE?

This chapter contributes an autoethnography to clarify the concept. Autoethnography is a qualitative research method that builds on the ethnographic heritage and autobiography (Anderson & Glass-Coffin, 2022; Doloriert & Sambrook, 2012; Ellis et al., 2011). Autoethnography focuses on social embeddedness in a specific time and place and on experiences made by the autoethnographer. Autoethnographers write in the first person about their experiences by reflecting and integrating research related to the researched topic. The autoethnographer of this chapter is one person in different roles: researcher, practitioner, author, designer, artist, consultant, and creative entrepreneur.

As the autoethnographer and writer of this chapter, I will now continue in the first person and contribute examples from my professional experience as a consultant and creative entrepreneur. I have been self-employed since 1994, starting with a design studio which developed into a communication consultancy in Germany. I have worked for clients with local, national, and international business models in various sectors such as banking and engineering – all with headquarters or a subsidiary in Germany. I also indite my business models, bring them into existence – to the market – and run them as the founder and owner of these start-ups. One is a service, and one is a physical product. I am writing from my memory which means that I have observed, experienced, and remembered specific situations, but I maintain the anonymity of those concerned.

Limitation – while a strength – is also the method of autoethnography. As a qualitative method performed by a single individual, it might overlook or even point to relevant issues. A restriction was that I focused on inditing outcomes because I know how I indited them. An inditer could also contribute to other's business models, for example, as a consultant, or indite a collective outcome, for example, as a member of an innovation team. These processes are even more complicated and hard to disentangle. Therefore, I draw in this introductory and conceptual chapter on my theoretical and experiential knowledge. The next part contributes three autoethnographic examples of inditation: (a) inditing the basics: originality and uniqueness, (b) inditing multiplication: the mould for a material prototype of a physical product, and (c) inditing variation: the model for a service.

3.1. Inditing the Basics: Originality and Uniqueness

If you indite a unique result, such as an artwork, you need different skills from someone who indites a prototype such as knowledge of colours, materials, and long-term training. As an author, you would need to be able to write a narrative. In an inditation process, you will include your experience and apply your knowledge, which might be expert knowledge. You need to know how to start, decide which material – or genre – would be appropriate, where, when, and how you could influence details, and you must decide when to stop. You will then work out what you do not know and need to know and solve this issue by obtaining relevant knowledge. You know when the brainchild is 'ready', or time will tell as you might have set a deadline. To some inditers, the 'ready' brainchild is not interesting anymore, and they let it go with the 'birth', for example, a drawing, painting, or a text, such as a poem. They focus on inditing the next brainchild, and sometimes they work in parallel on some brainchildren. This is a snippet of text I indited as an unpublished outline of an essay, I preliminarily called 'just words':

> Words even transcend time, such as the words on Trajan's column. Words store meaning over time. Just words. I read a lovely story of 'just' sitting together, having a wonderful evening. No words were necessary. Just words. Not even necessary.

This is a combination of letters. They constitute words and sentences and transport meaning through time and space. Other visualisations, such as paintings, also transcend time and space. Inditers might like the process of inditing as an end in itself and eventually do not reflect overly on the outcome as a means to an end in their business model. They might prefer collaborating with gallerists and publishers and delivering the outcome to management so that they, as the artists or authors, could focus on their strengths, which might be inditing a unique outcome: a novelty. Novelties are crucial in research and researchers also indite. They might contribute to private organisations that then use the outcome to sell it as a product or a service or to the public sector, and get paid, for example, by a state. Several inditers, such as artists like Warhol or Hundertwasser, thought deeper about their business model, for example, on inditing prototypes and serial processes, such as serigraphy or lithography. Today, social media and self-publishing might be a chance for inditers to exclude the 'middle man' and sell directly to clients. However, this takes time, effort, and knowledge. I see this development as a chance and challenge in terms of the 'right to exist' for management – especially gallerists and publishers – to deliver solutions that work in selling the brainchildren of the artists, authors, and researchers, who might want to be more aware of the value of their intellectual capital.

3.2. Inditing Multiplication: The Mould for a Material Prototype of a Physical Product

For inditing prototypes, you need specific knowledge and experience in designing and producing prototypes, for example, as an engineer or designer. This is an example of inditing a prototype of a physical product, a table:

> I needed a standing desk on wheels for one person for meetings and seminars and could not find such a thing as a 'ready-made' product to purchase, although I had searched the internet. So, I decided to bring what I needed into existence. The table needed enough space for

a laptop and space to store something, for example, materials, such as papers and boxes in design thinking processes. As it is a standing desk, it needed to be robust, so it did not fall over. I started by sketching, made some drawings, and then searched for appropriate materials and craftspeople: metalworkers and carpenters. The wheels needed to be arrestable. When the table was not needed, it could stand somewhere it would not disturb. As the principle was one person, one table, it needed to be flexible for just a few people and many people in seminars. The tables could stand together or with a space between, which is comfortable in Covid-times. This inditation process included the production of prototypes that I discussed with people who could work with them in seminars or meetings and then optimized the construction based on their feedback. This inditation process took about two to three years and cost a five-figure sum, not including my time. This brainchild 'got born' and could be ordered on a website. The tables are produced by a small German company and delivered directly to the client.

Inditing means investing time and money, which means taking risks since you do not know whether the 'born' brainchild will run successfully. You might see problems during the process that were or unknown at the beginning.

3.3. Inditing Variation: The Model for a Service

Inditing a service might need more visualisation because it could be 'invisible' to a future client, so you need to make it perceivable. You could therefore think of the visual identity right from the outset. You must consider your client's needs and future experience. There is also a strong narrative and different parameters to be met. For example, if you have a website, you need to decide at the beginning whether your service will be available, for example, locally or globally, what languages you will use and what software meets your needs. You must know, for example, marketing automatisation and payment providers in designing a marketing funnel, which means to include thinking about the business model. Inditing a service is like 'building the plane while flying'; an expression you hear everywhere in Silicon Valley. Such a brainchild could be indited quickly. During the inditation process, the inditer makes decisions such as local/regional/ national/international, visualisation, knowledge and experience in terms of what works for the clients, for example, content management systems, website architecture/navigation. The service must be perceivable and meet the needs of the client.

Overall, this first part is an initial inditing stage where I play with thoughts, develop options, and decide on an outcome. I then work more specifically towards the outcome, which might still happen in the imagination and could add practice unless the brainchild is 'ready' to see the light of day. Much research is 'out there' in different disciplines and fields including tacit knowledge (Arthur et al., 2002; Nonaka & Von Krogh, 2009; Polanyi, 2009), philosophy, intuition, and reflection (Nishida, 1987). Inditation might be a theory, and part of former research and existing methods could belong to a theoretical framework of inditation. Creative entrepreneurs indite in various sectors. They could indite a unique outcome such as original artwork, a prototype for a material product, or a service. An inditation process includes the framework of a business model (Osterwalder & Pigneur, 2010) because the creative entrepreneur has the outcome in mind. Inditers could indite their own business (founders, owners) or contribute to other businesses in business-to-business (b2b) and business-to-consumer (b2c), for example, as creative consultants. In all these examples, creative entrepreneurs run a business which is a means to an end (must earn money) and not an end in itself (a hobby). Creative entrepreneurs indite in novelty creation, and they could work in the creative industry. The process is the same, and only the parameters might be different. The business model might be part of an inditation process whether you indite a unique result, prototype, and/or service. As a creative entrepreneur, you want to understand your future customers or clients to balance their needs and your needs with your brainchild. If a brainchild is born, it is the founder, owner, manager, and stakeholder's task to help run it professionally and successfully. It is then beyond the inditation process because it is management.

4. ESTABLISHING OR REJECTING THE CONCEPT OF INDITATION: AN OUTLINE OF A ROADMAP FOR FURTHER RESEARCH

This chapter introduced the concept of inditation as a creative, complex process used by creative entrepreneurs to bring 'intellectual brainchildren' into the world as unique results, products, or services.

The last part provides an outline of a roadmap for further research to reject or establish the concept of inditation. It serves as an invitation to the research community to constitute a theoretical framework (Alvesson & Kärreman, 2011; Carlile & Christensen, 2005; Rivard, 2014, 2021; Saetre & Van de Ven, 2021; Weick, 1989, 1995, 1999; Whetten, 2002) of inditation within the field of creative entrepreneurship.

This conceptualisation is an invitation to the academic community for further inquiry. Hence, I will start by preparing a broad outline of a roadmap and topics for further research to establish and implement the concept of inditation within creative entrepreneurship. Further research is needed to understand the process in detail.

There are challenges for research: it is still unclear whether inditation might eventually be a wide-ranging process of bringing 'the new' into the world. The process so far appears vague and unclear: why, where, when, and how does it start? The concept of an entrepreneurial idea, or any idea, seems to be somewhat fuzzy and obscure even in philosophy.

Further investigation is required to understand and describe an eventually non-linear, creative logic of inditation. It might be possible to have a closer look at parts of the process such as the influence of visualisation to clarify thinking. Complexity, visualisation, anticipation, processual thinking, and reasoning towards an outcome might be more relevant than seen so far in research.

It is not understood how a creative entrepreneur navigates and orients in such a complex process as inditation. They might indite in contemplation. They might even miss the point of receiving financial rewards – or be highly successful. So, what does success mean to an inditer?

The creative entrepreneur could have been much faster by exclusively focusing on inditation. An inditer might need courage and trust that the outcome will
work and provide economic success. The – invisible – act of contemplating and
focusing might be seen by others as hanging around, which it might be if there
were no outcome.

Inditation needs time; Kant indited for 10 years and wrote his text down in a
few months. It could also mean setting up a service business model in a day or
painting a picture in minutes – while acquiring the relevant knowledge could have
taken much more time, usually years.

Inditers might contribute to the socio-economic and cultural heritage of a
society. As the contributors, they need to survive economically. There are schemes
for grants, and there might be solutions to support inditers to enable and support
them to indite 'the new'. The outcome might be economically relevant.

Part of the process of inditation might be a kind of experiential mould for a
prototypical framework. Inditers gain experience and knowledge they could apply
to future prototypes. Like a blueprint, this kind of mould-like knowledge might
be embodied, implicit and tacit, experiential knowledge, serving as a pattern.

It seems that the process of inditation ends when management begins.
Unfortunately, this is not exactly clear. Therefore, further research is needed to
describe a possible transition from the process of inditation to the process of
management, for example, is it a smooth, gradual, abrupt, controlled process, and
how might it work best?

Furthermore, what is the right time to stop an inditation process? You know
when a brainchild is ready to reach the light of day, but how do you know and
why? It might be that the inditation process does not end with the 'birth' of the
brainchild but continues for a while. For example, an owner and founder of a
start-up might want to ensure that the child 'runs successfully' and contributes
to management. This individual might still sense responsibility as 'the mother' of
the brainchild and would also decide differently than other managers because of
the deep and thorough knowledge of the brainchild and a sense of responsibility.
Managers would eventually decide differently, causing potential conflicts.

There could also be several 'mothers'. For example, if an innovation team
indited together, there might be a collective brainchild. There is the issue of intellectual property and responsibility.

The intention towards meeting future clients' needs might be necessary.
Research on needs could be provided regarding inditation processes because it
might be that both the needs of the creative entrepreneur in the inditation process
(e.g. independence and freedom) and the needs of the future clients (e.g. fun and
health) need to be met so that the brainchild can 'run' successfully. Additionally,
knowledge about business models and knowledge about choices and decisions
such as willingness and consequences of scaling a business model might be helpful, which is a critical entrepreneurial decision right from the outset.

There might be existing methods that serve well in an inditation process. For
example, Poe's method could be analysed. There are methods for inventing and
innovating. The process of inditation might start by thinking 'backwards'. What

could the creative entrepreneur provide to make their ideal customer 'happy'? What kind of problem or conflict would they like to solve and whose needs could be met by the indited outcome? If you want to make a lot of money you might think about scaling straight away. If you are happy with 'enough' to make a living then you might like to be supportive to your local community and think of an outcome to meet the needs of 'your' local people. These are entrepreneurial decisions right at the start, and they might even depend on the onto-epistemological stance and mindset of the creative entrepreneur. It would also be interesting to know whether creative entrepreneurs consider sharing part of the sum they earn from the outset in the inditation process and what they do later. Additional knowledge, for example, of different kinds of media, such as social media and cross-media production, might be needed to successfully set up distribution and marketing channels. These might be specific skills needed for individuals working as creative entrepreneurs who develop their own services or products. If Handel, Poe, and Kant had lived nowadays, they might have had trouble identifying grant frameworks, proper media, and publishing channels for their brainchild, for example, social media, podcasting, traditional, or self-publishing. Who might be supportive of an inditer regarding the manifestation of the outcome? What could management contribute?

An inditer might start alone and could collaborate with others in a team. Research on groups and teams regarding inditation processes in creative entrepreneurship might be interesting to understand collective inditation processes. However, how would a team contemplate: each member alone or altogether? Might time and space be crucial as an overlooked source for contemplation to let the brainchild develop and grow? The time regarding pauses, even stillness for contemplation and space as a supportive and safe environment for the inditer might be more important than recognised. It would be interesting to see research regarding a possible difference between contemplation and meditation in the inditation processes.

This chapter introduced the concept of inditation within the creative entrepreneurship field. It also conceptualised an outline of a theoretical framework of inditation. In the future, a theory of inditation might provide a methodological framework for bringing 'the new' into the world by creative entrepreneurs.

ACKNOWLEDGEMENTS

I want to thank my supervisors, Dr Sue Williams and Dr Henning Große of the University of Gloucestershire, for their support, and PD Dr Wolfgang Kienzler of the Friedrich-Schiller-University Jena for pointing to Wittgenstein.

REFERENCES

Alvesson, M., & Kärreman, D. (2011). *Qualitative research and theory development: Mystery as method.* Sage.

Anderson, L., & Glass-Coffin, B. (2022). Learn by going autoethnographic modes of inquiry. In T. E. Adams, S. L. Holman Jones, & C. Ellis (Eds.), *Handbook of autoethnography* (2nd ed., pp. 57–83). Routledge

Arthur, W. B., Day, J., Jaworski, J., Jung, M., Nonaka, I., Scharmer, C. O., & Senge, P. M. (2002). Illuminating the blind spot. *Leader to Leader*, 24, 11–14.

Bible King James Version Standard (2011). *Biblica Inc.®*. Retrieved, January 5, 2022, from https://www.kingjamesbibleonline.org/Psalms-Chapter-45/

Campsie, P. (2015). *Designer of the invisible*. Retrieved, May 6 2022, from https://parisianfields.com/2015/10/11/designer-of-the-invisible/

Carlile, P. R., & Christensen, C. M. (2005). *The cycles of theory building in management research.* Harvard Business School. Retrieved, June 9, 2022, from https://hbswk.hbs.edu/item/the-cycles-of-theory-building-in-management-research

Christensen, C. M. (1997). *The innovator's dilemma: When new technologies cause great firms to fail.* Harvard Business School Press.

Christensen, C. M., & Euchner, J. (2020 [2011]). Managing disruption: An interview with Clayton Christensen. *Research-Technology Management, 63*(3), 49–54.

Doloriert, C., & Sambrook, S. (2012). Organisational autoethnography. *Journal of Organizational Ethnography, 1*(1), 83–95.

Elias, S. R., Chiles, T. H., & Crawford, B. (2022). Entrepreneurial imagining: How a small team of arts entrepreneurs created the world's largest traveling carillon. *Organization Studies, 43*(3), 203–226.

Ellis, C., Adams, T. E., & Bochner, A. P. (2011). Autoethnography: An overview. *Historical Social Research, 36*(4), 273–290.

Fox, M. (2015). Adrian Frutiger dies at 87. *The New York Times*. Retrieved, February 28, 2021, from https://www.nytimes.com/2015/09/20/arts/design/adrian-frutiger-dies-at-87-his-type-designs-show-you-the-way.html

Handel, G. F. (1727). *My heart is inditing* (Coronation Anthem No. 4, HWV 261). https://catalogue.nla.gov.au/Record/1714353

Merriam-Webster (n.d.). *Indite*. Retrieved, May 2, 2022, from https://www.merriam-webster.com/dictionary/indite

Nishida, K. (1987). *Intuition and reflection in self-consciousness.* V. H. Viglielmo, Y. Takeuchi, & J. S. O'Leary, Trans.). State University of New York.

Nonaka, I., & Von Krogh, G. (2009). Perspective – Tacit knowledge and knowledge conversion: Controversy and advancement in organizational knowledge creation theory. *Organization Science, 20*(3), 635–652.

Osterwalder, A., & Pigneur, Y. (2010). *Business model generation: A handbook for visionaries, game changers, and challengers.* Wiley.

Poe, E. A. (1846a). *Marginalia – part 05*. Edgar Allan Poe Society of Baltimore. Retrieved 24th April 2024 from https://www.eapoe.org/works/pollin/brp20405.htm

Poe, E. A. (1846b). *The philosophy of composition*. Graham's American Monthly Magazine of Literature and Art. https://www.eapoe.org/works/essays/philcomp.htm

Polanyi, M. (2009 [1983]). *The tacit dimension.* University of Chicago.

Purcell, H. (1685). *My heart is inditing; written for the coronation of James II*. https://imslp.org/wiki/My_heart_is_inditing%2C_Z.30_(Purcell%2C_Henry)

Rivard, S. (2014). Editor's comments: The ions of theory construction. *MIS Quarterly, 38*(2), iii–xiv.

Rivard, S. (2021). Theory building is neither an art nor a science. It is a craft. *Journal of Information Technology, 36*(3), 316–328.

Saetre, A. S., & Van de Ven, A. H. (2021). Generating theory by abduction. *Academy of Management Review, 4*(46), 684–701.

Sartre, J.-P. (2004 [1940]). *The imaginary.* Taylor & Francis.

van Manen, M., & van Manen, M. (2021). Doing Phenomenological Research and Writing. *Qualitative Health Research, 31*(6), 1069–1082.

Weick, K. E. (1989). Theory construction as disciplined imagination. *Academy of Management. The Academy of Management Review, 14*(4), 516–531.

Weick, K. E. (1995). What theory is not, theorizing is. *Administrative Science Quarterly, 40*(3), 385–390.

Weick, K. E. (1999). Theory construction as disciplined reflexivity: Tradeoffs in the 90s. *The Academy of Management Review, 24*(4), 797–806.
Whetten, D. A. (2002). Modelling-as-theorizing: A systematic methodology for theory development. In D. Partington (Ed.), *Essential skills for management research* (pp. 45–71). Sage.
Wittgenstein, L. (1998 [1977]). *Culture and value [Vermischte Bemerkungen]* (P. Winch, Trans.) (2nd ed.). Blackwell.

CHAPTER 5

THE SLIPPERINESS OF ENTREPRENEURIAL INTENTION IN NARRATIVES OF CULTURAL AND CREATIVE INDUSTRIES ENTREPRENEURSHIP

David Sharpe

ABSTRACT

Entrepreneurial intention – the decision to, and subsequent practice of, launching a business – is often referred to as a planned, considered act. Factors influencing the decision to embark on entrepreneurial ventures have been identified and used to create models of entrepreneurial intention. Do these models, which emerge primarily from behavioural psychology, hold true for participants in the cultural and creative industries (CCIs)? Narrative research conducted with 18 CCI entrepreneurs from Australia indicates that the intention to start their ventures is neither clearly identified nor defined. These narrative accounts present intention as a slippery notion – difficult to define, to separate from other factors, and to rely on with certainty. In these accounts, the founding of CCI ventures is revealed as a gradual, organic process, less distinct than existing models of entrepreneurial intention suggest. Three themes that impact on entrepreneurial intention are identified from these accounts – desire for personal growth, progression from freelancing, and realisation of creative projects – to further illuminate how venture creation takes place in the CCIs.

Creative (and Cultural) Industry Entrepreneurship in the 21st Century
Contemporary Issues in Entrepreneurship Research, Volume 18A, 59–72
Copyright © 2024 by David Sharpe
Published under exclusive licence by Emerald Publishing Limited
ISSN: 2040-7246/doi:10.1108/S2040-72462023000018A005

Keywords: Creative industries; cultural industries; entrepreneurship; entrepreneurs; entrepreneurial intention; small business; business founders; entrepreneur stories; entrepreneur narratives; narrative research

1. INTRODUCTION

The decision to launch an entrepreneurial venture has been positioned as a planned, intentional act (Bird & Jelinek, 1989; Krueger & Carsrud, 1993). Businesses are not started by reflex, but after a consideration of the operating environment and the opportunity at hand (Krueger et al., 2000). This understanding of entrepreneurial intention as careful and deliberate emerges from behavioural psychology frameworks such as Shapero and Sokol's (1982) Entrepreneurial Event Model (EEM) and Ajzen's (1991) Theory of Planned Behaviour (TPB).

Does this view of entrepreneurial intention as a product of planning and consideration hold true for the CCIs? Research into the experiences of 18 entrepreneurs from a range of CCIs in Australia indicates personal intentions to start a venture (for-profit or not-for-profit) are more fluid and spontaneous than existing models of entrepreneurial intention suggest. In recounting the establishment of their CCI ventures through narrative interviews, entrepreneurial intention is presented as a gradual and organic progression. Many interviewees recount the iterative, almost unintentional nature of starting a venture, challenging the idea of venture creation as precise and clearly defined.

Through this research, three dominant themes around entrepreneurial intention emerge: personal growth, progression from freelancing, and project realisation. Each is presented as a fluid process rather than as a deliberate act of entrepreneurial instigation. In each case, entrepreneurial intention proves slippery – difficult to define, to separate from other factors and to rely on with certainty. The use of narrative inquiry offers the opportunity to examine the experience of entrepreneurial intention post hoc and finds that it is emergent, tentative, and entangled with many other diverse factors. In presenting insights on the lived experience of entrepreneurship, such narratives offer a nuanced consideration of how entrepreneurial intention works in the CCIs and its inherent complexities.

2. EXISTING MODELS OF ENTREPRENEURIAL INTENTION

Entrepreneurial intention is well established as a concept that helps explain the cognitive processes people undertake when embarking upon an entrepreneurial venture. Moriano et al. (2012) describe it as 'the conscious state of mind that precedes action and directs attention toward a goal such as starting a new business'. It is useful to look briefly at the predominant models of entrepreneurial intention and their key characteristics (see Table 1 for a summary). Liñán and

Fayolle (2015) note two distinct strands within the literature on the topic. The first is influenced by social psychology, in particular Ajzen's TPB, which considers factors that influence behaviour generally. The second strand focuses on Shapero and Sokol's EEM, which specifically considers new venture creation.

Ajzen's TPB positions cognitive elements as predictors for behaviour: intentions, attitudes, subjective norms (perceptions of others' attitudes towards a behaviour), and perceived behavioural control (perceptions of one's ability to perform a behaviour). In a review of research papers which used TPB to examine entrepreneurial intention, Lortie and Castogiovanni (2015) found that it was most commonly used to explain and predict new venture creation. In practical application, this model has frequently been used to predict venture creation by university students and to examine entrepreneurial intention within specific industries sectors.

Shapero and Sokol's model (1982), the EEM, considers the lead up to the formation of a company – the 'entrepreneurial event' in its name. It too identifies cognitive factors such as perceptions of desirability (the value placed on entrepreneurship by peers, family, colleagues, etc.). However, it also considers the role of precipitating events which prompt a person to consider an entrepreneurial venture. Such events can be negative displacements (such as losing a job or forced emigration), positive pulls (such as encouragement from other people) or being between career stages. Krueger et al. (2000) note the importance of a person's propensity to take action within Shapero and Sokol's model and consider the model superior to the TPB for assessing entrepreneurial intention.

That both these models have been used predominantly for predictive research is unsurprising, given that prediction of future behaviour is fundamental to both. Less research has considered how these models – or entrepreneurial intention more generally – relate to existing entrepreneurs; to, in essence, consider the entrepreneurial event post hoc.

Bird's work on the formation and execution of intentionality among entrepreneurs is a critical exception (Bird, 1988). Through interviews with 20 entrepreneurs, Bird found distinct and recurrent patterns of thought and behaviour. She identified the influence of contextual factors (social, political, and economic) and personal factors (personal history, current personality, and abilities), which influenced two contrasting types of thinking: rational and intuitive. These then result in entrepreneurial intention and action. Liñán and Fayolle (2015) note the surprising lack of empirical validation of Bird's model. However, it provides a less prescriptive model than the TPB and EEM and allows for greater consideration of contextual and personality influences on entrepreneurs.

Douglas considers the construct of entrepreneurial intentions – largely dependent on models such as the TPB and EEM, and to a lesser extent, Bird's – too broadly defined and lacking clarity (Douglas, 2013). For Douglas, means, motive, and opportunity drive the choice to pursue entrepreneurial action and entrepreneurs will choose an opportunity based on its potential to deliver the greatest positive utility.

Douglas's model adds practical aspects of the entrepreneurial experience, such as opportunity and risk, to a consideration of the cognitive influences on

Table 1.   Selected Theories of Entrepreneurial Intention.

Source	Theory	Key Points
Ajzen (1991)	TPB	Intentions, attitudes, subjective norms (perceptions of others' attitudes towards a behaviour), and perceived behavioural control (perceptions of one's ability to perform a behaviour) are predictors of behaviour (such as the decision to start a business)
Shapero and Sokol (1982)	EEM	Precipitating events, perceptions of desirability, and perceptions of feasibility prompt entrepreneurial action
Bird (1988)	Influence of contextual and social factors	Contextual factors (social, political, and economic) and personal factors (personal history, current personality, and abilities) influence rational and intuitive thinking. This prompts entrepreneurial intention and then action
Douglas (2013)	Individual-opportunity nexus prompts entrepreneurial intention.	The nexus point between opportunity and individual skills prompts entrepreneurial intention. The opportunity is then evaluated by its potential benefits and weighted by the individual's attitudes to those benefits

individuals. He positions Shane and Venkataraman's concept of the individual–opportunity nexus as central to his model (Shane & Venkataraman, 2000). The nexus point is where an entrepreneurial opportunity is seized by an individual who can realise it. Douglas argues that each nexus point causes the formation of entrepreneurial intention. The opportunity is then evaluated by the opportunity's potential benefits and weighted by the individual's attitudes to those benefits.

These theories of entrepreneurial intention are attempting to define a process which in practice may be undefinable or be subject to so many differing and competing influences to make it impossible to reduce to a simple model. Such is the nature of model making – that, at best, a model will capture a majority of the experience of intending to start a business – but perhaps there will always remain something alchemical about the process. It is here where we can see the slipperiness inherent in entrepreneurial intention emerging.

In narrative research with CCI entrepreneurs in Australia – those who have grown and exited their ventures and those who are still in the middle of building them – entrepreneurial intention is apparent, but more complicated than these existing models indicate. In these accounts, it is rarely as simple as having an intention to start a business and then doing so. Before looking at specific examples of where the boundaries of entrepreneurial intention start to blur, it is useful to consider the narrative inquiry technique employed with this sample set and review how this method accounts for the slipperiness of entrepreneurial intention by allowing for nuance and complexity in its execution.

3. NARRATIVE INQUIRY

Narrative inquiry is the practice of collecting and analysing the experiences of individuals, as lived and told (Creswell & Poth, 2018). The telling of stories constructed from the lived experience of the teller is an inherent human practice, which happens repeatedly and iteratively, in attempts to give meaning, as Polkinghorne puts it, 'to their experience of temporality and personal actions' (Polkinghorne, 1988, p. 11). As Clandinin (2016) points out, this practice is not simply about recording information about these experiences but is also a transactional and relational exchange with listeners, influenced by a range of social, cultural and institutional forces which shape the living and telling of the story. The collection of narrative accounts from entrepreneurs and the subsequent analysis of those accounts has prompted multiple studies; Foss (2004), Roy (2016), and Lindström (2016) provide useful examples from within the CCIs.

Narrative inquiry lends itself to entrepreneurship's inherent complexities. Narrative accounts become exercises in constructing meaning from past events and the jumbled, non-linear nature of personal experience, when viewed in retrospect can clarify the significance of events and their ramifications. The construction and recounting of a narrative are imprecise, allowing the subject to select the parts of the story they see as significant to the overall sense-making of the exercise in the order and with the emphases they select.

The challenge for researchers undertaking narrative inquiry is to account for various moving parts: the context in which narratives are constructed and collected, the social and cultural influences brought to bear by teller and audience, and the various levels of meaning created, consciously and unconsciously. Narratives are not precise and authoritative accounts of real events, but collages of memory, personal perspective, interpretation and performance. The social and cultural influences on the teller and their process of narrative creation mean that neither objectivity nor exactness can ever be fully achieved.

Applying such a method to the topic of entrepreneurial intention might seem at odds with the categorical approach of the existing models outlined above. However, narrative research offers a chance to explore the intricacies of entrepreneurship by considering complex and sometimes contradictory accounts. This allows a nuanced portrait of the entrepreneurial event to emerge – one that encompasses cognitive factors and precipitating events, and also the elements of the human experience that fit less neatly into the existing frameworks.

In undertaking narrative research with 18 Australian entrepreneurs working within the CCIs, care was taken to select participants from a broad range of industries sectors (see Table 2 for participant details). Definitions of CCIs abound, but a recent Australian definition includes music and performing arts; film, television and radio, advertising and marketing; software development; writing, publishing and print media; and architecture, design and visual arts (Trembath & Fielding, 2020). Nine men and nine women who founded enterprises in one or more of these sectors provided narrative accounts of their entrepreneurial journeys, and these accounts provide a vivid picture of the challenges and successes experienced in the founding of ventures in creative fields in Australia. The comparability of CCI subsectors is an ongoing challenge for researchers, but a concentration on one element (venture creation) provides a common experience to be analysed despite the differences across fields of expertise. By identifying thematic trends which emerge through the retelling of those experiences, an indication of areas of commonality emerges rather than a definitive result that can be applied across all CCI subsectors.

Table 2. Interviewees.

Gender	Age Range	Creative Activity	For-profit or Not-for-profit	Number of Years Trading	Location	Highest Annual Turnover Reached ($AUD)
Male	30–39	Web and graphic design	For profit	18	Sydney	1,000,000–1,999,999
Female	50–59	Commercial and residential architecture	For profit	29	Sydney	500,000–999,999
Male	50–59	Music distribution	For profit	19	Sydney	Over 20M
Male	50–59	Circus production	For profit	25	Multiple locations	10,000,000–19,999,999
Male	Over 59	Feature film maker	For profit	12	Sydney	0–499,999
Female	40–49	Visual arts classes	For profit	3	Regional New South Wales	0–499,999
Female	Over 59	Jewellery design and retail	For profit	35	Sydney	2,000,000–4,999,999
Female	40–49	Web and campaign design	For profit	14	Sydney	2,000,000–4,999,999
Female	Over 59	Children's literature publishing	For profit	8	Regional New South Wales	0–499,999
Male	30–39	Advertising campaign production	For profit	10	Sydney	500,000–999,999
Male	30–39	Games and interactive content	For profit	7	Multiple locations	1,000,000–1,999,999
Female	50–59	Film and TV content makers	For profit	12	Melbourne	Over 20M
Female	50–59	Children's choir	Not-for-profit	32	Multiple locations	2,000,000–4,999,999
Male	40–49	Sunglasses design	For profit	3	Sydney	0–499,999
Male	30–39	Sculpture and public art	For profit	11	Sydney	0–499,999
Female	Over 59	Experimental theatre	Not-for-profit	17	Regional Victoria	0–499,999
Female	50–59	Web and graphic design	For profit	21	Brisbane	1,000,000–1,999,999
Male	20–29	Theatre and opera	For profit	8	Sydney	0–499,999

Another challenge is to recognise and account for the role of not-for-profit enterprises within CCIs. These enterprises make up a significant proportion of organisations within arts-related subsectors. Entrepreneurship manifests itself through the founding and growth of not-for-profit organisations as CCI enterprises. These ventures may sit comfortably under definitions such as art entrepreneurship (Callander & Cummings, 2000), cultural entrepreneurship (Hausmann & Heinze, 2016), non-profit entrepreneurship (Camarena et al., 2001), or social entrepreneurship (Roper & Chaney, 2006), all of which seek to articulate how individuals pursue entrepreneurial activities without an individual profit motive.

The CCIs, therefore, is a concept that includes for-profit and not-for-profit organisations, and entrepreneurship is evident in each. To accommodate this, a definition of entrepreneurship must move beyond dependence on business and/or profit drivers to incorporate a wider range of motivations. Shane and Venkataraman's (2000, p. 18) widely referenced definition – 'the scholarly examination of how, by whom, and with what effects opportunities to create future goods and services are discovered, evaluated, and exploited' – is broad enough to encompass the scope of the CCIs. As is that of Stevenson et al., who define entrepreneurship as 'a process by which individuals – either on their own or inside organisations – pursue opportunities without regard to the resources they currently control', where opportunity is defined as a future situation that is deemed desirable and feasible (Stevenson et al., 2000, p. 5).

From these starting points, I define a CCI entrepreneur as an individual undertaking an entrepreneurial process within a CCI subsector, with 'entrepreneurial process' defined as the creation of a new venture, which incorporates opportunity recognition, resource gathering, innovation, risk, and results in a new creative product or service. Consequently, the sample includes two founders of long-standing not-for-profit arts organisations.

4. FINDINGS

4.1. Personal Growth

The desire for personal growth emerges through the narratives collected as influential to decisions by CCI entrepreneurs to start businesses. Sometimes, these influences express the expectations of others (as suggested in the TPB), but sometimes they are linked to personal existential concerns about purpose.

This was the case for Jim,[1] who started his music distribution business with a box of records in his front room and grew it to over \$20M in annual turnover. Having worked in record stores and having some familiarity with music distribution, Jim identified a demand for independent music, left unmet by mainstream retailers. But beyond this market gap, there was also an expectation that he should do something with his life. As recorded in his narrative:

> [I felt] my stepfather's voice breathing down the back of my neck. I was like, what the hell am I going to do? I just felt it was important to do. It was personal because ... there was a real need for me to do something.

Jewellery brand founder Beth felt a similar need for personal direction. Having travelled extensively, she developed a love of fine silver jewellery, and on her return to Australia, initially sold her jewellery at markets. Establishing her business fulfilled a personal need for Beth to direct her energies into a meaningful activity.

> I'd always been desperately searching for a direction in my life. I was really quite distraught about not having a direction. I felt very bad about myself and this was a way of giving myself a direction and that really psychologically was the best for me.

In addition, she had a drive to share her passion for her product with others.

> My love was fine jewellery ... like Jensen or some of the Scandinavian silversmiths... that was my determination to bring that sort of ... designed jewellery and make it my own.

That sense of 'making it my own' is an indication of how closely entrepreneurial intention was not just tied to her own identity, but also helping form it.

Other stories of seeking a level of personal growth show elements of the negative displacement influences identified by Shapero and Sokol (1982). For some, like Charles, founder of a circus performance company, parting ways with a former employer was a catalyst. In his narrative, he notes:

> I was actually working for another company ... touring Shakespeare across Australia and I'd done that for about eight years ... [I thought] actually I don't think it's going to be able to change that much more within this context.

This experience of leaving an unfulfilling job would be familiar to many, but in choosing an entrepreneurial path Charles was also seeking to fill a personal need: 'Really, I needed to go and do my own thing ... We have the freedom to kind of choose the direction. Whereas I didn't have that option before'. As Charles explores this further in his narrative, a need to precipitate action and to 'not die wondering' also emerges: 'The main impetus was that I didn't want to sit around when I was 60 and went... what if I tried this and not done it'.

For Owen, a visual artist working in public art and industrial installation, business is tied to his creative practice and to his desire to develop that practice. After completing art school, he found that: 'industrialised production was something that I wanted to engage with and to do it kind of hands-on and deeply and ... affordably'. He discovered that as his work blurred pure art and industrial design, he could create commercial pieces which also suited his creative interests. 'I kind of had to bring it in-house and I guess industrial design ... meant that I could still engage with it and still do my art'.

In this observation, we see the importance of being able to 'still do my art' as an important driver for entrepreneurship. Owen also had a desire to use his art and design studio to explore an equitable model for multiple artists sharing a space.

> I had a couple of friends around me that wanted to also create small, creative businesses. I did the more equitable model and I tried to say, 'well as an encourager for me to pay my overheads, I'm going to split (the studio's costs) evenly'.

Graphic designer Kira also founded her business out of a desire for personal and creative growth, but in her case the prompt was technological: 'I hadn't thought of starting a business. It wasn't anything that I aspired to do, actually. I did it out of need'.

That need was a desire to adopt Apple computers and software to undertake her design work, whereas her employer wanted to stick with Microsoft equipment. This negative displacement meant that: 'I just knew that I had to jump on board ... the risk of not taking that step and staying in the role that I was in ... I just felt that I would get left behind'. For Kira, her own skill level provided a level of risk mitigation.

> The worst thing that can happen is, you know ... if I have no work. If business doesn't go well, then at least I've got the skills and I can go back and work for someone else.

4.2. Progression From Freelancing

Another common feature of the narratives collected from creative entrepreneurs is the gradual formation of a business out of a freelance career. In these cases, it is difficult to pinpoint the exact timing of an 'entrepreneurial event' as Shapero and Sokol's (1982) model posits. Rather, there is an imprecise transition from a creative practitioner undertaking project work, to gather people and infrastructure around them, to generate an amount of activity that looks and feels business-like. In some cases, this change would have happened before a company is established.

Pat, the owner of a web design company, experienced such a transition. His freelance career started while he was studying design. He found his skills in demand and customers seeking him out for work. For him, the shift to a business structure was about:

> just wanting to get a little bit more structured and formalised about being able to do things like invoicing ... hiring people ... just take care of the basics and become more tax efficient.

He also reflected on the change of attitude that came along with this progression.

> That became the mindset as I'm going ... take this more seriously and that's ... going to be my job with my role is to build this company.

In the case of Liz, an architect, her freelance career started through one of Shapero and Sokol's 'negative displacements', when her employer let her go due to a lack of available work. Her recollection of that time was:

> I don't think I thought about running a business. I just think I thought about, 'oh if there's going to be a gap here, I can speed up a couple of the private jobs I've got'.

The eventual transition to forming a business came, like Pat's, through the accumulation of bigger and more challenging work, but, for Liz, there was also an element of identity formation. In her narrative, she recalls the prospect of always being known as the employee of her previous boss. This crisis of identity – of needing to step out of her employer's shadow – was foundational:

> Who am I, if I'm not (his) employee? I'm just Liz. I was kind of terrified by that ... Not too long into me doing (freelance work) ... I realised, I wasn't going to go back and at that point.

For James, co-founder and owner of an advertising and marketing content agency, the path to establishing his business was more circuitous. As an actor and a producer/director, his original entrepreneurial intention was not to start a content business, but to make sketch comedy for TV. However, an approach from a local government organisation to create a campaign for waste management provided an opportunity to mix business with his creative ambitions.

> The idea was that we would put the profits from the commercial jobs into those longer form entertainment projects. Yeah, and we did that initially by reinvesting … the money, any of the profits back into equipment so that we could actually shoot sketches or short films with zero budget.

However, as he and his fellow creatives completed this project, further projects presented themselves. A business structure was formed not around the original creative intent but around content generation, which customers would pay for. 'We started in, you know, non-commercial and then we became [a] commercial production house and then we became [a] creative agency'. The pivot towards entrepreneurship, to creating and growing a business rather than making sketch comedy out of creative passion, happens somewhere in the middle of the process. It was prompted as much by the demands from potential customers than any individual entrepreneurial intention.

Sara, the founder and owner of a digital creative agency, discovered that her freelance career was morphing into entrepreneurship while working with a group of other freelancers. Her freelance career in marketing burgeoned while on a working holiday in the UK and was prompted by finding a group of like-minded collaborators with whom she could work on projects in the UK and Australia. Again, a significant project instigated the shift.

> I was in London for a holiday and that's when I … got the project. So, I actually came home to Sydney with the project and then started forming like a, you know, a group of people to work on the project which is kind of a part of my tribe.

For her and her collaborators, there was an excitement about working on digital projects which were cutting edge as well as finding a 'tribe' of collaborators. This prompted Sara to coordinate her freelance friends into a viable collective.

> I came back to Sydney to actually do the work. I was only over there … just on a holiday and then I came back with … this project that I quickly, it was like, you know said, 'yeah of course I could do that!' and then came home going, 'Holy shit. How am I going to do that?' Okay, let's put a team together and make it happen.

As in James' narrative, one project leads to more and then a selection of collaborators establish the company Sara runs today. For these former freelancers, the exact nature and timing of the intention to transition into a business is diffused over a number of such projects.

4.3. Project Realisation

For some CCI entrepreneurs, founding their ventures started not through a desire to create a company, or even to be in business, but because it was a procedural step enabling a creative project they wanted to pursue. In these cases, forming a company was prompted by external drivers such as government funding and taxation requirements.

This was the case for feature filmmaker Darcy, who has produced five features throughout his career, each with their own company. Because the Australian government's tax incentives for film production require a company structure (a 'special purpose vehicle'), choosing a freelance or self-employment status were not options. His accumulated body of work ('creature feature' genre films) sits under an umbrella brand, and the long tail of revenue generated by each title, each with its own company, contributes to the overall sense of one business rather than a collection of individual projects.

For Darcy, the entrepreneurial intent came from his experience as a script analyst for a government funding body and wanting to make films of his own.

> In my lunch times, I'd grab a script and sit down with my sandwich and just see what these scripts were like … most of them were pretty bad. I just went, well, I'm just going to make something low budget. I started looking around for survival, Australian survival stories.

As Darcy notes, his 'business' tends to stop and start with each film, with the financing arrangements and production coordination elements presenting entrepreneurial challenges of their own. In his narrative, entrepreneurship emerges from a creative urge, and from a desire to forge a filmmaking career, rather than from a desire to build a business with a standard product offering and an ongoing revenue stream.

A contrasting screen industry narrative is offered by Harriet, a producer of broadcast TV series. Having started her career in much the same way as Darcy –founding a company for each production – Harriet undertook a business planning process that led her to establish one company to house multiple productions: 'I said, I can have a company that holds the intellectual property (IP) … So, I'm not having to … do this every time and just have a slightly … different model'.

Later, she took a further step in this direction by co-founding another company with the specific aim of building a brand for television crime drama and building a more traditional business that would have a life beyond the careers of the founding producers. 'I suppose [the first company] was an IP holding company … [the second company], this is a business now, rather than a vehicle for a project'. In Harriet's story, we can see the progression from a project-centric model to a more traditional 'business building' model.

Similarly, children's press publisher Verity was prompted to start a business to publish a title (a reworking of classic European folk tales) she could not sell to another publisher.

> [...] the next publisher we took it to also said the same thing … 'oh look, it's a lovely story, beautiful illustrations, not quite commercial enough for us' … we need to have, start a little … publishing house … We decided, okay, we will start with our story because we didn't want to risk anyone else's work on it.

In other examples, the desire to produce a creative project forces a business structure into existence, even without an external driver. For example, Eleanor's desire to start a children's choir led to the establishment of a multi-million-dollar not-for-profit organisation. Her motivation was a 'quest to work with young people to create a very high level of artistry and the belief that children ... had this innate artistry'. Thoughts of personal gain or monetary reward were less important than the need to explore children's choral work to a highly professional level. 'It needed to be created. I thought, they're a great thing. There aren't any in [this city]. Let's make one!'

This level of entrepreneurial vision in a not-for-profit arts context is also apparent in Rose's story of setting up a hybrid arts company in a regional town. For her, the motivation was being able to continue to undertake creative work she had explored in Europe and apply it to a regional Australian setting.

> I knew the [local] area. There wasn't anyone doing anything experimental, even site-specific work ... I just tried to pull the best together of what I had experienced overseas.

Rose's process was to take six months to survey the local cultural landscape and understand what existing infrastructure she could utilise. Basing herself out of a local co-working space, she established a 'community of practice', which grew into an internationally recognised company merging visual and performing arts. As with Eleanor, the entrepreneurial skill sets of managing risk, attracting funding and building networks, and relationships are all in evidence. However, the entrepreneurial intention is driven by the creation of work rather than the creation of a business.

To what extent did these creative entrepreneurs intend to start businesses? In the narratives outlined above, venture formation is presented as secondary to more fundamental intentions: to produce a creative work, to embark on personal growth, or to formalise an existing freelance practice. Entrepreneurship may in some cases be 'a planned, deliberate act'. But in these accounts, planning is limited, and deliberateness is specifically questioned. Narrative inquiry cannot offer a definitive answer on the true nature of intent; selective recall or self-deprecation may be evident within these accounts. However, a commonality in these recollections of the experience of entrepreneurship in the CCIs is that the specific intention to start a business is difficult to identify, conflated with other motivations and, in some cases, absent.

5. CONCLUSION

The more the narratives of CCI entrepreneurs are explored, the slipperier the notion of entrepreneurial intention becomes. Few position the founding of a business as an aim in and of itself; it is more likely that an entrepreneurial event will be couched in terms of personal growth or creative need. In some cases, the intention to start a business as a considered deliberate act is specifically denied. What the narratives of these entrepreneurs point to is a level of complexity in the decision to start a business which existing models of entrepreneurship only partly allow for.

Unsurprisingly, the impetus to produce fulfilling creative work is missing from existing entrepreneurial models, but these narrative accounts from CCIs consistently point to this as a factor. Sometimes this means adopting business structures to realise that work. At other times, personal creative growth or unfulfilled ambition fuel entrepreneurial intent. In the case of freelancers who evolve their creative practice into a business, the gradual progression of that journey means specific intent is harder to pin down. The implication is that the traditional concept of entrepreneurial intention needs expansion to truly fit the experience of creative entrepreneurs. For these founders of CCI ventures, creative drive, personal growth and the vagaries of government funding for CCIs need to be factored in. If entrepreneurship is worthwhile fostering within the CCIs, a deeper understanding of what drives the decision to start enterprises is crucial. Doing so requires a recognition of the slipperiness of this concept as it applies to creative practitioners, in the hope of being able to grasp it fully.

NOTE

1. Pseudonyms used throughout.

REFERENCES

Ajzen, I. (1991). The theory of planned behavior. *Organizational Behavior and Human Decision Processes*, *50*(2), 179–211.
Bird, B. (1988). Implementing entrepreneurial ideas: The case for intention. *Academy of Management Review*, *13*(3), 442–453.
Bird, B., & Jelinek, M. (1989). The operation of entrepreneurial intentions. *Entrepreneurship Theory and Practice*, *13*(2), 21–30.
Callander, A., & Cummings, M. (2021). Liminal spaces: A review of the art in entrepreneurship and the entrepreneurship in art. *Small Business Economics*, *57*(2), 739–754.
Camarena, L., Feeney, M., & Lecy, J. (2021). Nonprofit entrepreneurship: Gender differences in strategy and practice. *Nonprofit and Voluntary Sector Quarterly*, *50*(6), 1170–1192.
Clandinin, D. (2016). *Engaging in narrative inquiry*. Routledge.
Creswell, J., & Poth, C. (2018). *Qualitative inquiry & research design: Choosing among five approaches* (4th ed). Sage.
Douglas, E. (2013). Reconstructing entrepreneurial intentions to identify predisposition for growth. *Journal of Business Venturing*, *28*(5), 633–651.
Foss, L. (2004). 'Going against the Grain …' Construction of entrepreneurial identity through narratives. In D. Hjorth & C. Steyaert (Eds.), *Narrative and discursive approaches in entrepreneurship* (pp.80–104). Edward Elgar.
Hausmann, A., & Heinze, A. (2016). Entrepreneurship in the cultural and creative industries: Insights from an emergent field. *Artivate*, *5*(2), 7–22.
Krueger, N., & Carsrud, A. (1993). Entrepreneurial intentions: Applying the theory of planned behaviour. *Entrepreneurship and Regional Development*, *5*(4), 315–330.
Krueger, N., Reilly, M., & Carsrud, A. (2000). Competing models of entrepreneurial intentions. *Journal of Business Venturing*, *15*(5), 411–432.
Liñán, F., & Fayolle, A. (2015). A systematic literature review on entrepreneurial intentions: Citation, thematic analyses, and research agenda. *International Entrepreneurship and Management Journal*, *11*(4), 907–933.
Lindström, S. (2016). Artists and multiple job holding – Breadwinning work as mediating between bohemian and entrepreneurial identities and behavior. *Nordic Journal of Working Life Studies*, *6*(3), 43–58.
Lortie, J., & Castogiovanni, G. (2015). The theory of planned behavior in entrepreneurship research: What we know and future directions. *International Entrepreneurship and Management Journal*, *11*(4), 935–957.

Moriano, J., Gorgievski, M., Laguna, M., Stephan, U., & Zarafshani, K. (2012). A cross-cultural approach to understanding entrepreneurial intention. *Journal of Career Development*, *9*(2), 162–185.

Polkinghorne, D. (1988). *Narrative knowing and the human sciences*. State University of New York Press.

Roper, J., & Cheney, G. (2006). The meanings of social entrepreneurship today. In A. Kakabadse & M. Morsing (Eds.), *Corporate social responsibility* (pp. 255–267). Palgrave Macmillan.

Roy, V. (2016). *Navigating multiple identities: Identity work of creative entrepreneurs in the founding stage*. Ph.D. thesis, University of Warwick. http://webcat.warwick.ac.uk/record=b3022102~S1

Shane, S., & Venkataraman, S. (2000). The promise of entrepreneurship as a field of research. *Academy of Management Review*, *25*(1), 217–226.

Shapero, A., & Sokol, L. (1982). Social dimensions of entrepreneurship. In C. Kent, D. Sexton, & K. Vesper (Eds.), *Encyclopedia of entrepreneurship* (pp.72–88). Prentice-Hall.

Stevenson, H., Irving, G., Roberts, M., & Bhide, A. (2000). *New business ventures and the entrepreneur* (International edition). Irwin/McGraw-Hill.

Trembath, J., & Fielding, K. (2020). *Australia's cultural and creative economy: A 21st century guide*. Produced by A New Approach think tank with lead delivery partner the Australian Academy of the Humanities, Canberra. https://newapproach.org.au/wp-content/uploads/2021/08/5-ANA-InsightReportFive-FullReport.pdf

RESILIENCE AND ADAPTATION OF CREATIVE AND CULTURAL ENTERPRISES

CHAPTER 6

MASK-MAKERS AS EMERGING CREATIVE ENTREPRENEURS DURING COVID-19*

Hannah Grannemann, Jennifer Reis, Maggie Murphy and Marie Segares

ABSTRACT

Shortages of personal protective equipment (PPE) across the United States at the start of the COVID-19 pandemic created entrepreneurial opportunities for sewists and makers. In the United States in March and April 2020, masks were not readily available to the general public from existing retailers and PPE for medical use was being rationed for healthcare workers. Sewists and crafters, professionals and amateurs alike, began making and selling and/or donating masks. For individuals with sewing skills and time, sewing and selling masks became a lifeline financially, personally, and socially. To understand the experiences of people who made and distributed handmade masks during the early months of the pandemic in the United States, an interdisciplinary team developed an online cross-sectional survey instrument using a qualitative-dominated approach with both open and closed questions. This chapter explores themes identified from a sample of 94 participants, predominantly female-identifying, who created an enterprise or added a product line to an existing business. The sample includes individuals who did not identify as a 'creative entrepreneur' prior to the pandemic but did identify as an entrepreneur after starting

---

*All authors contributed equally to this chapter.

Creative (and Cultural) Industry Entrepreneurship in the 21st Century
Contemporary Issues in Entrepreneurship Research, Volume 18A, 75–89
Copyright © 2024 by Hannah Grannemann, Jennifer Reis, Maggie Murphy and Marie Segares
Published under exclusive licence by Emerald Publishing Limited
ISSN: 2040-7246/doi:10.1108/S2040-72462023000018A006

a mask-making venture. Informed by entrepreneurship literature, the authors observed that these nascent entrepreneurs articulated recognisable motivations for social entrepreneurship, showed signs of pre-existing entrepreneurial mindsets, and employed business models and marketing tactics of entrepreneurs, largely without any business training. Implications for the study include increased recognition of latent entrepreneurial readiness, interest of women in social entrepreneurship, and higher levels of business knowledge among women than previously recognised.

Keywords: COVID-19; mask-making; social entrepreneurship; creative entrepreneurs; nascent entrepreneurs; women entrepreneurs

1. INTRODUCTION

During the early months of the COVID-19 pandemic and continuing through much of 2020, a series of '[m]arket and government failures' led to widespread shortages of PPE throughout the United States (Cohen & Rodgers, 2020, p. 1). In early April 2020, the Centers for Disease Control and Prevention (CDC) recommended that Americans wear face coverings in public and reserve 'medical-grade' masks and respirators for healthcare professionals (Dwyer & Aubrey, 2020). Although not as effective as medical-grade PPE, cloth masks were more effective at stopping the spread of COVID-19 than not wearing a mask at all. However, large textile and medical manufacturing companies were not able to shift their production processes quickly enough to produce cloth masks. This created an extreme and sudden market opportunity for thousands of sewists to make, sell, and donate homemade masks to fill the need. Start-up costs (capital) were minimal, as existing hobby supplies commonly held by sewists such as cotton quilting fabric could be used to launch an enterprise using equipment they already owned such as sewing machines. Communities of sewists-turned-mask-makers shared information about where to source equipment and supplies when finding them was difficult due to supply chain problems triggered by the spike in demand for mask-making materials such as fabric, elastic, and wire.

In response to surging search demand for cloth masks after the CDC recommendation was announced, Etsy, an e-commerce platform for handmade and vintage products and craft supplies, contacted its sellers and urged them to list handmade masks on its site. Within weeks, Etsy had issued 'best practices' for selling handmade masks on its platform (VanderMey, 2020); by December 2020, sales revenue from handmade masks – just on the Etsy platform – amounted to $743 million (Dobush, 2021). Most Etsy sellers are women, with estimates ranging from 79% to 86% (Pengue, 2021; Snyder, 2015; Statista Research Department, 2022). Similarly, nearly 70% of hobbyists who sew in the United States are women (MaritzCX LLC, 2017).

We conducted a survey of mask-makers who made and sold and/or donated masks during 2020, asking them about their motivations and processes, and invited them to reflect on and share their experiences related to mask-making. Our respondents were overnight entrepreneurs who made thousands of masks. Our research could be used to better understand how to activate potential entrepreneurs and support them at the earliest stages of their ventures. Our research also has direct implications for research in business practices and the motivation of entrepreneurs in the social and creative/entrepreneurship sectors, an area that is currently lagging behind the research into entrepreneurs who are mainly motivated by profit. Our research adds to the literature on nascent entrepreneurs because the COVID-19 pandemic revealed a heretofore unknown base of thousands of ready entrepreneurs. Finally, since the vast majority of our respondents were women, researchers interested in gender dynamics will find the use for our research, especially as gender intersects with the other areas of entrepreneurship research we have named.

This chapter begins with a review of the extant literature on entrepreneurial motivations and mindsets, business models, and entrepreneurial marketing approaches. We then describe the methods we used to research mask-makers, who started making masks because PPE was not widely available to people outside of healthcare settings and their ventures. We introduce the sample this chapter will examine, present our findings, and discuss the limations of our study.

2. LITERATURE REVIEW

When our study began, mask-making during the COVID-19 pandemic was a novel phenomenon. Although there is historical precedent for women hobbyists to be mobilised during times of crisis to contribute 'volunteer labor' as part of the home front efforts during World War I and World War II (Martindale et al., 2020, p. 2), there is limited research on craft and artisan entrepreneurship during public health crises. Our literature review, therefore, covers relevant research on the four aspects of entrepreneurship we analysed in this chapter.

2.1. Motivations and Mindsets

Individuals engage in social and creative entrepreneurship for complex reasons. Intrinsic creative passion and desire for the autonomy to pursue a creative vision are the driving motivations for most creative entrepreneurs (Casulli et al., 2021; McKelvey & Lassen, 2018; Schulte-Holthaus, 2018; Toscher et al., 2020). Writing about crafts entrepreneurs at the nexus of 'professional' and 'amateur' who start online storefronts or sell wares on Etsy, Luckman (2013) observes 'self-fulfillment, autonomy, and flexibility have been identified as key reasons people undertake self-employed, pro-am work from home' (p. 165).

Financial crises, whether personal or systemic, have also historically motivated women who are amateur sewists, creative workers, or crafters to see 'their hobbies and artistry skills as a means to an income' (Russum, 2019, p. 124). Amateur artisans who go into business often cite receiving encouragement from friends and family as a motivating factor in their decision to sell their work (Close, 2014, 2016).

Jourdain and Naulin (2020) point to non-financial benefits, such as the desire for sociability and social recognition, as motivations for women in particular to convert creative hobbies into money-making ventures.

Most social entrepreneurs are driven by some form of prosocial motivation (Ruskin et al., 2016; Shaw & Carter, 2007; Stephan & Drencheva, 2017; Yitshaki & Kropp, 2016). Prosocial values and motivations are grounded in an individual's desire to help or benefit others and create positive change in society (Grant, 2009; Grant & Berry, 2011). Stephan and Drenchava found that social entrepreneurs often share motivations with commercial entrepreneurs including self-interest, profit, and 'the desire to seek out new situations and independence' (Stephan & Drencheva, 2017, p. 12). Both social and creative commercial entrepreneurs may also be motivated by the desire to develop or demonstrate self-efficacy, feel a sense of self-worth or value to others, or be part of a network or community (Aileen Boluk & Mottiar, 2014; Bacq & Alt, 2018; Mair & Noboa, 2006; McKelvey & Lassen, 2018; Toscher et al., 2020).

Understanding the entrepreneurial mindset as well as entrepreneurial readiness in creative makers is necessary as well. Eight domains of an entrepreneurial mindset have been defined as future orientation; creativity and innovation; comfort with risk; communication and collaboration; flexibility and adaptability; critical thinking and problem-solving; initiative and self-reliance; and opportunity recognition (Garman, 2020). Other literature has explored the continuum of entrepreneurship readiness and motivation in creative makers ranging from little interest to those ready to scale up into larger business structures (Bouette & Magee, 2015).

In a recent study of new and existing creative and social entrepreneurs who produced handmade masks during the early pandemic, Buford et al. (2021) found that mask-makers who 'were more entrepreneurial and saw mask-making as both beneficial for their local and global communities, as well as a source of supplemental income' and those that made masks out of a sense of obligation but refused any payment for their work shared the motivation of 'answering the call' (p. 38). Additional motivations of mask-makers included wanting to connect with a community during the crisis and finding an outlet for self-expression by making a political or artistic statement. Many of the mask-makers in the study were also motivated by a desire to contribute to the 'public good', both by helping their friends, family, and community, and by normalising mask-wearing (Buford, 2022; Buford et al., 2021).

2.2. Business Models

Business models were initially contextualised for the for-profit sector to describe a company's plan for becoming profitable (Kopp, 2020). Alternative business models have since emerged for social enterprises or companies that 'run commercial operations with the goal of addressing a societal problem' (Santos et al., 2015) to enable social enterprises to clarify how they view their purpose, value to customers/clients, and ways of earning income or becoming financially sustainable. Examples of business models in the social enterprise context include one-for-one

(Knowledge@Wharton, 2015), microfinance and entrepreneur support, employment, and service subsidisation (MaRS Discovery District, n.d.; Santos et al., 2015) models.

Creative makers inwardly or externally motivated to become entrepreneurial are unlikely to study entrepreneurship or business formally. Instead, they use mainstream books that focus on micro-enterprise and quick-to-launch 'side hustles' that recommend prototyping processes and fast market testing related to demand and financial viability (Guillebeau, 2015; Ries, 2011). Whitaker's popular book (2016) encourages 'portfolio thinking' in creative business ventures, viewing the approach as necessary in designing a viable business model that can withstand evolving market forces.

The Business Model Canvas by Osterwalder is a tool used by entrepreneurs and in entrepreneurship education (Osterwalder, 2004). Business models have also been adapted for use with the lean start-up approach which 'favors experimentation ..., customer feedback ..., and iterative design' (Blank, 2013). The Lean Canvas is a variation on the Business Model Canvas designed specifically for entrepreneurs with lean start-ups. It emphasises problems (of customers and/or society) and solutions (that the organisation can provide) and identifies the organisation's 'unfair advantage', which doesn't exist at the start but must be built into a competitive advantage (Maurya, 2012). The lean start-up approach also emphasises the development of a minimal viable product, one which is quickly developed with minimal work while future iterations are improved as knowledge about customers improves (Dennehy et al., 2019).

2.3. Marketing Approaches

The entrepreneurs were new, but their marketing tactics were well established. Entrepreneurial marketing tactics often rely more on using free or low-cost methods with the cost incurred in staff time than on high-cost methods such as purchasing advertising (Neck et al., 2018). To prevent losing ground to competition and to recognise emerging opportunities, environmental scanning is especially important for entrepreneurs in the early to middle stages of the product life cycle (Crane, 2010; Ruskin-Brown, 2008). Having an up-to-date understanding of a potential customer's circumstances is an advantage to an entrepreneur, as it gives them insight into how their product could fit the customer's needs (Christensen et al., 2016).

Pricing choices are affected by the availability and visibility of comparable products. Open markets with robust competition inspire the use of pricing tactics such as pricing at marginal or variable cost (Besanko et al., 1996; Ruskin-Brown, 2008) and competitive pricing, where prices are pegged to the prices of direct competitors (Kolb, 2015). Astute understanding of customer segments and their needs offers the opportunity to identify a way to offer value beyond basic needs and therefore increase price and profitability (Ruskin-Brown, 2008). Niche opportunities and smaller segments of customers with specific needs (Crane, 2010), offer the possibility of selling at 'prestige prices' (Kolb, 2015), more efficient and effective marketing efforts (Kolb, 2015) and higher profits (Ruskin-Brown, 2008). Artist entrepreneurs who directly sell their work and set their own prices often price their work taking into account the cost of materials and the time spent creating the work (O'Neil, 2008).

3. METHODS

As an interdisciplinary team, we developed a cross-sectional survey to be distributed online and asynchronously to explore the attitudes, opinions, and practices of individuals who made masks for distribution outside of the home during the early months of the COVID-19 pandemic (Segares et al., 2022). Although the survey included both closed and open questions, it was designed with a qualitative-first approach (Segares, 2022).

After receiving approval from the Institutional Review Board at the lead author's institution, we recruited participants through sharing a survey link with an invitation to participate on social network sites and through email and private messages to key informants. We encouraged sharing of the survey link with others who made handmade masks for distribution outside of the home to reach participants beyond our personal and professional networks. The survey was open for responses from mid-November 2020 through January 2021; 2,206 respondents began the survey, while 1,984 met the inclusion criteria. This chapter focuses on the responses of a sample of 94 participants who did not consider themselves to be 'creative entrepreneurs' in February 2020, but indicated they identified as 'creative entrepreneurs' after engaging in mask-making endeavours.

Establishing rapport in online research requires engaging enthusiastic participants through research that intrigues their interests (Mann & Stewart, 2003); this same passion may have introduced a limitation to our study. Because we recruited primarily through snowball sampling, which is non-randomised, it is possible that our sample is not representative (Atkinson & Flint, 2004) of the mask-making population as a whole. Though participants from across North America and in a range of income groups responded to the survey, the sample heavily favours White women.

4. FINDINGS

In this section, we share representative quotes from 17 participants included in our sample. We provide some summary demographic information of our sample of 94 respondents for context. The age distribution was as follows: 1% 18–24 years, 12% 25–34 years, 26% 35–44 years, 33% 45–54 years, 11% 55–64 years, and 17% 65 years and older. Ninety-seven percent of respondents identified themselves as female, 1% identified as male, and 2% identified as non-binary/gender non-conforming. An open text option for describing gender was available to respondents. Eighty-four percent of respondents identified themselves as White, 9% as Asian, 7% as Hispanic, Latinx, or Spanish Origin, 5% as Black or African American, 3% as Native American, American Indian, Alaska Native, Indigenous, or First Nation, and 1% as Native Hawaiian or other Pacific Islander. Respondents could choose more than one race or ethnicity and an open text option was also available. Of respondents from the United States, 27% of respondents were either from the Midwest or Southeastern, 23% of respondents were from the Northeast, 11% were from the West, and 8% were from the Southwest. Five percent of respondents were from Canada. The 2019 household income of the respondents was as follows: 7% less than $25,000, 12% $25–34,999, 18% $35–49,999, 14% $50–74,999, 14% $75–99,999, 32% $100–199,999, and 2% $200,000 or more.

While all 94 participants donated or gave away some of the masks they made, and 75 participants made both masks to sell and masks to distribute for free, the remaining 19 participants solely made masks to distribute for free. We assigned each respondent used in this sample a pseudonym.

5. ENTREPRENEURIAL MINDSETS: A MIX OF NECESSITY, OPPORTUNITY, AND PROSOCIAL MOTIVATIONS

Tens of millions of Americans lost their jobs in the early months of the pandemic, leading to severe financial difficulties. Lani made masks to help pay her bills, noting that she had never 'promoted my work for sale before', but that a friend encouraged her to sell them. Heather, who previously worked as a fabricator, set up an online store to sell her masks, which 'gave me a real boost economically and emotionally, to sell a good product that people were happy to pay me for', and plans to expand her offerings to other products after the demand for cloth masks waned.

The sudden widespread demand for PPE presented itself as an opportunity for our respondents to go into business for themselves. Crystal, who had made a New Year's resolution to make more art, reflected, 'I saw a wide open market to step into'. James similarly responded, 'I saw an opportunity and made it work for me'. Kristen, a nurse, explained that after she bought masks for her family members, she 'saw how they're made and thought, I can make these', going on to sell masks through Facebook.

Many participants articulated political and prosocial reasons for mask-making. Barbara, who learned to sew to make masks, explained, 'I did not see the administration supporting any kind of prevention, so saw many were taking it on themselves to do so. I did as it gave me a purpose and I felt like I had a role in helping'. Michelle, who operated a free mask distribution point that served thousands in her community before she started making masks for sale, was motivated by 'the desire to benefit the community and bring it together at a time when we were increasingly splintered'. Crystal articulated a similar motivation, 'Covid hit my Brooklyn neighborhood early and hard ... The morgue trucks were everywhere. I had COVID bad, myself. Action needed to be taken'.

Finally, many participants reflected on the impact mask-making had on their creative confidence and identity. Before the pandemic, Angela volunteered as a customer for a local theatre company and circus. However, after selling her handmade masks, she now states

Many more people now know that I sew and a few have asked me to do other projects. It has
also given me more confidence in my sewing and I have now had ideas about creating a small
business that would reach beyond masks and costuming.

Julie, a needlework hobbyist who made masks to supplement her income,
reflected, 'People want my items. Some people only use my masks exclusively. It's
a powerful feeling. And while I am stuck at home, it gives me an outlet'.

6. INNOVATIVE AND HYBRID BUSINESS MODELS

Participants used a range of business models in their mask-making ventures,
especially varieties of social enterprise models. Ashley used the one-for-one
model, noting that 'for each one I sold I donated one to my local church, where
they were distributed to the local homeless population and others in need' while
others aimed to recover supply costs while avoiding generating a profit. Another
common practice was exemplified by Amy, who used the proceeds from sales to
purchase more material for masks she would donate.

Some operated informally and asked prospective buyers to donate to charity
in lieu of payment. Lisa said she 'could not imagine myself charging for masks
during this time' and instead asked recipients of her masks to donate to charity.
Others developed formal non-profit organisations. Jessica shared, '[w]e built a
501c3 on the fly that is closing in on 100,000 masks donated, so I went from being
a home sewist to basically building a startup (except none of us are getting paid)'.

Social enterprise models do not prohibit retaining profits. Ten participants in
the sample specifically mentioned financial needs, including due to unemployment or furlough, as factoring into their decision to sell masks. Most who sold
masks used a retail selling business model, relying on word of mouth, e-commerce platforms such as Etsy, or social networking sites such as Facebook for
marketing and distribution. A few developed a wholesale model, selling masks in
bulk to local organisations to provide to employees.

Although she mentioned that she 'never had any ambition to sell my work ...
[and] still don't', Lisa now identifies as a creative entrepreneur because 'people
would pay for it if I charged. Also, people are often surprised that I don't charge
and try to encourage me to. And so, now I kind of think of myself as a very very
minor humanitarian'.

7. CUSTOMER NEEDS AND PRODUCT DEVELOPMENT

As the pandemic continued, mask-makers adapted their products to match the
changing interests of their customers. Customers began observing the range of
quality available such as masks with wiring for a better fit over noses or to prevent
fogging glasses. Many mask-makers showed pride in the quality of masks, using
quality as a differentiating point. Rachel wrote: 'Some people say they feel safest
using mine, and I want them to feel as safe as possible'. Kristina wrote: 'People
are aware now that we will be in masks for quite a while and want comfortable,

attractive ones instead of cheap'. A popular choice was to use different patterned fabrics to reflect the interest of their customers, such as cartoon characters or sports teams. Sara wrote: 'If we've got to wear them, make them fun to wear! (I do a lot of character masks like Mickey [Mouse])'. Rachel wrote: 'What I make now we call "luxury masks"... people have all they need, so they are not a necessity but more for self-expression. I like to think people enjoy my designs and my fabric choices'.

These product improvements and differentiations came with the ability of the mask-makers to command a higher price and increase profits. Kimberly shared: 'I am now selling premium masks with all the bells and whistles to help supplement my income'. Some makers who were using the profits from their masks to purchase supplies remarked that it allowed them to fund making masks for people who could not afford them. Sara wrote, 'Any extra $[*sic.*] went towards buying more expensive material with characters or custom material ... I could make unique masks and still make a little $[*sic*] on the side'.

8. DISCUSSION

We identified three dominant themes in the comments from the participants in our sample that illuminate their entrepreneurial approach: entrepreneurial motivations and mindset, business model innovation and hybridisation, and marketing approaches that are low cost and emphasise cooperation.

8.1. Motivation and Mindset: Affective Benefit, Market Opportunity, Necessity Entrepreneurship

The extreme market demand during the COVID-19 pandemic encouraged entrepreneurial thinking in makers who had limited to no economic activity previously related to their creative practice. Participants described a wide range of motivations and mindsets for engaging in mask-making, all consistent with the literature on creative micro-enterprise and social entrepreneurship. From this, a few clear trends emerged.

Some participants' initial motivations for making masks overlapped with their motivations for engaging in creative entrepreneurship because they saw these activities as one and the same. Many mask-makers who were entrepreneurially minded from the outset were motivated by the need for income replacement due to the economic interruptions caused by COVID-19. These participants, who previously had little interest in monetising their creative practice or taking the skills from their creative profession into a 'side hustle' space, provide a clear demonstration of the necessity entrepreneurship and entrepreneurial mindsets such as initiative and self-reliance. Many participants who were out of work during the pandemic noted that making and selling masks helped them pay rent as well as childcare, medical, and veterinary bills, among other expenses. At the same time, a major shift to entrepreneurial thinking was abruptly brought about through participants' opportunity recognition from the extreme market demand.

Political activism and communitarian ideals were major motivations behind many respondents' social and creative entrepreneurship, whether distinct from or intersecting with profit motivations. However, whether initially motivated by profits, politics, or prosocial ideals, making masks provided many participants with new opportunities for creative expression, skill validation, and personal growth. These experiences in turn served as motivators for these mask-maskers to develop new creative entrepreneurial identities and/or ventures. Many pivoted the experience of developing and managing a mask-making business into other creative entrepreneurial activities. Pride in creativity and innovation were apparent in responses about selling for the first time, which may mean that these entrepreneurs will continue to develop their businesses even as the acute need for masks wanes.

8.2. Business Models Innovation and Hybridisation

Within this sample, all participants included donating or giving away masks within their business models. Twenty percent developed what we categorised as purely social enterprise business models where they did not sell any masks, while the remaining 80% operated hybrid models wherein they both donated/gave away masks and sold masks. Participants who donated all of the masks they made used a variety of social enterprise business models including donating free masks directly to non-profit organisations, providing free masks to individuals in exchange for donations to charitable organisations, joining collectives where mask-makers were matched with people in need of PPE, and creating formalised non-profit organisations.

Among the participants who developed hybrid models, the one-for-one and sliding scale or 'pay what you wish' models were most common. In the one-for-one model, participants would donate a mask for each mask sold. In the sliding scale or 'pay what you wish' models, some participants kept their earnings as profits while others reinvested in supplies to make more masks for donation.

Because demand for PPE was so high during the early months of the pandemic, many participants found mask-making to be profitable as a full-time business or side project. Others were able to sustain the social enterprise elements of their business through donations. As the pandemic wore on and PPE became more widely available, some participants began to develop and exploit an 'unfair advantage' (Maurya, 2012) to incorporate into their business models. Participants discussed using specialised fabrics, developing mask designs that were more comfortable or better fitting, and creating seasonal product offerings (e.g. Halloween or Christmas masks).

8.3. Marketing: Cooperation and Low-cost Tactics

The mask-makers' marketing approaches were in alignment with their social entrepreneurship business models and prosocial motivations. They were primarily pursuing social goals to reduce the spread of COVID-19, not maximise profits or push competitors out of the market.

Utilising low-cost marketing tactics is typical of early-stage entrepreneurs. Mask-makers did not maximise or invest significantly in their marketing opportunities because there was a large demand and easily accessed customers. In fact, many mask-makers describe feeling overwhelmed and burnt out in their mask-making, often not able to handle all the requests. Motivated by prosocial goals to increase mask-wearing by the general public, there were very few responses about trying to edge out competitors and many shared ways they were cooperating with other mask-makers. There was a great deal of imitation of competitors on pricing, but not undercutting on prices to gain more market share. Many respondents describe their products as higher quality than competitors, so competed on quality rather than price. The demand for homemade masks in early 2020 was so high that there was not a great need for marketing; a mask-maker needed only to put the word out that they were making and donating or selling masks and they were inundated with requests. Listing their masks on sales platforms such as Etsy, relying on word of mouth through friends and family, and posting on social media were plenty effective for this group to meet its goals. Word of mouth (used by 75% of respondents), followed by Facebook (used by 69% of respondents), were by far the most popular options for mask-makers in our study to choose for the promotion of their masks. Promotion on Facebook was a grassroots effort, which took the form of posting in neighbourhood, professional, or interest groups and using the platform to reach personal connections to increase awareness about the availability of masks they had made.

As the pandemic continued into 2020, after it became clear that the situation would last longer than a few weeks or a couple of months, people began to amass a personal collection of masks. With this shift, mask-makers in our study began to create differentiated products to match the interests of their customers.

9. CONCLUSIONS

Though they may have discovered an interest in entrepreneurship in their own right while making and selling/donating masks, creating a new business was not the intention for most of the entrepreneurs in our study, even if it was an outcome. The social enterprise model was dominant among the new entrepreneurs in our study. Further, we observed that these entrepreneurs often engaged in a two-phase process within the rapid timeframe between March 2020 and when they completed our survey in late 2020 or early 2021. At the beginning of the COVID-19 pandemic, mask-makers made basic masks. Later, they transitioned to making and selling more complex masks. This is similar to entrepreneurs who begin with a 'minimum viable product' to test their product idea and market, then iterate and continue to develop their products, and learn more about their customer base. Additionally, we observed a trend where respondents eased their way into entrepreneurship by first donating masks, then shifting to selling (many while continuing to donate) masks. For many participants, the experience of increased confidence and skill validation from mask-making served as an on-ramp for developing an entrepreneurial identity. These entrepreneurs had the full ability to start a venture, but hadn't done so prior to the COVID-19 pandemic. In this way, our study has implications for future research on latent entrepreneurship, nascent entrepreneurs, and entrepreneurial identity. Groups interested in increasing entrepreneurial activity, such as local governments or non-profits supporting entrepreneurship, may take note of the existence of these thousands of social entrepreneurs who seem to have had a high level of entrepreneurial readiness, most of whom are women, and use our research to improve their understanding how to empower and engage the potential entrepreneurs in their communities.

Furthermore, future research on how these entrepreneurs chose and used their business strategies could inform how entrepreneurs are educated inside and outside of higher education; clearly, they had internalised many business theories without a formal business education. Our research warrants more examination of existing motivation for social entrepreneurship and how it can be activated. Finally, our sample was vastly dominated by women and may specifically inform future research on women entrepreneurs in all of the categories we explore here: necessity, social, and creative entrepreneurship, and all the permutations of those categories.

ACKNOWLEDGEMENTS

We thank the thousands of participants in our survey who shared their stories graciously and used their sewing skills to support public health.

REFERENCES

Aileen Boluk, K., & Mottiar, Z. (2014). Motivations of social entrepreneurs: Blurring the social contribution and profits dichotomy. *Social Enterprise Journal, 10*(1), 53–68. http://dx.doi.org/10.1108/SEJ-01-2013-0001

Atkinson, R., & Flint, J. (2004). Snowball sampling. In M. Lewis-Beck, A. Bryman, & T. Futing Liao (Eds.), *The SAGE encyclopedia of social science research methods*. Sage Publications, Inc. https://doi.org/10.4135/9781412950589

Bacq, S., & Alt, E. (2018). Feeling capable and valued: A prosocial perspective on the link between empathy and social entrepreneurial intentions. *Journal of Business Venturing, 33*(3), 333–350. https://doi.org/10.1016/j.jbusvent.2018.01.004

Besanko, D., Dranove, D., & Shanley, M.. (1996). *The economics of strategy*. John Wiley. http://digitool.hbz-nrw.de:1801/webclient/DeliveryManager?pid=1545160&custom_att_2=simple_viewer

Blank, S. (2013). Why the lean start-up changes everything. *Harvard Business Review*, May. https://hbr.org/2013/05/why-the-lean-start-up-changes-everything

Bouette, M., & Magee, F. (2015). Hobbyists, artisans and entrepreneurs: Investigating business support and identifying entrepreneurial profiles in the Irish craft sector. *Journal of Small Business and Enterprise Development, 22*, 337–351.

Buford, M. (2022). Beyond crisis couture: The creative resilience of mask makers in the pandemic and how we can shape our futures. *XRDS: Crossroads, The ACM Magazine for Students, 28*(2), 46–50. https://doi.org/10.1145/3495261

Buford, M., Nattar Ranganathan, V., Roseway, A., & Seyed, T. (2021). Crisis couture: A study on motivations and practices of mask makers during a crisis. In *Designing interactive systems conference 2021* (pp. 31–47). Association for Computing Machinery. https://doi.org/10.1145/3461778.3462016

Casulli, L., Knox, S., MacLaren, A. C., & Farrington, T. (2021). Art-identity founders, venturing processes, and entrepreneurship: Implications for policy. *Journal of the International Council for Small Business*, 2(4), 303–312. https://doi.org/10.1080/26437015.2021.1944794

Christensen, C. M., Hall, T., Dillon, K., & Duncan, D. S. (2016). Know your customers' "Jobs to Be Done." *Harvard Business Review*, September 1. https://hbr.org/2016/09/know-your-customers-jobs-to-be-done

Close, S. (2014). Crafting an ideal working world in the contemporary United States. *Anthropology Now*, 6(3), 68–79.

Close, S. (2016). The political economy of creative entrepreneurship on digital platforms: Case study of Etsy.com. In *49th Hawaii international conference on system sciences* (pp. 1901–1908). https://doi.org/10.1109/HICSS.2016.241

Cohen, J., & Rodgers, Y. M. (2020). Contributing factors to personal protective equipment shortages during the COVID-19 pandemic. *Preventive Medicine*, *141*, 106263. https://doi.org/10.1016/j.ypmed.2020.106263

Crane, F. (2010). *Marketing for entrepreneurs: Concepts and applications for new ventures*. SAGE Publications, Inc. https://doi.org/10.4135/9781452274836

Dennehy, D., Kasraian, L., O'Raghallaigh, P., Conboy, K., Sammon, D., & Lynch, P. (2019). A lean start-up approach for developing minimum viable products in an established company. *Journal of Decision Systems*, *28*(3), 224–232. https://doi.org/10.1080/12460125.2019.1642081

Dobush, G. (2021, March 8). *Etsy's blockbuster pandemic year*. Craft Industry Alliance. https://craftindustryalliance.org/etsys-blockbuster-pandemic-year/

Dwyer, C., & Aubrey, A. (2020). CDC now recommends Americans consider wearing cloth face coverings in public. *NPR*, April 3. https://www.npr.org/sections/coronavirus-live-updates/2020/04/03/826219824/president-trump-says-cdc-now-recommends-americans-wear-cloth-masks-in-public

Garman, K. (2020). *The entrepreneurial mindset: Preparing our next generation for the future of work*. New Degree Press.

Grant, A. M. (2009). Putting self-interest out of business? Contributions and unanswered questions from use-inspired research on prosocial motivation. *Industrial and Organizational Psychology*, 2(1), 94–98. https://doi.org/10.1111/j.1754-9434.2008.01113.x

Grant, A. M., & Berry, J. W. (2011). The necessity of others is the mother of invention: Intrinsic and prosocial motivations, perspective taking, and creativity. *The Academy of Management Journal*, 54(1), 73–96.

Guillebeau, C. (2015). *The $100 startup: Reinvent the way you make a living, dow what your love, and create a new future*. Pan Macmillan.

Jourdain, A., & Naulin, S. (2020). Making money out of leisure: The marketization of handicrafts and food blogging. In S. Naulin & A. Jourdain (Eds.), *The social meaning of extra money: Capitalism and the commodification of domestic and leisure activities* (pp. 61–95). Springer International Publishing. https://doi.org/10.1007/978-3-030-18297-7_3

Knowledge@Wharton. (2015). *The one-for-one business model: Avoiding unintended consequences*. Knowledge@Wharton. https://knowledge.wharton.upenn.edu/article/one-one-business-model-social-impact-avoiding-unintended-consequences/

Kolb, B. M. (2015). *Entrepreneurship for the creative and cultural industries*. Routledge. https://doi.org/10.4324/9781315778907

Kopp, C. M. (2020). Business models. *Investopedia*. https://www.investopedia.com/terms/b/business-model.asp

Luckman, S. (2013). The aura of the analogue in a digital age: Women's crafts, creative markets and home-based labour after Etsy. *Cultural Studies Review*, *19*(1), 249–270. https://doi.org/10.5130/csr.v19i1.2585

Mair, J., & Noboa, E. (2006). Social entrepreneurship: How intentions to create a social venture are formed. In J. Mair, J. Robinson, & K. Hockerts (Eds.), *Social entrepreneurship* (pp. 121–135). Palgrave Macmillan. https://doi.org/10.1057/9780230625655_8

Mann, C., & Stewart, F. (2003). Internet interviewing. In J. Gubrium & J. Holstein (Eds.), *Postmodern interviewing*. SAGE Publications, Inc. https://doi.org/10.4135/9781412985437

MaritzCX LLC. (2017). *2016 Creative products size of the industry study UPDATE Q4 2016 – Q3 2017.* Association for Creative Industries.

MaRS Discovery District. (n.d.). *Social enterprise business models.* MaRS Discovery District. https:// learn.marsdd.com/article/social-enterprise-business-models/

Martindale, A. K., Armstead, C. C., & McKinney, E. C. (2020, December 28). Knit your socks and sew your masks: Hand knitting in the world wars compared with home sewing masks for COVID-19. *Pivoting for the pandemic.* https://doi.org/10.31274/itaa.12047

Maurya, A. (2012, February 27). *Why lean canvas vs business model canvas?*LEANSTACK. https:// blog.leanstack.com/why-lean-canvas-vs-business-model-canvas/

McKelvey, M., & Lassen, A. H. (2018). Knowledge, meaning and identity: Key characteristics of entrepreneurship in cultural and creative industries. *Creativity and Innovation Management, 27*(3), 281–283. https://doi.org/10.1111/caim.12293

Neck, H. M., Neck, C. P., & Murray, E. L. (2018). *Entrepreneurship: The practice and mindset.* SAGE.

O'Neil, K. M. (2008). Bringing art to market: The diversity of pricing styles in a local art market. *Poetics, 36*(1), 94–113. https://doi.org/10.1016/j.poetic.2007.12.002

Osterwalder, A. (2004). *The business model ontology: A proposition in a design science approach.* Ph.D. thesis, University of Lausanne. http://www.hec.unil.ch/aosterwa/PhD/Osterwalder_PhD_BM_ Ontology.pdf

Pengue, M. (2021, June 30). *Etsy statistics: Buyers demographics, revenues, and sales.* Writer's Block Live. https://writersblocklive.com/blog/etsy-statistics/

Ries, E. (2011). *The Lean Startup: How today's entrepreneurs use continuous innovation to create radically successful businesses.* Crown Business.

Ruskin, J., Seymour, R. G., & Webster, C. M. (2016). Why create value for others? An exploration of social entrepreneurial motives. *Journal of Small Business Management, 54*(4), 1015–1037. https://doi.org/10.1111/jsbm.12229

Ruskin-Brown, I. (2008). *Practical pricing for results* (Vol. 1–1 online resource (xiv, 371 pages): illustrations). Thorogood; WorldCat.org. http://site.ebrary.com/id/10263883

Russum, J. A. (2019). Sewing entrepreneurs and the myth of the spheres: How the "Work at Home Mom" complicates the public-private divide. *Frontiers, 40*(3), 117–138.

Santos, F., Pache, A.-C., & Birkholz, C. (2015). Making hybrids work: Aligning business models and organizational design for social enterprises. *California Management Review, 57*(3), 36–58. https://doi.org/10.1525/cmr.2015.57.3.36

Schulte-Holthaus, S. (2018). Entrepreneurship in the creative industries: A literature review and research agenda. In E. Innerhofer, H. Pechlaner, & E. Borin (Eds.), *Entrepreneurship in culture and creative industries* (pp. 99–154). Springer International Publishing. https://doi.org/10.1007/978-3-319-65506-2_7

Segares, M. (2022). Qualitative online surveys: Lessons learned from COVID-19. In *SAGE research methods: Doing research online.* SAGE Publications. https://doi.org/10.4135/9781529601268

Segares, M., Grannemann, H., Reis, J. A., & Murphy, M. (2022). Mask-making and entrepreneurial opportunity in the time of COVID-19. *Journal of the International Council for Small Business, 3*(2), 153–161. https://doi.org/10.1080/26437015.2021.1971581

Shaw, E., & Carter, S. (2007). Social entrepreneurship: Theoretical antecedents and empirical analysis of entrepreneurial processes and outcomes. *Journal of Small Business and Enterprise Development, 14*(3), 418–434. https://doi.org/10.1108/14626000710773529

Snyder, B. (2015, July 23). *A huge percentage of Etsy sellers are women.* Fortune. https://fortune. com/2015/07/23/etsy-sellers-women

Statista Research Department. (2022, May 9). *Etsy – Statistics & facts.* Statista. https://www.statista. com/topics/2501/etsy/#dossierKeyfigures

Stephan, U., & Drencheva, A. (2017). The person in social entrepreneurship. In Ahmetoglu, G., Chamorro-Premuzic, T., Klinger, B., & Karcisky, T. (Eds.), *The Wiley handbook of entrepreneurship* (pp. 205–229). John Wiley & Sons, Ltd. https://doi.org/10.1002/9781118970812.ch10

Toscher, B., Dahle, Y., & Steinert, M. (2020). Get give make live: An empirical comparative study of motivations for technology, youth and arts entrepreneurship. *Social Enterprise Journal, 16*(2), 179–202. https://doi.org/10.1108/SEJ-03-2019-0016

VanderMey, A. (2020, April 7). *Etsy rallies its artisanal troops: 'Start making face masks': Some crafters are working 12-hour days to meet surging demand.* Bloomberg. https://www.bloomberg.com/news/articles/2020-04-07/face-masks-on-etsy-are-a-top-seller

Whitaker, A. (2016). *Art thinking: How to carve out creative space in a world of schedules, budgets, and bosses.* HarperCollins.

Yitshaki, R., & Kropp, F. (2016). Motivations and opportunity recognition of social entrepreneurs. *Journal of Small Business Management, 54*(2), 546–565. https://doi.org/10.1111/jsbm.12157

CHAPTER 7

FOSTERING CREATIVE ENTREPRENEURSHIP THROUGH SELF-HELP GROUP: POST-COVID RESILIENCE

Bhawana Bhardwaj, Balkrishan and Dipanker Sharma

ABSTRACT

Creative entrepreneurship is a vital concept that revolves around setting up a business that is novel, thoughtful, lucrative, and yet compassionate. The global pandemic has made people realise the significance and importance of creative entrepreneurship. Self-help groups (SHGs) play a pivotal role in boosting the rural economy and empowering people. Rural creative entrepreneurship has witnessed a significant transformation during the COVID-19 pandemic. The conventional concepts vanished due to the modern shift towards digitisation. Usage of the technology became the new normal and SHGs made all possible efforts to acclimatise promptly. Online virtual meetings, conference calls, and groups on WhatsApp made common people techno-savvy, facilitating work from home. The adoption of digitisation became a catalyst for the development of remote/rural areas. The present study is focused on the role of creative entrepreneurship in supporting and helping SHGs to function seamlessly during the COVID-19 pandemic. The authors aimed at analysing pandemic and post-pandemic creative entrepreneurship through SHGs in Himachal Pradesh (India). The authors identify that Creative Entrepreneurship initiatives have changed and supported the livelihood of rural people during the pandemic. This chapter also highlights challenges faced by the SHGs during the lockdown and their resilience strategies.

Creative (and Cultural) Industry Entrepreneurship in the 21st Century
Contemporary Issues in Entrepreneurship Research, Volume 18A, 91–104
Copyright © 2024 by Bhawana Bhardwaj, Balkrishan and Dipanker Sharma
Published under exclusive licence by Emerald Publishing Limited
ISSN: 2040-7246/doi:10.1108/S2040-72462023000018A007

Keywords: Creative entrepreneurship; self-help group; women; COVID-19; resilience; rural

1. INTRODUCTION

Creative entrepreneurship is one dynamic and still emerging area that entails establishing a firm that is unique, thoughtful, lucrative, and compassionate (Bhardwaj & Sharma, 2022). The words creative and entrepreneurship are dovetailed to form creative entrepreneurship. The term 'creative' refers to something unique in its origins or an original idea. Entrepreneurship, on the other hand, is creating a business on one's own and taking on the risk and profit factors. Jean Baptiste Say and Joseph Schumpeter were pioneers in the field of entrepreneurship. Joseph Schumpeter, coined the term entrepreneurship and defined it as 'Entrepreneurship is a creative activity' (Schumpeter, 2000). It is also defined as 'the combination of productive factors and objectify the same as a creative social-economic factor' (Long, 1983).

Furthermore, Jean Baptiste first coined the word 'entrepreneur' in the eighteenth century (Steiner, 2002) defining 'entrepreneur' as 'someone who anticipates the optimal use of resources in such a way that it progresses towards a profitable conclusion while encountering challenges along the way'. Entrepreneurship allows flexibility, energy, invention, and, above all, novelty. Art merchants, wedding photographers, musicians, and bloggers are a few examples of creative entrepreneurship. The concept has a long history and has been clarified by researchers who have refined the phrase regularly to contribute to the research (Landström, 2005). As a result, to succeed in those undertakings, one needs to have a wide range of managerial skills (McKelvey & Lassen, 2018).

A SHG is a small group of people voluntarily and mutually established to achieve a specific purpose. The members of the group pool their resources and assist one another (Katz, 1976). Members' contributions are minimal, and women are typically included in the informal group. These organisations assist women in developing saving habits and increasing their income (Kondal, 2014). SHGs are important for the development of the rural economy and for empowering people (Cord, 2021; Nordberg et al., 2020). Creative industries play a role in rural development, and SHG acts as a source of finance for starting such industries. Like other industries, rural creative entrepreneurship has faced transformation during the COVID pandemic (Bodh, 2020). Due to the modern shift towards digitisation, traditional techniques have transformed. Technology is the new normal, and SHGs have sought to adapt as quickly as possible. Common people are techno-savvy as a result of online virtual meetings, conference calls, and WhatsApp groups, allowing them to work from home to work from anywhere. Digitisation has aided the development of isolated and rural places (Myovella et al., 2021).

India is a densely populated country with around 1.21 billion population, having a variety of cultural diversity (Census India, 2022). Situated in the Himalayas,

Himachal Pradesh is a hill state of India, with a total population of 6.8 million where the majority lives in the rural areas, amounting to 6.1 million (Census India, 2022). With such a vast population, people in rural areas often keep themselves busy with their household works. Extant literature significantly discusses their survival during pandemic. Rural creative industries, on the other hand, have played a significant role that has gone unappreciated (Khlystova et al., 2022).

The current study has focused on rural creative industries and their role in assisting rural people in surviving during pandemics and lockdowns. Our research aims to address this gap and contribute to the literature on rural creative entrepreneurship. We observe the role and importance of creative entrepreneurships among SHG members in Himachal Pradesh, India. Specifically, our study tries to answer the following research questions:

RQ1: How have SHGs supported rural people during COVID-19 by fostering creative entrepreneurship?
RQ2: What are the basic creative activities that SHGs introduced during COVID-19 pandemic?
RQ3: How have the lives of members of SHGs changed as a result of the creative industries?

To answer the above questions, we have taken women SHGs as a sampling unit and the role of creative entrepreneurship in their survival journey during a pandemic. We use a case study approach taking into consideration the role of SHGs under the Aegis of CORD (Chinmay Organisation for Rural Development). CORD is an NGO that is actively involved in Managing and Supporting SHGs. Using secondary sources, this paper highlights the creative industry, its features, and its significance in Rural India. We identify the role of creative entrepreneurship in the upliftment of the rural population through SHGs in Section 2. Section 3 discusses the role of SHGs Initiatives in Lockdown during pandemic. Sections 4 discusses the results of the case study method adopted to understand the role of creative entrepreneurship among SHGs. The last section (Section 5) discussed the results and future scope of the study.

2. CREATIVE ENTREPRENEURSHIP: AN OVERVIEW

The term Creative Entrepreneurship means the art of establishing a business in an industry that is novel as well as creative in nature. Being an entrepreneur is a risky task, yet rewarding sometimes, so the entrepreneur who is practicing this must be master in the said field on his own or can leverage assistance in the task (Bujor & Avasilcai, 2014). Creative entrepreneurship is related to creative industries whose driving force is the entrepreneur. The creative industries are basically the ones that work in the arena which involves thinking and make others involve in the process too through their work (Bujor & Avasilcai, 2016). The creative entrepreneur through his creativity, ideas, and passion makes money out of it. The unique selling proposition in this case deems to be creative and generates uniqueness (Bujor & Avasilcai, 2014). Sustainability is the key to creative indus-tries for the long run survival, as it is being guided by fashion, young people, and taste preferences (Bakoğlu & Yıldırım, 2016).

2.1 Features of Creative Entrepreneurship

2.1.1. Related to Something New
Novelty is constantly encouraged in creative entrepreneurship. When there is newness, it brings uniqueness. The fresh ideas make everything interesting, but they also make everything risky (Henry et al., 2011).

2.1.2. Entrepreneur as the Main Doer
The entrepreneur is the protagonist of the story. He develops the concept and applies it to the business. The concept is at the centre of his profession, and the entrepreneur is a facilitator (Wu et al., 2021).

2.1.3. Sustainability
When starting a creative enterprise, the entrepreneur must keep one thing in mind and that is appropriateness. The ability to survive for prolonged periods of time is based on the combination of adaptation and resource alignment (Parrish, 2008).

2.1.4. Continuous Thinking Process
Creative Entrepreneurship is a never-ending process that evokes critical thinking. It generates ideas that are novel and causes others to shift their ways of thinking or, more likely, to think in a whole other way (Tehseen & Haider, 2021).

2.1.5. Investor of Talent
Creative entrepreneurs are individuals who invest in talent. They do so on their own or with the support of others (Bujor & Avasilcai, 2016). Just because of their talent, it became the way to earn the money (Mickel et al., 2013).

2.1.6. Significance of Creative Entrepreneurship
Creative entrepreneurs are the enablers of innovation. The thing that should be kept in mind while innovating is that it must not only satisfy the actual demand of the people but also exceed it (Yeşil et al., 2013). The other importance of being a creative entrepreneur is that it has evolved the thinking of others and let them consider the same scenario in an entirely different way. This will open up the horizon for new things and further will anchor more (Rahim & Mohtar, 2015). The new way of doing things always has an impact on productivity. The outcome surely increases whenever a new or creative idea is posted in a picture. The impor-tant thing that has to be taken care of is the skill set of the entrepreneur as well as the people employed under him. The new always brings further problems, and if there is no proper mechanism, the risk of failure will be evident (Poschke, 2013).

Creative entrepreneurship fosters organisational ambidexterity. As it not only explores innovation but also lets the people working under the employer exploit its potential to the fullest. The employees always have an ocean of information and ideas that can be a sustainable plus for the creative industries (Volery et al., 2015). Creative entrepreneurship makes boundaries collide and makes the discipline interdisciplinary (Ripsas, 1998).

2.2. Types of Creative Entrepreneurship

2.2.1. Entrepreneurs as Creative Service Providers
End users receive exclusive services from these types of entrepreneurs. Because the consumer is king, they must have direct contact with them to inform them of their current requirements. They profit from their one-of-a-kind services. The key characteristic of this type of entrepreneur is that they rely heavily and exclusively on technology and digitisation. The majority of their work is project-based and self-funded. Creative service providers include advertising agencies, design consultancies, and architecture firms, to name a few (Bujor & Avasilcai, 2014).

2.2.2. Entrepreneurs as Creative Content Producers
Creative entrepreneurs in this arena are engaged in the development of creative projects. Just like creative service providers, they are also highly influenced by the usage of digitisation. The basic limitation faced by them is falling into the threat of piracy. Film, television, music labels, and fashion designers are a few examples of the same (Bujor & Avasilcai, 2014).

2.2.3. Entrepreneurs as Creative Experience Providers
The entrepreneurs are basically providing their lifelong experiences to the clients. They basically pay for the others' copyright. The technology is used as a tool for communication to reach out to the end users.

2.2.4. Entrepreneurs as a Creative Original Producers
They are the ones who bring things into existence from concept to actuality. As the creators are small craftspeople, their work is largely funded by non-governmental organisations. However, because the work is primarily a work of art, it is not mass manufactured due to restricted resources. Typically, such work is done on a contract basis and is less commercialised. Visual arts, crafts, and designer-maker antiques are examples (Bujor & Avasilcai, 2014).

3. CREATIVE ENTREPRENEURSHIP AND COVID-19: ROLE OF SHGs

The pandemic has thrown the global economy into disarray. The pandemic provided possibilities for people to strive for the best in their own lives (Sharma, Chaudhary,

Jaswal, & Bhardwaj, 2022; Song & Zhou, 2020). Due to the modern shift towards digitisation, traditional conceptions are disappearing. Technology is the new normal, and SHGs have sought to adapt as quickly as possible (Herath & Herath, 2020). The use of the internet in private spaces is beneficial for society. It not only gave individuals confidence but also allowed them to unite on a worldwide scale (Fisher, 2020).

India is a rural society, with rural areas housing half of the population (Census 2011). People rely on agricultural pursuits to make a living. People were stressed by the lockdown since they were confined within the four walls of their homes. Due to a technological divide, the communication medium was disrupted. The public was terrified in the initial period of the pandemic. There was anarchy, and people were struggling for their everyday survival in the midst of it. They were feeling helpless because there was a standstill scenario all around them. Getting groceries and other necessities has become a difficult undertaking.

The collective strength of women's SHGs has come into focus as 1.3 billion Indians face an extraordinary 40-day lockdown to battle the COVID-19 situation. SHG women are involved in Creative entrepreneurship such as mask-making, running community kitchens, distributing crucial food supplies, and sensitising people about health and cleanliness in about 90 per cent of rural districts of India. As of today, around 67 million Indian household women are members of SHGs. Looking at the facts and figures, around 19 million masks have been made by 20,000 SHGs across 27 Indian States. SHGs have established 10,000 community kitchens around the country. SHG members were actively using their WhatsApp group to reduce the uncertainty and mayhem caused by rumours and misinformation. SHG members assisted the elderly and those who were quarantined by distributing vital meals (World Bank, 2020).

Himachal Pradesh's state government has given the Himachal Pradesh State Livelihood Mission (HPSRLM) 50,000 rupees to help support the masks' production. The self-help organisation produced roughly 32,000 masks, with the majority going to rural local bodies, police agencies, IPH departments, and other departments across the state's several districts (Govt. of Himachal Pradesh, 2020). In addition, SHG was producing 100 personal protective equipment kits every day to combat the crisis (Times of India, 2022).

4. METHODOLOGY

This study is qualitative in nature, and we have used the case study method. The reason for choosing the case study over other methods is that it provides in-depth, comprehensive detailed knowledge about the area and its contextual position. As the study focused on the role of SHG in fostering creative entrepreneurship through various means in the midst of the pandemic. Hence, we have gathered the secondary data and presented in a more meaningful form. To understand the role of creative entrepreneurship, we used the case study of an organisation called CORD.

5. RESULTS

To understand the role of creative entrepreneurship, we used a case study of an organisation called CORD). CORD is a non-profit organisation based in Himachal Pradesh, India. CORD was established in 1983, with the primary purpose of providing maternity and childcare services to the rural tribe under the blessings of Swami Chinmayananda. Later in 2003, Swami Tejomanyanda created a separate entity who practices the development of rural people on a national level through a free dispensary, which later became the Chinmaya Rural Primary Health Care and Training Centre (CRPHC & TC). CORD is funded by USAID and works in partnership with the Indian Government and the National Institute of Health and Family Welfare. Dr. Kshama Metre has been the director and founder of Chinmaya Rural Primary Health Care and Training Centre since 1984. Locals who work at CORD refer to her as 'Dr. Didi'.

Swami Swaroopananda has been the chairperson and trustee of Cord since 2017. Currently, he serves as the global leader of the Chinmaya Mission. In a resource team at CORD Training Centre, in addition to these, he is working assiduously on their specific and accurate programmes for the betterment of the rural people. CORD operates 2,250 SHGs around the country, with a total of 29,652 members. Through bank linkages, 151 SHGs were granted a loan of Rs. 4,74,22,000 in 2020 (CORD Report, 2020). The following section discusses the creative activities undertaken by the CORD with the help of the SHGs involved.

5.1. Case Study 1: Creative Leadership in a SHG Under CORD

According to the annual report of CORD, the NGO's primary focus was on maternal and child health care for rural influxes who were destitute and unable to support their families. In 1987, the Mahila Mandals were founded with the purpose of empowering women. Mahila Mandals is a rural women's organisation that supports women in their pursuits. According to Swami Chinmaynanada, founder of CORD, the long-term development can only be realised if women in rural regions are empowered and actively endeavour to make their families and communities prosperous. Dr. Metre worked tirelessly to realise her dream, and the NGO now serves 27,000 consumers in 900 tiny towns, providing a variety of services to improve people's lives (Handy et al., 2004). Empowerment has had far-reaching implications for norms, values, and community legislation (Page & Czuba, 1999).

They essentially gather a small amount of money from the other females in the group and invest it in necessities once a significant amount has been amassed. CORD now operates 2,250 SHGs around the country, with a total of 29,652 members. Through bank linkages, 151 SHGs granted a loan of Rs. 4,74,22,000 in 2020. For 7,893 SHG members, 955 field training sessions on effective and sustainable SHG management were conducted. The members of the SHG group were able to earn a living through Creative entrepreneurship activities such as mushroom farming, sewing, knitting, and pine needle products. A total of 152 SHG members were trained in activities such as soap manufacturing and mask creation. Fig. 1 highlights various creative entrepreneurial activities facilitated by SHGs with the support of CORD. Creative entrepreneurship activities such as making yarn and blankets from sheep wool, basket making, and mask making have helped remote people in surviving and fighting the difficult phases of COVID-19.

Fig. 1.   Type of Creative Entrepreneurship Initiatives by SHGs. *Source*: Developed by authors in line with secondary data, CORD Report 2021.

5.2. Challenges Faced by Creative Entrepreneurs During the Outbreak of COVID-19

In December 2019, the most obnoxious news about COVID-19 disease came out, which affected every nation worldwide and whose epicentre was marked in Wuhan, China. The people around the world felt helpless and unable to help their loved ones during the hard times. SHGs faced challenges in connecting to the people in remote areas due to the severe lockdown. There was a precise challenge in respect of adapting to the culture and location. As everything was shut down, the people fought for the daily survival (WHO COVID-19 Dashboard).

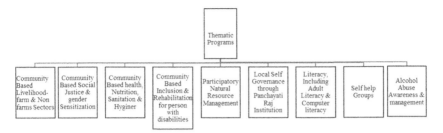

Fig. 2. List of Creative Entrepreneurship Initiatives by SHGs. *Source*: Developed by authors in line with secondary data, Cord (2021).

Convincing people to stay indoors and follow the nation's guidelines of social distancing, self-quarantines, and wearing the mask strictly was a challenge. Moving freely in the village without mask, mixing up with fellow peers, and playing cards at the tea shops were few of the things noticed by the Pradhan, and despite formal request by Pradhan, the localities still continued to repeat the same, even sometimes involved in fights and quarrels too. Pradhan is a formal authority, generally an individual, who is elected by the rural people for the welfare and development of the rural area. As depicted in Fig. 2, CORD took various creative initiatives to facilitate the same and SHG members played a vital role in running such campaigns. Table 1 shows the role of Creative entrepreneurial activities in the form of social campaigns to facilitate the fight against COVID-19.

5.3. Creative Activities Practiced by SHGs

5.3.1. E-Sanjeevani App
This application assists patients in remote locations. According to the Code Report 2020–2021, this E-application was used to train 454 Mahila Mandals who served 117 patients.

Table 1. Composition of Programme Components in CORD to Facilitate the Campaign.

S. No.	Particulars of Outreach	Total Number of Members
1.	Mahila Mandal's	1,173
2.	Self-help Groups	2,250
3.	Adolescent Girls Group	181
4.	Bal Vihars	295
5.	Farmer Club/Men's Club	70
6.	PWD (person with disability) Groups	150
7.	Gram Sabha Facilitated	26
8.	Up Gram Sabha Facilitated	179

Source: Cord Annual Narrative Report (1 April 2020–31 March 2021).

5.3.2. Vegetable and Dairy Production

The SHGs have established a microfinance programme for their members. According to the facts in CORD's Annual Report, Chinmaya Ganesh SHG obtained a loan of Rs. 6 lakhs, which appears to be a silver lining in people's lives. This money can be put to good use in businesses such as vegetable and dairy production. The loaned money can be used to buy seeds and fertilisers in the case of vegetable farming, whereas the dairy production is concerned, the member of SHG can buy mitching cattle stock so that they can reap money from it.

5.3.3. Swadhyaya Classrooms

Digitisation acted as a catalyst for transformation, particularly in rural schools and institutions. Mobile phones, document files, or pdfs have supplanted the traditional use of pen and paper, and physical space has been replaced by google or zoom courses. During the pandemic, CORD launched the Swadhyaya classrooms, which were exclusively for young girls' educational academics. The NGO's main thrust area was the application of digitalisation. Virtual celebrations were becoming a tradition in addition to the studies. Independence Day, Republic Day, Environment Day, and Deepawali are just a few examples.

5.3.4. CBL-FAS

CORD helped farmers in their entrepreneurial endeavours through the Community-Based Livelihood-Farm and Allied Sector initiative (CBL-FAS). The following were the main areas of focus in this programme:

1. To improve the farmers' skills and give appropriate training.
2. To keep the cost of input products low.
3. To look into alternative innovative ways to make a living.
4. To introduce novel natural farming practices and technology as well as to involve women farmers in farm decision-making, with a special focus on marginal and small farmers.

Aside from this initiative, an NGO coordinated and formed the Gurudeva Himalaya Farmer Producer Company, through which farmers were trained in a variety of farm-related activities such as pickle-making, jam-making, and other agricultural outputs.

5.3.5. Community-based Inclusion and Rehabilitation Programme

This programme facilitated the People with Disabilities (PWD). Therapeutics, rehabilitation, education, accessibility, community-based livelihood, and advocacy are the topics covered under this curriculum.

5.3.6. Chinmaya Shanta

An initiative by the name of Chinmaya Shanta whose focus is on the mental health and well-being of rural communities. The teams were basically helping the concerned person and their families in coping techniques so that they can manage their mental health and well-being during pandemic.

5.3.7. Seven J's

Seven J's provide an awareness about the management of natural resources in communities in Himachal Pradesh's localities. They were primarily interested in the interplay between the seven Js: Jal (Water), Jungle (Forest), Jameen (Land), Jan (People), Janwar (Cattle Stock), Jivika (Earning), Jalvayu (Climate), and the others pleaded with the people to look after them with utmost care.

5.4. CORD Pandemic Programme Interventions

The SHG and Mahila Mandals of various regions of the district Kangra, Himachal Pradesh, had undertaken activities to help the native people in collaboration with CORD (Table 2).

5.5. Technological Change and the Dealing Mechanism

COVID-19 made digitalisation possible at a faster pace. Because of this change, everything became simple but not for the people who did not know how to use the technology at all. This was the challenge to be undertaken by the CORD. The CORD trainer taught the SHG members how to operate their phones and how to participate in online meetings using their phones. Using technology was a struggle for them, as they were unable to type their messages and related things.

Table 2. Contribution by Mahila Mandal Amidst of COVID-19.

S. No.	Name of Mahila Mandal	Region Name	Contributions
1.	Chinmaya Jayanti Mahila Mandal	Kangra	Rural residents received 5,000 face masks (handmade)
2.	Chinmaya Shiva Mahila Mandal	Passu	5,000 Handmade face masks were distributed to rural communities
3.	Chinmaya Mahila Mandal Nichla Chetru	Chetru	Rs 31,000 was donated to the Prime Ministers CARES (Citizen Assistance and Relief in Emergency Situations) fund
4.	Chinmaya Shiva Mahila Mandal	Bhuner	15 Migrant labourer's who were under the local administration's institution quarantine were given cooked food
5.	Chinmaya Chudpur Mahila Mandal	Indora	1,100 Handmake face masks were provided to migrant workers harvesting wheat in farmer's fields
6.	Chinmaya Kurdsan Mahila Mandal	Indora	Two migrant labourers were given food and cash assistance to meet their family's basic necessities
7.	Chinmaya Bojpur Mahila Mandal Ghoran Panchayat	Indora	700 Handmade masks were distributed to residents in their own Panchayat, which had been sealed owing to COVID-19

Source: CORD's Comprehensive Panchayat-based Micro Level Action Report on COVID-19 (Till 30 June 2020).

However, the voice search feature of Google helped people and they were searching their quires through their voice. Members of the SHG group then pass on their wisdom to their fellow indigenous people. This was a slow procedure and a daunting task, but CORD was successful in some ways, albeit not entirely. Just like people were using mobile phones and learning the usage of technology, now they can sell their products via online. Their audience for the potential product has extended and hence making money.

6. DISCUSSION AND CONCLUSION

The present study has focused on the role of SHGs in fostering Creative entrepreneurship. We discovered that SHGs encourage creative entrepreneurship. The study revealed that SHGs have aided people through difficult times. People who do not have a solid source of income benefitted greatly from the actions launched during the pandemic. People's lives have altered dramatically, as everything is accessible with a single click of a finger on their smartphone, allowing for a simpler life. Various Creative industries such as mask-making, soap manufacturing, and The Social awareness programmes have supported rural people during COVID-19.

The research looked into creative entrepreneurship and how SHGs dealt with implementing activities throughout the epidemic. It also looked at how creative outlets improved the lives of rural people who worked hard with SHGs to ensure the survival of their families and the progress of the country as a whole. Despite the obstacles faced by SHGs linked through NGOs, the post-COVID brought radical transformation to the life of SHG members. The members of the SHG group were able to earn a living through Creative entrepreneurship activities such as sewing, knitting, and pine needle products. A total of 152 SHG members were trained in activities such as soap manufacturing and mask creation. The current research will aid in the exploration of creative entrepreneurial opportunities and improve the lives of rural people.

There are certain limitations to our research as well. We used secondary sources of data for data collection; therefore, future research can focus on primary data collection sources. The study's generalisations can be a source of concern because the implementation region may be culturally diverse. Future studies can be undertaken to empirically explore the experience of SHGs to assess the success of these creative entrepreneurship programmes.

REFERENCES

Bakoğlu, R., & Yıldırım, O. B. A. (2016). The role of sustainability in long term survival of family business: Henokiens revisited. *Procedia-Social and Behavioral Sciences, 235*, 788–796.

Bhardwaj, B., & Sharma, D. (2022). Migration of skilled professionals across the border: Brain drain or brain gain?. *European Management Journal*. https://doi.org/10.1016/j.emj.2022.12.011

Bodh, A. (2020). Himachal woman self help groups contributing in fight against coronavirus. *Times of India*, April 9.

Bujor, A., & Avasilcai, S. (2014). Creative entrepreneurship in Europe: A framework of analysis. *Annals of the Oradea University, Fascicle of Management and Technological Engineering, 23*(XIII), 151–156.

Bujor, A., & Avasilcai, S. (2016). The creative entrepreneur: A framework of analysis. *Procedia-Social and Behavioral Sciences, 221*, 21–28.

Censusindia.gov.in. (2022). Population Finder 2011. Retrieved, August 18, 2022 https://census india.gov.in/census.website/data/population-finder

Cord. (2021). Reports on the CORD India social activities. Retrieved December 30, 2021, from https://cordindia.in/resources/report

Fisher, R. (2020). Build more sustainable business in a post-Covid world. *HR Future, 9*, 36–37.

Government of Himachal Pradesh. (2020). SHGs of Rural Development Department manufactures 32,000 masks to mitigate the demand. Retrieved, April 4, 2022, http://himachalpr.gov.in/PressReleaseByYear.aspx?Language=1&ID=17079&Type=2&Date=01/05/2020

Handy, F., Kassam, M., & July, T. C. (2004). Women's empowerment in rural India. *ISTR Conference, 4*(3), 1–39.

Henry, C., & De Bruin, A. (Eds.). (2011). *Entrepreneurship and the creative economy: Process, practice and policy*. Edward Elgar Publishing.

Herath, T., & Herath, H. S. (2020). Coping with the new normal imposed by the COVID-19 pandemic: Lessons for technology management and governance. *Information Systems Management, 37*(4), 277–283.

Katz, A. H. (1976). The strength in us: Self-help groups in the modern world. New Viewpoints.

Khlystova, O., Kalyuzhnova, Y., & Belitski, M. (2022). The impact of the COVID-19 pandemic on the creative industries: A literature review and future research agenda. *Journal of Business Research, 139*, 1192–1210.

Kondal, K. (2014). Women empowerment through self help groups in Andhra Pradesh, India. *International Research Journal of Social Sciences, 3*(1), 13–16.

Landströn, H. (2005). *Pioneers in entrepreneurship and small business research*. Springer.

Long, W. (1983). The meaning of entrepreneurship. *American Journal of Small Business, 8*(2), 47–59.

McKelvey, M., & Lassen, A. H. (2018). Knowledge, meaning and identity: Key characteristics of entrepreneurship in cultural and creative industries. *Creativity and Innovation Management, 27*(3), 281–283.

Mickel, A. E., Mitchell, T. R., Dakin, S., & Gray, S. (2003). The importance of money as an individual difference attribute. *Emerging Perspectives on Values in Organizations, 3*,123–150.

Myovella, G., Karacuka, M., & Haucap, J. (2021). Determinants of digitalization and digital divide in Sub-Saharan African economies: A spatial Durbin analysis. *Telecommunications Policy, 45*(10), 102224.

Nordberg, K., Mariussen, Å., & Virkkala, S. (2020). Community-driven social innovation and quadruple helix coordination in rural development. Case study on LEADER group Aktion Österbotten. *Journal of Rural Studies, 79*, 157–168.

Page, N., & Czuba, C.E. (1999). Empowerment: What is it?*Journal of Extension, 37*(5), 24–32.

Parrish, B. D. (2008). *Sustainability-driven entrepreneurship: a literature review*. University of Leeds, School of Earth & Environment.

Poschke, M. (2013). Who becomes an entrepreneur? Labor market prospects and occupational choice. *Journal of Economic Dynamics and Control, 37*(3), 693–710.

Rahim, H. L., & Mohtar, S. (2015). Social entrepreneurship: A different perspective. *International Academic Research Journal of Business and Technology, 1*(1), 9–15.

Ripsas, S. (1998). Towards an interdisciplinary theory of entrepreneurship. *Small Business Economics, 10*(2), 103–115.

Sharma, D., Chaudhary, M., Jaswal, N., & Bhardwaj, B. (2022). Hiding Behind The SWOT: Gender Equality and COVID-19. *Journal of Positive School Psychology*, 730–740.

Schumpeter, J. A. (2000). Entrepreneurship as innovation. University of Illinois at Urbana-Champaign's Academy for Entrepreneurial Leadership Historical Research Reference in Entrepreneurship. https://ssrn.com/abstract=1512266

Song, L., & Zhou, Y. (2020). The COVID-19 pandemic and its impact on the global economy: What does it take to turn crisis into opportunity? *China & World Economy*, *28*(4), 1–25.

Steiner, P. (2002). *Jean-Baptiste Say: The entrepreneur, the free. Studies in the history of French political economy:* From Bodin to walras (p. 196). Routledge.

Tehseen, S., & Haider, S. A. (2021). Impact of universities' partnerships on students' sustainable entrepreneurship intentions: A comparative study. *Sustainability*, *13*(9), 5025.

The Times of India (2022). *Himachal woman SHGs contributing in fight against coronavirus | Shimla News – Times of India*. Retrieved, August 18, 2022 from https://timesofindia.indiatimes.com/city/shimla/himachal-woman-self-help-groups-contributing-in-fight-against-coronavirus/articleshow/75066270.cms

Volery, T., Mueller, S., & von Siemens, B. (2015). Entrepreneur ambidexterity: A study of entrepreneur behaviours and competencies in growth-oriented small and medium-sized enterprises. *International Small Business Journal*, *33*(2), 109–129.

World Health Organization, WHO Coronavirus (COVID-19) Dashboard (2022). Retrieved, July 31, 2022, from https://covid19.who.int/

World Bank. (2020). In India, women's self-help groups combat the COVID-19 (COVID-19 virus) pandemic. Retrieved, May 2, 2022, from https://www.worldbank.org/en/news/feature/2020/04/11/women-self-help-groups-combat-covid19-coronavirus-pandemic-india

Wu, Y. J., Yuan, C. H., & Chen, M. Y. (2021). From thinker to doer: Creativity, innovation, entrepreneurship, maker, and venture capital. *Frontiers in Psychology*, *12*, 649037.

Yeşil, S., Büyükbeşe, T., & Koska, A. (2013). Exploring the link between knowledge sharing enablers, innovation capability and innovation performance. *International Journal of Innovation Management*, *17*(4), 1350018.

CHAPTER 8

THE RESILIENCE AND ADAPTABILITY OF AN INNOVATIVE ECOSYSTEM OF CREATIVE ENTREPRENEURS DURING CRISIS TIMES: BALTIC CREATIVE CIC – A CASE STUDY

Fiona Armstrong-Gibbs and Jan Brown

ABSTRACT

This empirical chapter explores the case of Baltic Creative Community Interest Company (BC CIC), *a creative hub that enabled and demonstrated intrapersonal entrepreneurial capitals (Pret et al., 2016) to adapt quickly and develop novel offers for their tenants during an unprecedented period of crisis and change in the wider ecosystem. BCCIC is a community-owned property development company established to regenerate an underused post-industrial area in Liverpool and support the Creative and Digital community. Over the past decade, they have become a creative hub where small, unique micro-businesses thrive alongside more established enterprises.*

Using an organisational ethnographic approach, the authors highlight the complexity in the conversion of entrepreneurial capitals and how this has demonstrated resilience and adaptability in the CIC *during the global coronavirus pandemic in the 2020s. During the first coronavirus lockdown in 2020, The CIC responded swiftly to tenants by providing a wide variety of business support*

Creative (and Cultural) Industry Entrepreneurship in the 21st Century
Contemporary Issues in Entrepreneurship Research, Volume 18A, 105–118
Copyright © 2024 by Fiona Armstrong-Gibbs and Jan Brown
Published under exclusive licence by Emerald Publishing Limited
ISSN: 2040-7246/doi:10.1108/S2040-72462023000018A008

initiatives. Regular communications on sector-specific COVID-19 operational guidance and a support programme to help tenants apply for Liverpool City Council Small Business Support grants.

The establishment of this hub for creative entrepreneurs prior to the recent disruption proved invaluable. Although they were severely tested, emerging behaviours, such as agility, adaptability, and resilience during periods of crisis, were identified. This chapter offers key insights for scholars and those leading on creative hubs and cluster policy development and economic initiatives for creative sector support regionally, nationally, and internationally.

Keywords: Ecosystem; resilience; adaptability; entrepreneurial capitals; entrepreneurs; hub

1. INTRODUCTION

Given the unavoidable impact of the global coronavirus pandemic, it has and will continue to have a profound effect on every organisation including the creative sector. As Walmsley et al. (2021, p.4) noted:

> [...] the pandemic has impacted the creative and cultural industries more globally and traumatically than any other crisis in living memory. It has wrought a seismic shock across the cultural sector in particular.

This chapter explores the resilience and adaptability of an innovative hub of creative entrepreneurs during crisis times in Liverpool, UK. Its contribution is its contemporary insights of the creative industries applicable to practitioners, policy-makers, and academics as identified by Khlystova et al. (2022).

Through an organisational ethnographic approach, the research seeks to identify activities of intrapersonal entrepreneurial capital conversions, the interactions, and experiences between *Baltic Creative CIC* and their tenants and the significance of being part of a resilient and adaptable creative ecosystem.

2. THE LIVERPOOL CONTEXT

The late twentieth-century urban decline, regeneration, and subsequent renaissance of the northern city of Liverpool in the UK have been well-documented with commentary and critique from a variety of perspectives and scholars, most recently (Campbell, 2019; Couch & Fowles, 2019; Heap et al., 2017; Thompson et al., 2020). Since the 1990s, large-scale structural developments and funds such as ERDF (European Regional Development Fund) helped to refurbish buildings and upgrade infrastructure in Liverpool. However, this appeared to have been to the detriment of local clusters and creative ecosystems and resulted in fragmented creative entrepreneurial communities across the city. An urban landscape is not just physical assets; its social and cultural capital are equally important for it to thrive. Ragozino (2016) suggests that a social enterprise business model, with a hybrid approach to profit and purpose such as a CIC is well-suited to nurture and sustain relationships among people as well as between people in the urban landscape.

Baltic Creative Community Interest Company (referred to as *the CIC*) was established in 2009 and quickly became a hub for the Creative and Digital community to coalesce. Through a grant funding agreement with the Northwest Development Agency and ERDF *the CIC* received just under £5m to purchase and refurbish a site with a remit to regenerate the area by creating the much-needed environment for the creative and digital sectors to grow.

By 2012, *the CIC* had refurbished 18 warehouses (45,000 sq. ft.) and developed a central hub with a café. This satisfied growing market demand and allowed a variety of small companies from the creative and digital sectors to come together. The CIC was a key driver in reviving the area now known as the Baltic Triangle. Importantly, the buildings were owned by the community through an asset lock and represented by a board of trustees who retained control. This empowered them to make a permanent change to the creative infrastructure on behalf of the community. The local authority, commercial property owners, and speculators could not increase rents or move the community on once the area became more inviting and affluent. This practice of gentrification has been seen many times before in the global north and post-industrial areas that have benefited from regeneration driven by artists and creatives (Valli, 2021).

By 2020, the CIC housed over 200 businesses with 650 employees and had extended its footprint in the area to over 180,000 sq. ft. alongside many more businesses in the adjacent streets and buildings. With a management team of five people and a non-executive voluntary board of eight members, the CIC draws on a wide range of skill sets to ensure the original vision of the CIC is maintained.

In March 2020, the global coronavirus pandemic forced the closure of indoor public spaces, offices, and communal workspaces and those who could work from home were required to do so by law (Johnson, 2020). Only essential workers were allowed to travel and enter their workplace, people who could not work from home were supported by the UK governments furlough scheme or later the Self-Employed Income Support Scheme (SEISS). The government directive posed a huge challenge to the *CIC*, from the perspective of a public health crisis, duty of care, and safety to staff and tenants, but also operationally as the core revenue stream was generated through rental income from the community of creative entrepreneurs. This chapter will now explore how the management approach and tenants used their entrepreneurial capitals to continue to work together in the ecosystem.

3. LITERATURE/THEORETICAL FRAMING

The popularity of hubs and clustering in the cultural field has led to multiple forms and scales of clusters being developed (Cooke, 2008; Mommaas, 2004; Picard & Karlsson, 2011; Pratt, 2004, 2021; Wen, 2018). The development of creative clusters in vacant factory buildings and warehouses driven by local authorities' desire to repopulate and regenerate inner city spaces has led to innovative forms of clusters that act as physical hubs for creative practitioners. These physical hubs allow creative entrepreneurs to form their own unique ecosystems while at the same time remaining part of the wider creative ecosystem (Pratt, 2021).

The exploration of the cultural and creative industries using ecological thinking has been growing in recent years (de Bernard et al., 2021). Although terminology is still being debated, in this study the ecosystem is defined as 'all … [actors] in a particular area considered in relation to their physical environment' (Hornby & Cowie, 1995 cited in de Bernard et al., 2021, p. 9) with the ecosystem being the object of study. In this ecosystem, importance is placed on the relations among actors (Foster, 2020) and the ecosystem is described as 'a developing set of interconnections and interdependencies' among the actors (Gross & Wilson, 2019, p. 7). Different creative physical hubs and ecosystems are configured to suit diverse needs (Avidikos & Pettas, 2021; Jiménez & Zheng, 2021; Lee et al., 2019; Virani & Gill, 2019). As identified by Mert (2019), some creative physical hubs and ecosystems are created with a community and social focus and *the CIC* is an example of this.

It is proposed here that as tenants agree to rent a space in *the CIC* (a creative hub), they also form part of a unique creative ecosystem, and they have chosen to become members of that specific field (Bourdieu, 1993). For a creative hub to form, develop and survive an appreciation of how that specific ecosystem of actors operates is needed (Pratt, 2021). This includes how the processes and practices between the management and the various actors within the ecosystem operate. During periods of crisis these structures, processes, and practices need to be rigorous enough to support the ecosystem but also adaptive enough to be able to change to meet the unplanned for circumstances. The ability of the ecosystem to respond to both internal and external changes not only in periods of crisis but also in post-crisis are crucial factors for the long-term success and viability of the ecosystem.

At an individual actor level during periods of crisis, an individual's self-efficacy, that is, an individual's belief in the personal capability to accomplish a job or a specific set of tasks, will be tested in unforeseen ways (Bandura, 1977; Gist & Mitchell, 1992; McGee et al., 2009). The individual's choices, level of effort, and perseverance may be influenced and supported by being part of a functioning creative ecosystem rather than operating alone (Chen et al., 2004).

Using Bourdieu's (1990) approach to practice theory and drawing on the research from Pret et al. (2016) relating to intrapersonal entrepreneurial capitals and capital conversions, the types of capitals and how they were combined prior to, during, and post-crisis was explored in detail. Entrepreneurial capitals defined by Hill (2021, p.101) as '… only those aspects of capitals brought into doing business' can be categorised into economic, social, symbolic, and cultural capitals and can be converted into distinct types of capital by combining various capitals together.

Economic capital, for example, financial assets, can be '… immediately and directly convertible into money' (Bourdieu, 1986, p. 242). Although important, economic capital is only one type of capital that is required in entrepreneurial practice and as Hill (2021, p. 100) states there are a '… wide variety of capitals [are] involved in creative production'.

Cultural capital presents itself in three forms: objectified, institutionalised, and embodied behaviour. Cultural capital objectified in material objects and media is transmissible in its materiality (Bourdieu, 1986). In institutional form, cultural capital is objectified into qualifications and skills training. In terms of cultural capital in an embodied state and it presupposes embodiment and '… implies a labour of inculcation and assimilation, costs time, time which must be invested personally by the investor' (Bourdieu, 1986, p. 244), for example, the work experience of entrepreneurs.

Social capital is defined by Bourdieu (1986, p. 248) as '… the aggregate of the actual or potential resources which are linked to possession of a durable network of more or less institutionalised relationships of mutual acquaintance and recognition'. It refers to an individual's network of social exchange relations and is the sum of all actual and potential resources that can be accessed through a durable network of relationships.

Symbolic capital has been defined by Bourdieu (1984, p. 291) as '… a reputation for competence and an image of respectability and honorability'. Individuals can draw on and can be associated with the possession of prestige, status, and positive reputation.

Although the different types of capitals can be seen as being distinct, they can be converted into other types of capital. For example, social capital can be converted into cultural capital through the process of relational learning. Social capital into symbolic capital through the affiliation with reputable others can create a spill-over effect, while association with unreliable partners can impede reputation-building (Hill, 2021). Symbolic capital can be converted into social and cultural capital by facilitating access to social networks and exclusive education (Pret et al., 2016). The conversion of capitals is not an automatic process, and as Bourdieu (1986, p. 253) notes, it should be taken '… into account both the labour-time accumulated in the form of capital and the labour-time needed to transform it from one type into another'. During the process of conversion '… the (apparent) incommensurability of the different types of capital introduces a high degree of uncertainty into all transactions between holders of different types', and this uncertainty can increase the risk of loss of capital during the process of conversion (Bourdieu, 1986, pp. 253–254).

By defining the actors within the creative physical hub and ecosystem as individual and group entrepreneurs who have consciously agreed to work collaboratively as part of that ecosystem allows these actions to relationally create entrepreneurial capitals through situated practices which can be developed and adapted over time (Reid, 2020).

4. METHODS

Organisational ethnography provides insights and pays attention to the complexity of everyday life in organisations – in this study, it is within the creative hub known as Baltic Creative CIC. This method also considers how the CIC is positioned in the ecosystem – the wider political, cultural, social, spatial, and temporal dimensions and the activities and interactions that shape entrepreneurial activity. This approach allowed us to move beyond accounts which frame an organisation or enterprise as pre-ordained, ready-to-use, or a decontextualised business model (Watson, 2011). We used this approach to gather data as one of the co-authors is a founder director, now Chair of *the CIC* and positioned in the organisation throughout the pandemic.

4.1. Data Collection and Analysis

As an exploratory study, this qualitative approach is iterative and flexible, and it captured both the lived experience of the crisis through two key interviews with the Chair in 2022, her reflections of the organisational response and analysis of the activities published by *the CIC* on the website. Engagement with data was a cyclical process, where data collection, analysis, and interpretation often took place concurrently. Using template analysis (King, 2012; Waring & Wainwright, 2008) encouraged data generation at the same time as reviewing literature, so the most relevant and meaningful theoretical framework was identified early on. These preliminary findings were captured in a table outlining first-order concepts and then second-order themes, a similar approach used by Hill (2018). This gave a sense of the relationships emerging which we then considered to be the 'capital conversions' between the four entrepreneurial capitals (economic, social, cultural, and symbolic). We then applied the capital conversions theoretical framework devised by Pret et al. (2016) to form the discussion section.

We are mindful to protect the anonymity and confidentiality of the tenants, the findings, data, and quotes are from an organisational perspective (intrapersonal) – management reflections rather than tenant feedback directly between each other (interpersonal). The intention is to add to a growing body of research and learn from the crisis to create stronger more resilient creative communities rather than a tenant narrative at this stage (Guillemin & Gillam, 2004).

5. FINDINGS

The data collected suggests new activities and behaviours in *the CIC* both from management and tenants as a direct response to the pandemic (first-order concepts). Drawn from that are six second-order themes of operational and strategic activity managed by the CIC. This allowed us to identify the entrepreneurial capital conversions, and from that we identified the core activities that relate to resilience and adaptability of the CIC (see Table 1).

6. DISCUSSION

The findings clearly demonstrate resilient and adaptable behaviour as a response to the pandemic. In unprecedented circumstances, the value of being part of an

Table 1. Coding Scheme – Actions and Conversions of Capital Relating to Resilience and Adaptability.

First-order Concepts	Second-order Themes (Operational and Strategic Activity Managed by the CIC)	Capital Conversions (Pret et al., 2016)
Formal and experienced management structure (CIC) UK Government compliance Physical and communal space and safety – public health Asset and building closure (lockdown) COVID support strategy Operational guidance	1) Operational compliance and guidance RESILIENCE	Cultural × social: *management skills and knowledge were combined with existing strong relationships to keep tenants and staff safe and regularly updated.*
Letting strategy and tenant turnover Information/data gathering Tenant survey Staff furlough/redundancy Working from home	2) Understanding tenant behaviour RESILIENCE	Cultural × economic: *Management knowledge of government and financial support (furlough scheme, etc.) was used to spotlight cash flow challenges for CIC and tenants*
New product development Tenant activity and innovation Shift to digital/online offers	3) Innovation, opportunity, and change ADAPTABILITY	Cultural × symbolic: *Tenant skills, digital innovative practice as well as a strong sector reputation combined to enable tenants to adapt and innovate as lockdowns continued*
CIC-led regular communication statements with tenants Website updates/slack/emails BLM statement Messaging – tenants shift to offer online services and new market offers	4) Communication from the CIC ADAPTABILITY	Symbolic × social: *a solid sector reputation and a strong network were combined to communicate tenant services as lockdowns continued, enabling tenants to test the market and develop new products and income streams (economic).*
External relationships with support agencies Local authority (Liverpool City Council) LCR CA European Hub toolkit	5) Local and regional partnerships and advocacy ADAPTABILITY	Social × cultural: *a strong network and sector reputation created an opportunity for entrepreneurial learning (cultural) and dissemination/knowledge sharing and reinforcing symbolic capital.*
Access to government financial support LA Small business support grants £10k CBILS and payment 'holidays' Furlough/SEISS Deferral of VAT and other payments Rental income – voids and non-payment of rent Legal action	6) Government financial support and internal cash flow/revenue generation RESILIENCE	*Economic x cultural: financial support (furlough and grants) and the skills to apply this to the management of the CIC* *Economic x social: tenant income streams guided by the CIC and the ability to disseminate this to the network created an opportunity for cash flow and avoided some rent arrears*

agile creative hub and ecosystem is clear. All actors, whether they were tenants, part of the management team, or on the non-executive voluntary board harnessed, developed, and consolidated their entrepreneurial capitals efficiently and effectively for the benefit of both individuals and the collective whole. To achieve these multiple forms of capital conversions were identified, and these have been discussed further below.

7. RESILIENCE

Evidence of resilience can be found in the capital conversions of three key areas of the six themes as discussed below. The formation of the Baltic Creative CIC prior to the COVID pandemic and the established practices that had been embedded prior to the crisis period had allowed them to form a robust physical hub and ecosystem. The reactivity of the creative ecosystem as a whole and the roles which the various members played demonstrated the connected nature of the ecosystem and these connections remained resilient and adaptable to change to suit the ecosystem's needs (Gross & Wilson, 2019). With the closure of the physical hub the CIC members needed to move all practices online and rely on the capitals of individual and group members of the ecosystem to provide guidance, leadership, and solutions to challenges based on various capital conversions (Pret et al., 2016).

7.1. Operational Compliance and Guidance: Keeping Trading (Theme 1)

Cultural capital was developed in several ways. New specialised knowledge was obtained, efficiently gathered from external expert sources by the management team and collated via a central online platform. The ability of the CIC to act as a hub allowed it to react quickly to changing advice, this meant that consistency was maintained, all information was kept up to date and tenants were confident that their focus could remain on their own specific organisation's operational needs during a highly turbulent time.

> It was essential that we did everything we could to communicate with tenants quickly when the [lockdown] news broke and a couple of weeks later our survey showed how important and reassuring this was to many of the tenants. (Operations Manager)

Online COVID guidance was provided one week before lockdown commenced on 23 March, preparing as well as possible the tenants and community for the change to come. The online platform was accessible to all and provided support and links. A safety guidance booklet for tenants around office working and using communal spaces safely was created, updated, and re-distributed each time restrictions changed. The CIC was involved with the 2021 UK Government testing initiative to provide tenants with lateral flow testing kits, again position themselves ahead of the changing COVID landscape.

7.2. Understanding Tenant Behaviour: Adapting to Suit Tenants Needs (Theme 2)

As the operating conditions changed, it was vital that the CIC understood changing tenants needs. As the physical hub of the CIC closed due to Government compliance, the ecosystem was maintained digitally using online social meetups and events that provided information on specific COVID support, for example, local grant funding and a four-part series for tenants returning the workplace in partnership with a local social enterprise.

> We helped micro businesses and artists, [with tenancy agreements below the local council business rates threshold] apply for a £10k grant. If they hadn't been with us at the CIC they may not have been entitled to it and it had a significant impact on the community economy (estimated £900k) this was a massive support for people when their incomes disappeared without knowing when things would change. (Operations Manager)

Regular tenant surveys were undertaken to identify the challenges, allowing the CIC to mitigate for potential non-payment of rents and assuring the board that *the CIC* remained financially viable. Responding to demand from both management and tenants' health and well-being support was provided with free online health and well-being sessions including Pilates being provided.

To build resilience, existing management cultural capital was converted into both social and cultural capital to keep tenants safe. What would have previously been physical interactive relationships became strong online interactions. The tenants' financial situations were considered when making decisions for *the CIC* as a whole (Bourdieu, 1986).

7.3. Government Financial Support, Internal Cash Flow, and Revenue Generation: Maximising the Financials (Theme 6)

Prior to the COVID pandemic, the CIC had strong economic capital, shown the ability to competently manage its finances including accessing European and UK funding since its inception. The very formation of the CIC was built on a financial model that considered the need to efficiently bid for such funding. This historical reputation for financial competency reputation was heavily drawn upon during the COVID pandemic. Support with accessing funding, a recognition of various tenants' financial viability during specific time periods and the ability to communicate with funders proved to be vital for many tenants to remain viable during this challenging period. The ability for tenants to confidently gain support in financial matters allowed tenants to place much of their focus on keeping their own organisations viable and ensure their products and services were adapted to suit the customers' needs.

Online workshops were held that ensured that tenants were up to date with local grant funding initiatives and regular surveys were held to ensure that any challenges tenants were facing were captured and any potential problems for the *Baltic Creative CIC*, for example, non-payment of rents were identified as soon as possible so that planning could be undertaken to mitigate for circumstances were possible.

> We shifted the 'Baltic Brew' get togethers online – the first one was really about bringing people together and checking in, we managed to share some great advice about financial planning, grants and wanted to create an environment for peer-to-peer engagement. (Marketing Manager)

Many tenants were eligible for a small business 'Local Restrictions Support Grant' of £10,000 issued by the local authority but for several reasons the application was considered difficult to navigate. Working with the City Council rates office the *CIC* helped tenants secure the grant which helped with fixed costs like rent and electricity.

Economic capital was also converted into cultural and social capital by the increased knowledge gained relating to financial support and by the ability to share tenant stories of success despite cash flow problems (Bourdieu, 1986).

8. ADAPTABILITY

As well as building resilience the efficient conversion of capitals also allowed *the CIC* to adapt to new opportunities. Evidence of adaptability can be found in three key areas of the six themes as discussed below. Existing cultural capital was harnessed to innovate and change which provided a high level of symbolic capital for both individual actors within the CIC and for the CIC as a whole operating in the ecosystem (Bourdieu, 1986). This increased level of symbolic capital has been maintained post-pandemic restrictions as the buildings are fully let in 2022 despite a reluctance for many other sectors to return to the workplace.

Existing symbolic capital was also converted into social capital so that new services were communicated effectively, and social capital was converted into cultural capital by the building of a strong reputations that the Baltic Creative CIC's creative ecosystem was innovative, reactive, supportive, vibrant, and willing to share their entrepreneurial learning (Bourdieu, 1986). This reputation, and thus the symbolic capital, continues to be developed with a healthy rate of enquiries from potential new tenants and new opportunities for collaborations with the wider creative ecosystem being further developed post-pandemic.

8.1. Innovation, Opportunity, and Change (Theme 3)

Turbulent times created an uncertain business environment and forced tenants to adapt to survive. With over 50% of tenants innovating, this became an important focus for the *CIC* management to support. To ensure this was effective the *CIC* broadened its contacts and network creating events online with partners.

> Before the pandemic we had over 1,000 visitors coming to see us in Liverpool and we missed those connections and wanted to reach out to other people and places. We designed series of events with Ethos magazine (a tenant) – it helped us to reflect and consider where we could be in the future, they were really inspiring, and these global partnerships and visits are starting up again. (Chair)

8.2. Communication From the CIC: Strong Communications Both Internally and Externally (Theme 4)

It was vital that there remained efficient internal and external communications. A key priority of the CIC was the further development of the online communication systems. As a collective with strong social roots face-to-face communication supported by online support had always been the standard operating model. However, with the need to reduce unnecessary socialisation and strict social distancing rules put into place nationally the CIC management team and board had to convert all their communications online. With high levels of digital literacy within the CIC all communications were transferred online by the marketing manager with support from an external PR agency. This led to multiple award nominations and awards for tenants and CIC from BIMA and Liverpool City Region Combined Authority. Greater use of digital communications also enabled the CIC to issue important public statements. Good news stories were shared internally and externally, and good practice shared with the wider creative community.

8.3. Local and Regional Partnerships and Advocacy: Connecting the Networks Online and Powerful Advocacy (Theme 5)

The UK Government imposed lockdown restrictions on all non-essential businesses in the UK. This meant that for most organisations all networking with partners, whether local, regional, national, or international, was transferred online. To ensure that tenants were supported effectively the CIC team explored numerous resources and networks that were available online and consolidated information on the main CIC website.

The use of existing networks such as the European Creative Hubs Network (ECHN) also allowed the learning and support created by the Baltic Creative CIC to be shared with the wider ECHN so that mutual learning and understanding could gained as the CIC responded to challenges that emerged because of the pandemic.

Advocacy was also used to show solidarity with critical issues such as the Black Lives Matter movement in 2020. This also led to several strategic decisions being made by the CIC.

> It was important to the board to make a public statement on BLM in 2020, not just to show solidarity but to be held accountable by our creative community and make a real commitment and change in 2021 and beyond …. Strategic decisions such as developing an EDI policy and embedding it in practice also took place. As we emerge from the pandemic, so are our partnerships – Taste Ramadan. What we learn as a CIC and as we work with different partners, we share that with tenants. (Chair)

Online network events highlighted professional business services such as legal, Health & Safety, etc., the Kickstarter scheme support: supporting young people into the workplace and sector-specific opportunities: BIMA bespoke affiliate membership for tenants with access to awards programmes, conferences, and training. The combination of symbolic capital and social capital ensured that the CIC adapted to a changing ecosystem remained a hub for its community to coalesce around.

9. CONCLUSIONS

To date the analysis of the capital conversions in the CIC has only been undertaken at an intrapersonal level (Pret et al., 2016). To explore if and how specific capital conversions occurred, and continue to occur, on an interpersonal level

(Hill, 2021) further research is needed that focuses specifically on individuals with the creative hub and ecosystem.

Baltic Creative CIC is a creative hub within a wider ecosystem in which the physical hub is the buildings, and the ecosystem is the actors the types of capital that were converted during a period of unprecedented disruption can be analysed in detail.

The efficient conversion of capitals allowed the CIC to not only remain resilient but to also adapt, change, and pivot during a period when all actors were being severely tested. Despite these challenging times key learnings have been made. The CIC focused on being 'as safe a space as possible'. One of the key learnings is the resilience and adaptability of the actors came from the fact that they saw themselves as an identifiable creative ecosystem. They looked out for each other, and it was the conversion of their capitals that kept that ecosystem healthy. This was evident when the physical hub had to close, and they ecosystem pivoted quickly online.

It should be noted that data were collected only during the pandemic period and further research will be needed to explore how the creative hub and ecosystem adapt and change in the future. The conceptualisation of a cluster of creative entrepreneurs as its own distinct creative hub and ecosystem offers the potential of further research as the agility of such ecosystems to adapt to changing circumstances could offer an interesting contribution when considering the development of thriving creative communities in the future.

REFERENCES

Avidikos, V., & Pettas, D. (2021). The new topologies of collaborative workspace assemblages between the market and the commons. *Geoforum, 121*, 44–52.

Bandura, A. (1997). *Self-efficacy: The exercise of control*. Freeman

Bourdieu, P. (1984). *Distinction: A social critique of the judgement of taste*. Routledge

Bourdieu, P. (1986). The forms of capital. In J. Richardson (Ed.)., *Handbook of theory and research for the sociology of education* (pp. 241–258). Greenwood.

Bourdieu, P. (1990). *The logic of practice*. Stanford University Press.

Bourdieu, P. (1993). *The field of cultural production*. Polity Press.

Campbell, P. (2019). *Persistent Creativity* (1st ed.). Palgrave Macmillan UK. https://doi.org/10.1007/978-3-030-03119-0_2

Chen, G., Gully, M. S., & Eden, D. (2004). General self-efficacy and self-esteem: Toward theoretical and empirical distinction between correlated self-evaluations. *Journal of Organizational Behavior, 25*, 375–395.

Cooke, P. (2008). Culture, clusters, districts and quarters: Some reflections on the scale. In P. Cooke & L. Lazzeretti (Eds.), *Creative cities, cultural clusters and economic development*. Edward Elgar Publishing.

Couch, C., & Fowles, S. (2019). Metropolitan planning and the phenomenon of reurbanisation: The example of Liverpool. *Planning Practice and Research, 34*(2), 184–205. https://doi.org/10.1080/02697459.2018.1548237

De Bernard, M., Comunian, R., & Gross, J. (2021). Cultural and creative ecosystems: A review of theories and methods, towards a new research agenda. *Cultural Trends, 31*(4), 332–353. doi:https://doi.org/10.1080/09548963.2021.2004073

Foster, N. (2020, January). From clusters to ecologies: Rethinking measures, values and impacts in creative sector-led development. Conference Paper. Creative Industries Research Frontiers Seminar Series, London.

Gist, M. E., & Mitchell, T. R. (1992). Self-efficacy: A theoretical analysis of its determinants and malleability. *Academy of Management Review, 17*, 183–211.

Gross, J., & Wilson, N. (2019). *Creating the environment: The cultural eco-system of creative people and places*. https://www.artscouncil.org.uk/creative-people-and-places/learning-creative-people-and-places

Guillemin, M., & Gillam, L. (2004). Ethics, reflexivity, and "ethically important moments" in research. *Qualitative Inquiry, 10*(2), 261–280. https://doi.org/10.1177/1077800403262360

Heap, H., Southern, A., & Thompson, M. (2017). The scale, scope and value of the liverpool city region social economy. *Heseltine Institute for Public Policy and Practice, November 2017*.

Hill, I. R. (2018). How did you get up and running? Taking a Bourdieuan perspective towards a framework for negotiating strategic fit. *Entrepreneurship and Regional Development, 30*(5–6), 402–417.

Hill, I. R. (2021). Spotlight on UK artisan entrepreneurs' situated collaborations: Through the lens of entrepreneurial capitals and their conversions. *International Journal of Entrepreneurial Behavior & Research, 27*(1), 99–121.

Hornby, A. S., & Cowie, A. P. (1995). *Oxford advanced learner's dictionary* (Vol. 1430). Oxford University Press.

Jiménez, A., & Zheng, Y. (2021). Unpacking the multiple spaces of innovation hubs. *The Information Society, 37*(3), 163–176.

Johnson, B. (2020). Prime Minister's statement on coronavirus (COVID-19): 22 March 2020. https://www.gov.uk/government/speeches/pm-statement-on-coronavirus-22-march-2020

Khlystova, O., Kalyuzhnova, Y., & Belitski, M. (2022). The impact of the COVID-19 pandemic on the creative industries: A literature review and future research agenda. *Journal of Business Research, 139*, 1192–1210. https://doi.org/10.1016/j.jbusres.2021.09.062

King, N. (2012). Doing template analysis. In G. Symon & C. Cassell (Eds.), *Qualitative organizational research* (pp. 426–450). SAGE Publications.

Lee, D., Gill, R. C., Pratt, A. C., & Virani, T. E. (2019). Creative hubs, cultural work and affective economies: Exploring 'unspeakable' experiences for young cultural workers. In R. C. Gill, A. C. Pratt, & T. Virani (Eds.), *Creative clusters in question* (pp. 171–187). Palgrave Macmillan.

McGee, J. E., Peterson, M., Mueller, S. L., & Sequeira, J. M. (2009). Entrepreneurial self-efficacy: Refining the measure. *Entrepreneurship Theory and Practice, July*, 965–988.

Mert, C. (2019). In Istanbul's sounds and its 'Creative' hubs. In R. C. Gill, A. C. Pratt, & T. Virani (Eds.), *Creative clusters in question* (pp. 69–88). Palgrave MacMillan.

Mommaas, H. (2004). Cultural clusters and the post-industrial city: Towards the remapping of urban cultural policy. *Urban Studies, 41*(3), 507–532.

Picard, R. G., & Karlsson, C. (Eds.). (2011). *Media clusters*. Edward Elgar.

Pratt, A. C. (2004). Creative clusters: Towards the governance of the creative industries production system? *Media International Australia, 112*, 50–66.

Pratt, A. C. (2021). Creative hubs: A critical evaluation. *City, Culture and Society, 24*, 1–7.

Pret, T., Shaw, E., & Drakopoulou Dodd, S. (2016). Painting the full picture: The conversion of economic, cultural, social and symbolic capital. *International Small Business Journal, 34*(8), 1004–1027.

Reid, S. (2020). The generative principles of lifestyle enterprising: Dialectic entanglements pf capitals-habitus-field. *International Journal of Entrepreneurial Behavior and Research, 27*(3), 629–647.

Thompson, M., Nowak, V., Southern, A., Davies, J., & Furmedge, P. (2020). Re-grounding the city with Polanyi: From urban entrepreneurialism to entrepreneurial municipalism. *Environment and Planning A: Economy and Space, 52*(6), 1171–1194. https://doi.org/10.1177/0308518X19899698

Valli, C. (2021). Artistic careers in the cyclicality of art scenes and gentrification: Symbolic capital accumulation through space in Bushwick, NYC. *Urban Geography, 43*(8), 1176–1198. https://doi.org/10.1080/02723638.2021.1902122

Virani, T. E., & Gill, R. (2019). Hip hub? Class, race and gender in creative hubs. In R. C. Gill, A. C. Pratt, & T. Virani (Eds.). *Creative clusters in question* (pp. 131–154). Palgrave Macmillan.

Walmsley, B., Gilmore, A., O'Brien, D., & Torreggiani, A. (Eds.). (2022). *Culture in crisis: Impacts of COVID-19 on the UK cultural sector and where we go from here*. University of Leeds.

Waring, T., & Wainwright, D. (2008). Issues and challenges in the use of template analysis: Two comparative case studies from the field. *The Electronic Journal of Business Research Methods, 6*(1), 85–94.

Watson, T. J. (2011). Ethnography, reality, and truth: The vital need for studies of "how things work" in organizations and management. *Journal of Management Studies, 48*(1), 202–217. https://doi. org/10.1111/j.1467-6486.2010.00979.x

Wen, W. (2018). Scenes, quarters and clusters: The formation and governance of creative places in urban China. *Cultural Science Journal, 5*(2), 8.

INSIGHTS INTO CREATIVE SUBSECTORS

CHAPTER 9

DADDY OR HUBBY? FAMILY AND FEMALE ENTREPRENEURSHIP IN THE INDIAN MOVIE INDUSTRY

Rajeev Kamineni and Ruth Rentschler

ABSTRACT

*Despite almost 50% of the Indian population being women, there is a signifi-
cant gap between the genders in movie production. Although there might be
several reasons attributed to the underrepresentation of women in the role of
a movie entrepreneur, it is a fact that female movie entrepreneurs are few and
far between. Most of the female movie producers in Indian movie industry tend
to be spouses or children of leading male actors who have taken up the mantle
to assist their husbands or fathers. This chapter, using interviews and life history analysis, examines reasons for low numbers of female entrepreneurs in the
Indian movie industry, a domain that has largely been overlooked.*

Keywords: Female entrepreneurship; role of family in entrepreneurship;
Indian movie industry; movie producer as entrepreneur; creative industry
women entrepreneurs; social capital in entrepreneurship; innovation and
risk taking

1. INTRODUCTION

Mary Pickford was one of the partners of United Artists, a studio formed with
the basic premise that artists should be allowed the freedom to control their own
interests. One hundred and three years ago, as a female entrepreneur in the movie

Creative (and Cultural) Industry Entrepreneurship in the 21st Century
Contemporary Issues in Entrepreneurship Research, Volume 18A, 121–133
Copyright © 2024 by Rajeev Kamineni and Ruth Rentschler
Published under exclusive licence by Emerald Publishing Limited
ISSN: 2040-7246/doi:10.1108/S2040-72462023000018A009

industry, Mary was a pioneer in many ways and was entrepreneurial in her outlook and believed in the potential of cinema as a medium of entertainment. Seven
years after United Artists, Fatma films was established in India by Fatma Begum
and Fatma is the first female movie producer in India. Fatma was a true pioneer
in the sense that she was not connected to the movie industry and was not the
daughter or wife of an established star, but she moved from theatre to cinema
and broke many conventions of acting as well as producing. Unfortunately, in the
past 96 years, not many female Indian producers followed the trail blazing path
of Fatma. Few studies have examined how entrepreneurial Indian movie producers juggle gender tensions by using their family ties and networks to advance their
careers, as most previous studies have examined the actor or 'star' in the movie
(Wallace et al., 1993) or the movie itself (Ravid, 1999). But the fact is that there is
a 6.2:1 gender ratio in the Indian movie industry (Walia, 2015). For every six men
in the industry, there is one woman and there are only 15% women producers in
the Indian movie industry.

   The Indian movie industry is of great economic importance to India, with
movie business generating close to US$13 billion (economictimes.indiatimes.com)
in gross box office revenue per year in India alone and generating 2.65 million jobs
(Deloitte, 2019). India's central board of film certification (CBFC) website states
that there are more than 2,000 movies released each year in India, significantly
higher than the 700 produced in the USA. Unfortunately, due to the impact of
COVID-19, the Indian media and entertainment industry (as classified by Indian
trade associations/bodies) reported a 24% decline in revenues and hence going
back to the 2017 figure of US$18.9 billion (FICCI EY 2021). The Indian movie
industry offers an opportunity to study female producers in Indian movies as
'socialized worker[s]' (Gill & Pratt, 2008). Movies are exceptional in their reliance
on family ties and networking (Kamineni & Rentschler, 2020) as the primary –
and in many cases only – tool for identifying the 'right' producer for the movie
(Blair, 2000a; Kamineni & Rentschler, 2020). The reliance on family ties and networks has different outcomes for men and women (Grugulis & Stoyanova, 2012).
Hiring on short-term contracts in the context of technological innovation, ambiguity, risk, uncertainty, and pro-activeness necessitates reliance on family ties and
networks, with outcomes that reinforce the status quo (Ratten & Jones, 2021), seeing few women partake as producers in the Indian movie industry. To overcome
gender inequality, we need to understand the mechanisms by which ecosystem is
sustained in institutional social arrangements (Xu & Dobson, 2019). This chapter
unpacks how family ties and networks that rely on 'connections' and 'affinities of
habitus' (Bourdieu, 1984, p. 151) can contribute to gendered outcomes that are
productive or perverse for producers.

2. LITERATURE/THEORETICAL FRAMING

2.1. Entrepreneurship in the Indian Movie Industry

There is increasing focus on entrepreneurship in the Indian movie industry
(KPMG India, 2017). Entrepreneurship consists of three central underlying

dimensions that are exploited by entrepreneurial individuals to harness opportunities: innovation, risk taking, and pro-activeness. For Indian movie producers, each product (i.e. movie) is new, requiring continuous innovation. In the creative industries, innovation is valued not only for its monetary value but also for its creative content, ensuring that tensions between culture and commerce are also to the fore (Strøm et al., 2020). For Indian movie producers, risk-taking is continuous, as they seek to find that next blockbuster that will bring them fame and fortune as well as creative recognition (Elberse, 2013), creating continual tensions for them. Risk-taking in Indian movies embraces commerce and creativity to see movies succeed in domestic and international markets. For Indian movie producers, their continuous pro-activeness, searching for novel ideas, financial backers, and innovating in the way they undertake each new project, highlights the tensions that they always face (Hausmann & Heinze, 2016). Entrepreneurial movie producers, as a type of artist, are pro-active, imaginative (Elias et al., 2022), being well-educated, with tertiary qualifications but their careers are risky and uncertain due to the portfolio nature of their careers.

2.2. Female Entrepreneurship

In the past two decades, there has been a significant increase in the research of women's entrepreneurship. It has been identified that there are differences among women entrepreneurs with respect to the approach they take to entrepreneurship and the strategies they pursue (Davis & Shaver, 2012). Underlying growth patterns that have an impact on the entrepreneurial decision-making of women have been identified amongst women-owned businesses (Bardasi et al., 2011). Feminist theory has been used as a grounding factor to explain that there are obvious cultural differences between men and women; however, these differences do not hinder women's entrepreneurial behaviour (Calas et al., 2009).

There is a stream of literature (Adom & Anambane, 2020; Banchik, 2019) that tends to suggest that women entrepreneurs tend to be conservative and risk-averse, thereby restricting themselves to sustaining an enterprise rather than planning for growth of the enterprise which naturally leads to firms constraining to small and medium size (Jennings & McDougald, 2007). Just like male entrepreneurs, women entrepreneurs also tend to temper their growth motivation and growth plans depending on the business life cycle stage of their venture. The stereotypical values attributed to women such as interpersonal sensitivity, tenderness, and expressiveness could be used to their firm's advantage in growing and sustaining growth (Johnsen & McMahon, 2005). Success and expansion of women entrepreneurs' ventures need not be measured just in dollar and market share terms but can also be measured in the scale of personal development and appreciation of social responsibility (Dalborg, 2015).

2.3. Family Ties and Networks

While women constitute the largest consumer base in the creative industries, they are not represented equally in leadership roles in them (Caust, 2018). Previous studies have examined the various aspects and status of men and women in different contexts. First, gender can affect career progression due to the dynamics of gender diversity that is dependent on producer attributes of family ties and networking for career progression, thus increasing risk and the need for proactiveness for those outside the circle (Azmat & Rentschler, 2015). While 'neutral' criteria of meritocracy and skills/experiences are common in organisations, gender bias can still exist, as men may have more access to social networks and support systems that circumvent criteria on which merit is based (Broadbridge & Simpson, 2011). If this is the case for female Indian movie producers, then they may experience increased tensions as they seek to progress their careers.

Tension through exclusionary practices has seen calls for the creative industries to refocus their approach to employment (Wreyford, 2015), extending beyond networking and family ties. Gender in Indian movie production, however, presents a complex somewhat contradictory matter. The existing literature highlights that efforts to increase gender diversity are compromised by a major social barrier which relates to the likelihood of favouring new producers with similar major demographic characteristics (Wreyford, 2015). Hence, our study is timely as entrepreneurial Indian movie producers remain under-researched, calling out for greater understanding of how they create their social capital.

2.4. Social Capital

Factors such as social capital have been found to have a significant influence on the level of growth in ventures owned by women. Entrepreneurial Indian movie producers, irrespective of gender and social background, have a stake in building their communities. This view seeks to provide a platform for them to develop their careers, participating fully, which derives from Bourdieu's (1984) social capital which signifies that social relationships are a source of human activities. Thus, Bourdieu's theory of capital provides a framework for examining entrepreneurial Indian movie producers and a consistent approach to studying the unequal opportunities for men and women in advancing their movie careers in India as producers through gender and class relations (Tatli & Özbilgin, 2011). Social capital entails actual or virtual resources such as personal relationships and networks, which accumulate for individuals or groups (Bourdieu, 1990; Hill, 2018). Hence, if an individual is part of a network or demographic, networks may help or hinder career opportunities. Social capital provides a framework to understand how entrepreneurial Indian movie producers use family ties and networks to benefit their career progression and the underlying tensions that can create.

3. METHODOLOGY

The first author continues his association with the Indian movie industry in a non-executive role after being a senior executive for close to a decade. We employed the philosophical position of interpretive lens, symbolic interactionism, and the life history (Gabrium & Holstein, 1998; Van Maanen, 2011) narrative as a strategy of ethnographic enquiry, life stories of failure, success, and resilience are analysed. We interviewed female, male producers, and female stakeholders in the Indian movie industry. Whether it was female or male movie entrepreneurs, innovation, and risk-taking with a pro-activeness that aids success is something that is presaged to still be necessary in this uncertain and turbulent industry of rapid change and digitisation. Producers, directors, financiers, main technical crew, additional crew, cast, the studio, marketing agency/team, distributors, and exhibitors/digital right holders were identified as the salient stakeholders for this chapter. To that end, between 2018 and 2022, we purposively interviewed, recorded, and transcribed 15 participants who fit into the 10 stakeholder categories in the Indian movie industry. Providing a rich foundation for interpretation, thematic analysis of the data inductively revealed three key themes around which the findings are structured: (i) innovation, risk-taking, and pro-activeness; (ii) family ties; and (iii) networks.

4. FINDINGS

4.1. Innovation, Risk-taking, and Pro-activeness

Risk-taking is central to the Indian movie business. A senior male producer who was forced to take a break due to financial setbacks shares the importance of having a fallback option:

The writer and I moved to the movie production hub, leaving our families behind as our children were in school. We thought that we should settle down first before we bring our families, production is not an ordinary venture, it is very risky. We wanted to try one or two ventures and then decide if it is worthwhile to shift our families.

Such a scenario is almost impossible to imagine for a female movie producer in India because with very limited support structures, it is simply not possible to leave her family behind. Furthermore, maintaining reputation was perceived as critical to success for Indian movie producers, one told us:

So, as a producer, are you prepared sufficiently to handle the failure financially as well as reputation? I was prepared, I prepared my ground for failure.

Often this means using the family ties as connectors to down-play risk, to build careers, as another producer informed:

I used to sit along with my father-in-law who was an established and successful producer in the editing table. I learnt from him, and my editors and that gave me a lot of confidence.

Though the above quotes are from male producers they highlight the risk of losing all money and reputation a male or female producer faces. However, there are many producers who want to insure themselves against failure and that is one of the major reasons for involving family members in the business.

4.2. Family Ties

There is a quirky statistic in the Indian movie industry, a majority of the female movie producers tend to be spouses or children of leading male actors and in a way thrust into the role so that they can assist their husbands or fathers. It is interesting to hear the female movie producer's perspective about how she ended up as a producer.

My husband is an actor, he wanted to direct a movie. He got the opportunity to direct a movie with a producer from the US. Production commenced and suddenly producer abandoned the project and left the country thus forcing my husband to take up the responsibility of completing the movie and releasing it. He went from pillar to post to arrange funds and release the movie and by default I ended up as the movie producer.

From the above statement, it is evident that this female producer became a producer by default and not by choice. This is the common refrain from many female producers in the Indian movie industry. They take up the role or they are thrust into the role to safeguard their husband's or father's financial investments.

India's leading female movie producer is Late Mrs Parvathamma Rajkumar. She has produced 80 movies with her husband and sons in leading roles. Mrs Rajkumar can be classified as a reluctant debutante who changed from a shy home maker to a very successful producer and came into her own from the shadows of her super star husband to command respect and admiration in the industry. Nevertheless, the fact that she became a producer for her husband and sons cannot be ignored. A majority of current female movie producers represent their husband's or father's financial interests. The list can be expanded by adding on to the earlier statement that the majority of female producers in India tend to be actresses who produce their own movies or continue producing after they stopped acting or are daughters of producers, directors, and actors or wives of producers, directors, and actors. The notable exception to this trend is Guneet Monga, winner of an academy award and a first-generation professional movie producer who has carved out a niche for herself by independently producing creative content that achieved commercial success as well as critical acclaim. Guneet stands out as a rare exception who has made a mark as producer by sheer commitment and effort and exemplifies the belief that risk is lowered if passion for the 'art of cinema', drives production. As a male senior producer who has produced more than 25 movies commented:

If you are in the movie industry just for money then the industry will not take care of you, but if you are in it for the passion of movie making then you will somehow survive and be looked after.

A senior second-generation producer has his son, and now his granddaughters taking up the mantle of production and continuing the legacy of that well-known brand. These young women have had their entrepreneurial journey anchored in a family business, reducing the risk for them as female producers, protecting them from the travails of a start-up and the difficulties of being a woman in a male-dominated industry. The grandfather summed it,

A new generation must take up the mantle and then only new ideas and new methods will come in and will ensure the survival of this industry.

When the risk of failure is high, the risk of pilferage and corruption also exists because there is no guarantee for long-term survival and growth.

This makes producers constantly look over their shoulders for any impending trouble. Involving kith and kin who can be trusted with financial responsibility plus building networks that open access to a support system are the two ways in which producers try to safeguard their investment.

4.3. Networks

A female producer shared her experience on the value of networks as a means of success in the Indian movie business. She presents her perspective about the need for access to the peak trade body in Indian movies, the Producers' council, as a means to success:

> The sad part was that I was pregnant at that time, I was going around asking for business settlement and this gentleman never gave any settlement and he said he owes several million rupees to all the distributors, I literally fought with him and I went to the Producers' council and that was when I joined the Producers' council. I know that we can sort out our problems only through the Producers' council. Of course, they helped me at that time. Because, one woman coming every day to sort out the problem, they felt bad for me, first time producer. I wanted to do the next film, unless this is sorted out I cannot start another movie, finally I cleared up everything.

Her voice would not have been heard without the support of the Producers' council. This quote exemplifies the fact female producers must go to that extra mile just to be heard, illustrating the centrality of networking ties to success. This female producer had to enrol into the peak trade body to have a voice and to feel empowered. In other words, she needed men of influence in powerful positions behind her to receive the money which was owed to her. There is a long way to go for female producers in India.

The role of women in Indian movie business is not limited to the husband-wife team but is also seen in the social influence of the mother on her son and his career choice. Indeed, this is a type of mentorship from an early age. For example, a male mid-career movie producer who worked as a senior executive in other industries before taking up movie production explains it,

> Movies was the only world that existed for me from the age of four when I used to accompany my mother to the movies. As I grew up my love for movies became a passion and anyone who knew me was not surprised as I became a producer because it was natural progression for me.

In summary, Fig. 1 provides an empirical framework of the entrepreneurial dimensions (i.e. risk-taking, innovation, and pro-activeness) operating in Indian movies, with representative quotes illustrating how they apply for women in Indian movies. Further, illustrates the other two dimensions of family ties and networking that are present for women in seeking to carve out success in a competitive and volatile industry, also with representative quotes from our study.

5. DISCUSSION

Contrary to our theoretical framing of women in entrepreneurship where it was indicated that women entrepreneurs tend to be risk-averse and conservative, hence, restricting themselves to sustaining an enterprise rather than planning

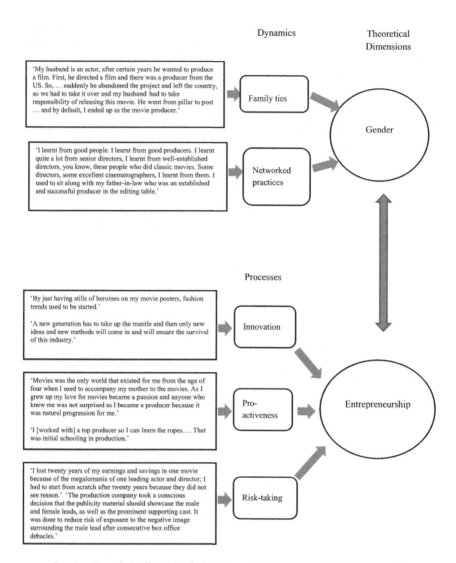

Fig. 1.   Female Indian Movie Producers' Entrepreneurship Framework.

for growth (Adom & Anambane, 2020; Banchik, 2019; Jennings & McDougald, 2007), we identified that by using family ties and networks as tools to manage their own time and family commitments (Byrne et al., 2019), female Indian movie producers are offering a way out of the dilemma women face in terms of the priority accorded to family and career.

Fig. 2 points out the dynamics and processes between entrepreneurship and gender that help us understand why as an industry standard, there are more flops than hits in the Indian movie business. In such a context, networks and family ties are all-important to getting a movie off the ground. If producers do not have access to networks and family ties then they need to work harder to build these so that they have a buffer to survive the vagaries of movie business cycles. Producers have a high chance of reputational damage occurring when a movie is a flop. Thus, where risk is high and rewards few and far between, Indian movie producers need to be pro-active in seeking work and ensuring success. Thus, entrepreneurial Indian movie producers mobilise social capital to develop their careers using networks and family ties due to the meagre formal channels for developing their careers (e.g. lack of formal education in movie making). We heard stories of opportunities and challenges and sought to understand the processes and dynamics that constitute the pool of creative resources using the Bourdieusian theory of capitals.

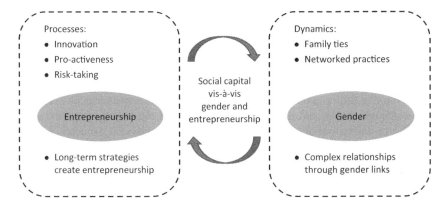

Fig. 2. Dynamics and Processes Within and Across Configurations (Linked to the Theoretical Dimensions of Fig. 1).

Social capital establishes how personal networks, relationships, and resources accrue to individuals or groups (Bourdieu, 1986; Hill, 2018), accruing a reputation that aids success. Social capital is an important means of legitimising creative people inside and outside their field. All producers and their circle whom we interviewed identified networks and family ties as essential to their career advancement. Indeed, internal networks within the family were critical to the success of entrepreneurial Indian movie producers' careers, while external networks outside the family were also crucial to their success. Furthermore, current female movie producers represent their husband's or father's interests in developing and extending networks. This reiterates the earlier statement that the majority of female producers in India tend to be actresses who produce their own movies or continue producing after they stopped acting or are daughters of producers, directors, and actors or wives of producers, directors, and actors. Through researching the reasons for low participation of women in the Indian movie industry, we identified that female participation as movie producers is influenced by the social capital, especially through family ties as a form of networking as well as through broader networks, such as professional bodies, like the Producers' council.

6. IMPLICATIONS AND FURTHER RESEARCH

There is a crying need for more female movie entrepreneurs; though the global percentage is low, it is much lower in Indian cinema, and a significant majority of Indian female movie producers tend to be wives and daughters of leading stars or producers. Though further research is essential to understand this trend from a cultural and social perspective, it is evident that movie production should be presented as a viable career option for female entrepreneurs. As pointed out by a female producer in this study:

> They have seen me in production every day and observers used to comment that I managed very well and took care of everyone. I felt proud, though it might be momentary, I feel that it is the credibility I have built.

This female producer rates credibility as a very important trait and with a sense of pride states that she has built it on her own. Such producers can be role models for other female producers to consider movie production as a viable career option. Though the number of female students enrolling in film and media courses in India is on the rise, the cascading effect of the increase in number of females donning behind the camera roles is not yet visible. With a population of close to half a billion women, only 18% of the total entrepreneurs in India are women (Singh, 2021), and this disparity is evident in the Indian movie industry also. With training and opening of entrepreneurial pathways for women in Indian movies and cultural change on the role of women in the movies slowly occurring, opportunities for Indian women behind the camera may open in the future. In brief, if entrepreneurial Indian movie producers could accumulate and deploy social capital effectively, with good support of peak trade bodies, skill development, formal movie education and training, building networks beyond family ties, career opportunities may open to more women, and women *and* men may find career opportunities improve.

Thus, our study extends Bourdieu's theory of capitals by applying his framework to careers of entrepreneurial Indian male/female movie producers at the individual level within a field that is rapidly changing in a dynamic social system. Tatli and Özbilgin (2011) argued that as Bourdieu's theory focuses on social class relations, it would benefit scholarship in gender studies by exploring how individuals own and distribute different capitals in organisational settings. Thus, we extend their study to a study of entrepreneurial Indian movie producers. We add to the literature on men and women in the creative industries, that is, movies (Elberse, 2013; Eliashberg et al., 2006), indicating that entrepreneurial Indian movie producers share common career experiences of accumulation and deployment of capital with others in the creative industries. We argue that entrepreneurial Indian movie producers, together with government and peak trade bodies, are responsible for using their capitals to optimise career opportunities for men or women.

For doing business, our findings have important implications for the development of female producers in the Indian movie industry. Based on distribution of capital, entrepreneurship is important to female Indian movie producers as they take responsibility for their own careers; however, they need skills in social capital as well as economic capital such as family ties and networking. Finally, their education can be boosted as well as being more focused by providing them with skills early before their worldview becomes fixed. These competencies enable entrepreneurial female Indian movie producers to move between different projects, groups, and events as part of building their careers, enabling women to grow in number and capability in an industry still dominated by men.

7. CONCLUSION

Though the limitation of interviewing a very limited number of female movie producers exists, the Indian movie industry does not reflect the makeup of society, providing an opportunity to examine family ties, networking practices and gendered outcomes for producers' working in it as they struggle to innovate, take calculated risks to create new products for each movie, and be pro-active in exploiting new business opportunities. Hence, we conclude that women face greater challenges than men, given their small number, reliance on family ties for networking and traditional social capital beliefs that favour men over women in business. Nonetheless, Bourdieu's theory of capitals offers rich insights on how entrepreneurial Indian movie producers use capital to progress their careers. Our study highlights stories of power and passion, missed opportunities and misunderstandings, struggle, and success in a field less dominant than Hollywood but more important economically and socially to the Indian and increasingly, the global economy.

REFERENCES

Adom, K., & Anambane, G. (2020). Understanding the role of culture and gender stereotypes in women entrepreneurship through the lens of the stereotype threat theory. *Journal of Entrepreneurship in Emerging Economies, 12*(1), 2053–4604.

Azmat, F., & Rentschler, R. (2018). Gender and ethnic diversity and corporate responsibility: The case of the arts sector. *Journal of Business Ethics, 141*(2), 317–336.

Banchik, A. V. (2019). Taking care and taking over: Daughter's duty, self-employment, and gendered inheritance in Zacatecas, Mexico. *Gender and Society, 33*(2), 296–320.

Bardasi, E., Sabarwal, S., & Terrell, K. (2011). How do female entrepreneurs perform? Evidence from three developing regions. *Small Business Economics, 37,* 417–441.

Blair, H. (2000a). Active networking: The role of networks and hierarchy in the operation of the labour market in the British film industry. *Management Research News, 23,* 20–21.

Bourdieu, P. (1984). *Distinction: A social critique of the judgement of taste.* Harvard University Press.

Bourdieu, P. (1986). The forms of capital. In J. G. Richardson (Ed.), *Handbook of theory and research for the sociology of education* (pp. 241–258). Greenwood.

Bourdieu, P. (1990). *The logic of practice.* Polity Press.

Broadbridge, A., & Simpson, R. (2011). 25 Years on: Reflecting on the past and looking to the future in gender and management research. *British Journal of Management, 22,* 470–483.

Byrne, J., Fattoum, S., & Diaz Garcia, M. C. (2019). Role models and women entrepreneurs: Entrepreneurial superwoman has her say. *Journal of Small Business Management, 57*(1), 154–184.

Calas, M. B., Smircich, L., & Bourne, K. A. (2009). Extending the boundaries: Reframing 'entrepreneurship as social change' through feminist perspectives. *Academy of Management Review, 34*(3), 552–569.

Caust, J. (2018). *To fix gender inequity in arts leadership we need more women in politics and chairing boards*. Retrieved from https://theconversation.com/to-fix-gender-inequity-in-arts-leadership-we-need-more-women-in-politics-and-chairing-boards-97782

Dalborg, C. (2015). The life cycle in women-owned businesses: From a qualitative growth perspective. *International Journal of Gender and Entrepreneurship, 7*(2), 126–147.

Davis, A. E., & Shaver, K. G. (2012). Understanding gendered variations in business growth intentions across the life course. *Entrepreneurship Theory and Practice, 36*(3), 495–512.

Deloitte Analysis. Retrieved, December 3, 2021, from https://www.mpa-apac.org/wp-content/uploads/2020/07/20200708_India-ECR-2019_Finalized.pdf

Elberse, A. (2013). *Blockbusters: Hit-making, risk-taking and the big business of entertainment*. Henry Holt and Co.

Elias, S. R. S. T. A, Chiles, T. H., & Crawford, B. (2022). Entrepreneurial imagining: How a small team of arts entrepreneurs created the world's largest traveling carillon. *Organization Studies, 43*(2), 203–226.

Eliashberg, J., Elberse, A., & Leenders, M. A. A. M. (2006). The motion pictures industry: Critical issues in practice, current research, and new research directions. *Marketing Science, 25*(6), 638–661.

EY. (2019). *A billion screens of opportunity*. Report published for Federation of Indian Chamber of Commerce and Industry (FICCI), Mumbai.

FICCI EY. (2021). *Playing by new rules: India's media and entertainment sector reboots in 2020*. Federation of Indian chambers of commerce and industry, Ernst and Young report.

Gabrium, J. F., & Holstein, J. A. (1998). Narrative practice and the coherence of personal stories. *Sociological Quarterly, 39*, 163–187.

Gill, R., & Pratt, A. (2008). In the social factory? Immaterial labour, precariousness and cultural work. *Theory, Culture & Society, 25*(7–8), 1–30.

Grugulis, I., & Stoyanova, D. (2012). Social capital and networks in film and TV: Jobs for the boys? *Organization Studies, 33*, 1311–1331.

Hausmann, A., & Heinze, A. (2016). Entrepreneurship in the cultural and creative industries: Insights from an emergent field. *Artivate: A Journal of Entrepreneurship in the Arts, 5*(2), 7–22.

Hill, I. (2018). How did you get up and running? Taking a Bourdieuan perspective towards a framework for negotiating strategic fit. *Entrepreneurship and Regional Development, 30*(5–6), 662–696.

Jennings, J. E., & McDougald, M. S. (2007). Family interface experiences and coping strategies: Implications for entrepreneurship research and practice. *Academy of Management Review, 32*, 747–760.

Johnsen, G. J., & McMahon, R. G. P. (2005). Owner manager gender, financial performance and business growth amongst SMEs from Australia's business longitudinal survey. *International Small Business Journal, 23*(2), 115–142.

Kamineni, R., & Rentschler, R. (2020). *Indian movie entrepreneurship: Not just song and dance*. Routledge.

KPMG India. (2017). *Media for the masses: The promise unfolds Indian media and entertainment industry report*. www.KPMG.com.in

Ratten, V., & Jones, P. (2021). Enhancing policies and measurements of family business: Macro, meso or micro analysis. *Journal of Family Business Management, 11*(3), 257–263.

Ravid, S. A. (1999). Information blockbusters and stars: A study of the movie industry. *Journal of Business, 72*(4), 463–492.

Singh, S. (2021). *Women run fewer than 13% of India's small businesses. Here's why*. Retrieved, April 19, 2021, from https://www.indiaspend.com/women/women-run-fewer-than-13-of-indias-small-businesses-heres-why

Strøm, H., Olsen, T. H., & Foss, L. (2020). Tensions for cultural entrepreneurs managing continuous innovation: A systematic literature review. *International Journal of Arts Management, 23*(1), 61–78.

Tatli, A., & Özbilgin, M., (2011). An emic approach to intersectional study of diversity at work: A Bourdieuan framing. *International Journal of Management Reviews, 14*(2), 180–200.

Van Maanen, J. (2011). Ethnography as work: Some rules of engagement. *Journal of Management Studies, 48*(1), 218–234.

Walia, S. (2015). *Don't let the success of Indian actresses fool you. Bollywood is still a man's world.* Retrieved, April 13, 2021, from https://qz.com/india/487104

Wallace, W. T., Seigerman, A., & Holbrook, M. B. (1993). The role of actors and actresses in the success of movies: How much is a movie star worth? *Journal of Cultural Economics, 17*(1), 1–27.

Wreyford, N. (2015). Birds of a feather: Informal recruitment practices and gendered outcomes for screenwriting work in the UK film industry. *The Sociological Review, 63*(S1), 84–96.

Xu, Z., & Dobson, S. (2019). Challenges of building entrepreneurial ecosystems in peripheral places. *Journal of Entrepreneurship and Public Policy, 8*(3), 408–430.

CHAPTER 10

BETWEEN PROFESSIONALISATION AND MARGINALISATION IN THE CREATIVE (AND CULTURAL) INDUSTRIES: A NEW LOOK OF THE WORK OF MUSICIANS IN A FRENCH LARGE CREATIVE CITY

Nathalie Schieb-Bienfait and Sandrine Emin

ABSTRACT

The policies in creative and cultural industries (CCIs) are often based on an implicit assumption that work in the cultural and creative sectors is 'good work' and dominant discourses tend to over-celebrate entrepreneurship. The authors argue that enough attention has been paid to the real work in CCIs. The stake is to better address the symptoms observed for a sustainable and inclusive economy in the CCIs. Through the entrepreneurship-as-practice perspective, the authors document the professionalisation difficulties in music sector, with a qualitative study in a French city, with a particular focus on the marginalisation experienced by the young artists. With the identification of their work specificities and the tendencies for the twenty-first century, the authors point out the diversity of the tasks, the multi-activity and collective practices and the need for some innovative support organisational forms to develop training and skilling (both artistic and entrepreneurial).

Keywords: Creative industry; cultural; musicians; France; professionalisation; marginalisation

Creative (and Cultural) Industry Entrepreneurship in the 21st Century
Contemporary Issues in Entrepreneurship Research, Volume 18A, 135–149
Copyright © 2024 by Nathalie Schieb-Bienfait and Sandrine Emin
Published under exclusive licence by Emerald Publishing Limited
ISSN: 2040-7246/doi:10.1108/S2040-72462023000018A010

1. INTRODUCTION

For the last 20 years, attention has been paid to the impact of the CCIs, in relation to the creative city concepts (Florida, 2002; Hall, 2000; Landry, 2000).
Starting from the seminal definition and the initiatives carried out in the UK by
the Department for Culture, Media and Sport Creative Task Force (see DCMS
reports), many scientific journals have underlined the contribution of the CCIs
to economic growth and organisational design. In developing the CCIs as means
of regenerating cities, establishing creative cities for a sustainable regional and
culture resilience (Cooke & Lazzeretti, 2018), City Councils have attempted to
make themselves more attractive by reinforcing their cultural assets (including educational institutions, festivals, theatres, places, etc.) (Schieb-bienfait et al., 2018).

Although these cities invested through a myriad of projects to supporting an
entrepreneurial CCIs workforce, their policies (Beirne et al., 2017) are often based
on an implicit assumption that work in the cultural and creative sectors is 'good
work' (Oakley, 2014), dominant discourses tended to over-celebrate entrepreneurship (Chapain et al., 2018; Ellmeier, 2003; McRobbie, 2002; Schieb-Bienfait
et al., 2018), with the frequent expressions of pleasure and commitment and
through the image of the cultural activities as a desirable place to work. For a
few years, more attention has been paid to this real work through some different
and contrasted situations – individual behaviours such as the freelancer and the
slasher[1] – in coordination with new kinds of collective action (alternative forms
of work, organisation and production practices) based on common projects
around evolutive and collaborative circles, creative collectives and cooperatives
(Boyle & Oakley, 2018; DeFillippi, 2015; Farrell, 2001; Haynes & Marshall, 2018;
Hennekam & Bennett, 2016).

Through an empirically grounded research on the work in a creative sector in
France (music sector), we want to give a new look and understanding in order to
deal with the following paradox and stakes for the twenty-first century. From one
perspective, some fragile situations, organisational bricolage and liminal practices
(sometimes, still unknown), a level of precariousness, and by contrast, the transition from cultural worker to cultural entrepreneur are the dominant forms of
work (Ellmeier, 2003; Menger, 1999, 2002, 2009).

We argue that this paradox is not well-documented because enough attention
has been paid to the real work in CCIs, particularly for the young people. The
stake is to better address the symptoms observed (substantial invisibilities, precarious situations) (Banks, 2017; Greenman, 2011; Hanage et al., 2016; Oakley &
O'Brien, 2016) for a sustainable and inclusive economy.

As contradictory voices are expressed, we denounce a form of instrumentalisa-
tion of culture and the arts for the benefit of the economy without measuring the
changes and impacts on artists and society in the twenty-first century. Therefore,
through the entrepreneurship-as-practice-perspective (Gartner et al., 2016; Teague
et al., 2021), we have explored in-depth the artists practices (here musicians)
anchored in different kinds of work in order to question their organising processes.

Through this chapter, we will document the professionalisation difficulties in
music, and particularly, the marginalisation experienced by the young artists. Let
us remind that professionalisation covers both the different processes aimed at

raising the degree of mastery of the different components of the profession of musician (i.e. the objectivist conception), and also we do integrate the relativist conception by taking into account the social processes that make it possible to organise the work and their wage relationship in the fields of the living arts. In the music sector, new occupational dimensions[2] have emerged for several years (particularly, with the new technologies and platforms online); moreover, the link between training and employment is increasingly uncertain and it varies according to the profession of the musician. With the identification of their work specificities and the tendencies for the twenty-first century, we point out new tasks, the diversity of these tasks, but also the multi-activity and collective practices. We identify the need for some innovative organisational forms, both light and reticular, where artists, institutions and formal organisations can build interactions and share knowledge to conceive new sustainable and inclusive paths for the professionalisation.

The characterisation of this work nurtures the knowledge for developing inclusive training practices to support the entrepreneurial practices and the need for continued artistic experimentation or for training both the artistic and entrepreneurial skills. In this perspective, the accompaniment of cultural workers could be considered as sustainable by considering the tensions between an increasing 'self-employment' with insecure work.

2. THEORETICAL BACKGROUND

2.1. Studying the Artistic Field Through the Lens of Entrepreneurship-as-Practice

Our research marks a theoretical shift in focus from the entrepreneur-individual to entrepreneurship as activity. Steyaert (2007) emphasises the processual character inherent in entrepreneurship by using the term 'entrepreneuring' rather than the noun entrepreneurship. This posture, this 'process thinking' (Hjorth & Steyaert, 2007), focuses on the act of doing on what is in the making. It tends to show how what happened has happened (Hjorth, 2017).

It encompasses process theories in entrepreneurship that focus on the creative and imaginative activity of human action, moving away from studies based on a linear, functionalist approach and a dual logic (actor/system). According to Steyaert, the concept of entrepreneuring also marks a shift in entrepreneurial studies from an individualistic vision towards a relational approach accounting for the multiplicity of actors involved and their integration into their environment. This approach is consistent with theoretical proposals such as theories of complexity, the interpretative approach (Gartner, 1993), the effectuation and pragmatic perspective (Sarasvathy, 2001) and the project-based view (Bréchet & Schieb-Bienfait, 2011; Lindgren & Packendorff, 2003).

It joins what is now referred to as entrepreneurship-as-practice (EAP) (Gartner et al., 2016; Teague et al., 2021) by applying to the field of entrepreneurship the 'practice turn' (Schatzki et al., 2001) that is already established in the social sciences. The EAP perspective is based on shared assumptions and core concepts of a practice-based approach applied to entrepreneurship. The EAP ontology and epistemology attempt to overcome classical and problematic dichotomies in entrepreneurship research (such as individual/collective, agent/structure and body/mind).

2.2. Theoretical Framing: Practices, Praxis and Practitioners to Identify Work

From a theoretical point of view, the research draws on the analytical frameworks proposed by Whittington (2006) and Rouleau (2013) around practices, praxis and practitioners to identify work and entrepreneurial practices. Through these practices, we set out to identify and to question whether the approach used for supporting artists needs in the twenty-first century.

This perspective focuses on actual practices, on what is underway. It studies actor-system interactions and productions through examining links and tangible and intangible artefacts. We have therefore taken a more in-depth look at these. In particular, we address the entrepreneurial and organisational practices designed and implemented by musicians to develop informal and temporary projects, partial organisations (Lingo & O'mahony, 2010; Lingo & Tepper, 2013) and certain forms of liminal practices (Lindkvist & Hjorth, 2015; Scott, 2012; Stjerne & Svejenova, 2016; Tarassi, 2018; Thomson, 2013) that are highlighted in institutional and non-institutional spaces (Evans, 2009; Garrett et al., 2017; Lange, 2011). We propose to more effectively identify the practices of artists from this perspective of 'entrepreneurship-as-practice' or of entrepreneuring (entrepreneurship being undertaken) (Steyaert, 2007) in order to answer the following questions: what are the entrepreneurial practices in these creative activities? What recommendations can we offer, particularly in terms of entrepreneurial support?

3. RESEARCH SETTING AND METHODOLOGICAL CHOICES

3.1. Approach, Design and Positionality

The CCIs encompass a wide range of professions and practices, which are oriented in varying degrees towards the commercial exploitation of artistic creation (Throsby, 2008). For this research, we narrowed the field of analysis to popular music (for the qualitative study). Projects pursued by musicians are in fact the furthest removed from traditional models of activity, thus adding complexity to the issues affecting the economic viability and sustainability of their activity. In France, these artists are subject to live performance legislation (intermittent employment, presumption of a salary, etc.) and in this sense experience specific difficulties in their professional and entrepreneurial careers.

Our aim is to study both the entrepreneurial and organisational work of musicians in a large French creative city in order to identify the unfamiliar and hidden aspects of their practices on the one hand and to study the circumstances surrounding marginalisation and emancipation (Naudin, 2018) and entrepreneurial support on the other hand. We want to achieve a clearer grasp of working practices by exploring individual trajectories (identity, training, career path), contexts (training establishments, workplaces, networks) and the stakeholders and structures involved in the support ecosystem, both institutional and on the fringes (liminal).

We selected methodologies which factored in these entrepreneurial and organisational processes to consider better for addressing the symptoms observed (invisibilities in the work, multi-activities, precarious situations…) (Banks, 2006, 2017; Greenman, 2011; Hanage et al., 2016; Oakley & O'Brien, 2016).

3.2. Data Collection

After our first longitudinal study of this French creative city (2009–2016), we have undertaken new data collection through semi-directed interviews with musicians and local support organisations focusing on these artistic activities. This new step in our research is based on an analysis of data collected between January 2018 and September 2020 from musicians and from artist support structures (specifically for musicians) and other support organisations in this large city in the Pays de la Loire region of France.

Our data is gathered from face-to-face semi-structured interviews with young musicians, with other musicians and artists entrepreneurs in different workplaces selected in the city (30 interviews) and with several support organisations, notably Trempo (see Box 1), the support organisation for musicians, which has developed two major initiatives: The Music Campus and The Music Incubation Platform (see Box 2 below). The interviews were conducted with musicians on the contemporary music scene (from September 2019 to February 2020) pursuing hybrid career paths. A recording and full transcription of the interview was made or comprehensive notes were taken. Interviews lasted between 1 and 2 hours, with an average length of 80 minutes.

Box 1. Presentation of Trempo,[3] The Support Organisation for Musicians.

Trempo is a highly original and innovative organisation which has developed a specific approach to supporting musicians. All music communities can be found in Trempo. Through its service offering, this structure can observe, analyse and compare the musician practices, trends and needs to create innovative solutions. Trempo also plays an essential role in the implementation of new public policies by building partnerships with local creative, social and business stakeholders, by engaging in dialogue with public authorities and by influencing the rise of a European music community. Trempo has a good overview of needs and practices in different fields: educational, technical and artistic (harnessing recording techniques, understanding stage performance issues), business (management, marketing, social networks, business plan), follow-up and community projects (collaborative processes, social inclusion and cultural mediation). The 28-strong team has a sound knowledge of the cultural environment – both in terms of the music industry and the territorial impact – and a clear vision of a musician's career, that is, an understanding of their career strategy. Trempo has developed many initiatives focusing on two main areas: The Music Campus and The Music Incubation Platform.

Box 2. Music Incubation Platform

The Music Incubation Platform supports career development, with a special focus on emerging musicians, bands and artist-entrepreneurs. It is based on complementary aspects: (1) rehearsal, residencies and recording studios; (2) mentoring and collective learning programmes for bands focusing on professionalisation and national and international market inclusion; (3) vocational and academic training programmes; (4) entrepreneurship and business programmes.

3.3. Data Analysis

Drawing on ethnomethodological approaches, we develop a comprehensive approach to occupational, entrepreneurial and organisational processes to better identify real practices and tensions. We selected the analytical frameworks proposed by Whittington (2006) and Rouleau (2013). The interview data was studied with a view to updating (themes analysis):

(1) The effect of practices (traditions, norms, rules for thinking and acting) on the work and entrepreneurial activity of artists.
(2) The praxis (daily and real practices) of their activity.
(3) The support practices of entrepreneurial artists (what stakeholders were mobilised, why and how) for their professionalisation.
(4) The connections between these three levels of analysis.

4. ANALYSIS AND FINDINGS: PRACTICES AND PRAXIS – STAKEHOLDER SUPPORT FOR MUSICIANS

In this section, results are organised from the frame of the EAP that means the following questions: to what extent do artistic sectorial practices effect musicians' organisational and entrepreneurial activities? How are their work and entrepreneurial actions characterised, and how diverse are their entrepreneurial practices (praxis)? What are the specific needs (musicians and support practices) for professionalisation? And what are the effects of connections between these different levels of analysis?

4.1. The Effect of Practices (Traditions, Norms, Rules for Thinking and Acting) on Artists' Work and Entrepreneurial Activity

4.1.1. The Influence of Public and State Authorities

In the artistic sector, local and public/legislative authorities play an important role by providing artists with support for entrepreneurial activities that helps to organise but also constrain careers and career paths (through the legal rules and restraints).

4.1.2. Project Economy, Intermittent Work

In France, intermittence (the main employment regime for artists and technicians) allows for a chain of multiple contracts that decrease in length and remuneration rate which leads to a deterioration in individual circumstances and unusual wage relations based on a multiplicity of contractual links (Langeard, 2013). Musicians' activity is therefore salary-based but carried out in a freelance capacity. Compared to the general workforce, musicians as an occupational group are, on average, younger, have a higher level of education, tend to be concentrated in a small number of metropolitan areas, show higher rates of self-employment, higher rates of unemployment and of several forms of forced underemployment (non-voluntary part-time work, intermittent work, fewer hours of work); more people have multiple jobs (Menger, 1999).

Over the past 20 years, the situation has deteriorated with increased uncertainty and non-continuous trajectories organised around project-based careers characterised by their 'reversible' nature (Langeard, 2013). Artistic work often tends to be presented as part of an employment dynamic typical of the projective city project of Boltanski and Chiapello (1999). The skills useful to the musician in the labour market correspond to the characteristics of the projective city: commitment, mobility, flexibility, employability, networking, adaptability, ability to generate projects and ability to integrate into projects. We report that there is thus a very uncertain link between the musician's training, his qualification, his real activity and his salary. The project economy dominates the musical sector, with strong consequences on the professionalisation processes, all the more so if the musician wants to be a project leader and potentially become an entrepreneur.

In this perspective, we can distinguish three types of situations that a musician can experiment on the same periods: (i) musician as participant, (ii) musician as employee (intermittent hours) and (iii) musician as manager of their own music group. Bringing each new artistic project to fruition presupposes that musicians seek out resources and skills and access the methods and facilities relevant to their career (training, educational institution, reputation, network, etc.). Musicians can access these resources through volunteering and self-production, for example. However, new skills may sometimes need to be acquired (administrative, technical, production, etc.), negotiations carried out with cultural institutions and recording label executives and regional programming must be mastered (festivals, cultural events, etc.).

4.2. The Paradox of the Intermittence Regime in France

With intermittence (intermittent work) and the associated legal presumption of a salary, an artist claiming benefits for being an intermittent (worker on casual contracts in the music sector) cannot be a company manager. Pursuant to Title III of the circular of 28 January 2010 drafted by the French Ministry of Culture:

'The exercise of the profession of musician with the presumption of a salary is incompatible with the regime of self-employment'. The exception to this rule is any activity unrelated to the activity usually carried out as an intermittent (under the terms of article L.7121-3 of the Labour Code).

Some musicians choose to practise their main occupation (related to live music and performance) only as an entrepreneur (using self-employed or other legal status); in this case, the regulatory framework entails holding a performance contractor licence. Artists who compose/write musical works cannot work under the micro-enterprise regime because their remuneration (sale of works, copyright, etc.) is de facto subject to the social welfare regime for artist-authors.

> What is schizophrenic is that in the music field we have project promoters who want to start a business, but at the same time the law tells them that as a musician/performer, there is the presumption of a wage. According to the law (labour code), you have to be paid to go on stage. (Interview 6)

> The head of the company is obliged to be an employee and if they want to apply for unemployment benefit for intermittents it's not in their interest to be a manager because this may invalidate their they can be rejected by the claims department of the employment centre for performers. So the most ambitious people and their team either find a tour organiser for the show component or for the editing-production-sound component, and that's where they set up a business in the music sector. (Interview 10)

The artist is therefore encouraged to be entrepreneurial (notably through a series of fixed-term contracts, otherwise known as contracts of use), but cannot create a company as an entrepreneur. Artists are multi-salaried and can rarely create their own business and become self-employed while working on a project.

4.3. Daily and Actual Musician's Practices

Most musicians must adopt various strategies during the first years of their career: concerts and entertainment are generally the best paid, whereas performances in bars, at dances and clubs are the most frequent but are often low-paid cash-in-hand jobs. In these different contexts, musicians do not have the same relationship with work (in a bar, a shopping mall or subsidised theatre); but for years, musicians have been pursuing these different strategies simultaneously and forging different networks and skills. Musicians try to perform as much as possible to train these skills and to create an identity at work, by moving from one strategy to another, from entertainer musician, to musician performing anonymously, or to solo artist-musician.

This ambivalence around work is reflected in the relationship to employment. With legal employment, dates accumulate and unlock the right to unemployment benefit under the intermittent scheme; with non-legal off-the-books employment, the remuneration supplements the intermittence or minimum wage. New modes of creation and distribution (beatboxing, IT, software, AI, web platforms, streaming, the Music-coin blockchain streaming platform, etc.) present risks as well as new opportunities for musicians, especially for composers and performers. Self-production can release major creative potential but it transfers all responsibility to the artist. Similarly, the widespread disintermediation and dissemination of works through platforms not only raise opportunities but also new problems relating to the creation/sharing of value processes and involves new interactions with downstream stakeholders. In general terms, the traditional system of associated remuneration is being challenged by new forms of creation. These professional challenges have begun to be addressed by the professionalisation structures (such as Trempo).

For a long time, production or consumption spaces for music were clearly defined and circumscribed (e.g. the composer's home was a place for creation, reflection and performance). Now, these spaces can merge or expand as new media introduces new temporalities and uses. Access to music is evolving with portable players and downloads. This privatisation of spaces has a dual effect on the artist's position and work: at the aesthetic level, the constraints created by these new media must be accepted, and at the economic level, the artist is directly responsible for the distribution of their work and for engaging with the portals and platforms concerned. Artists' skills are becoming increasingly hybrid, and they must sometimes take on new roles or cooperate with those who carry out these roles. New professionalisation approaches are therefore required.

4.4. Diverse Ways of Working and Being Enterprising

How musicians describe their work not only reveal the diversity of their activities, but also the reality of several permutations around invisible work, which in many aspects present entrepreneurial characteristics which are imposed to varying degrees. Looking beyond this report, the key to maintaining activity is multi-activity-based or requiring a variable and evolutive professionalisation approach: that means a combination of artistic, para-artistic and non-artistic performances, cumulative sources of income (work, copyright and related rights, public or private funding) and inclusion in networks. In-depth analysis of musicians' circumstances reveals a wide variety of approaches to imposed and voluntary slashing ranging from single to multi-activity in the particular music field(s)/sector(s).

Multi-activity can therefore drive the diversification of the business sectors in which the artist operates. Musician's activities can include singer-songwriter, composer for video games, the film industry and for sound space design projects, or diversification into tourism and heritage. This means that their sources of income are multiplied, enabling them to pursue their profession in line recommendations by the advocates of the business model. This can also be achieved through the multi-project approach, the simultaneous pursuit of two or three artistic projects as an author-composer-performer and registering as a musician or technician on two or three other parallel projects. Professionalisation stakes are changing; musicians must mobilise new and multiple skills. Alongside the activities that make up artistic practice (exploring, testing, experimenting/writing, sound/rehearsal work on the stage, in films, etc.), musicians must try to bring their artistic project(s) to fruition, seek artist residencies to experiment with their aesthetic approaches, mobilise collectives (artistic, technical, administrative, etc.), seek funding, make recordings of their projects to make them known to broadcasters, communicate about their projects, chase up event schedulers, deal with administrative tasks, etc.

Menger (2002) spoke of blurring boundaries between artistic work and its management. The following interview extract reflects this reality: '80% of my time is spent on communication, dissemination and fundraising. The time that I can devote to artistic activity, to creation, is limited' (interview 12). Finally, with this multi-activity, artist activities can include composer/musician/computer-assisted music facilitator or trainer/playlists and events scheduler, etc. As early as 1998, Catherine Paradeise showed that for the majority of artists, survival depended on a multi-activity approach. All these realities (multi-activity, multi-skill, multi-project) are often intertwined but do not overlap. They paint the picture of musicians who design, produce and market themselves with the tools and practices of their time and who also tend to be organisers of resources and skills.

5. DISCUSSION AND IMPLICATIONS

This research documents the real work of musicians in the French context and the difficulties associated with their professionalisation. The emergence of new professionalisation stakes has to be taken into account; otherwise the marginalisation experienced by the young musicians will be more significant and serious. First, beyond the French context, the research outlines the growing range of heterogeneous situations for musicians on this work continuum of the professionalisation. Moreover, emerging challenges are placing greater pressure on artists due to changes and new external factors (the aspects of the music value chain, the use of new technologies, such as IT, blockchain, web and streaming platforms, etc.) in the twenty-first century. By identifying different permutations and different ways of working and organising for musicians who have made the decision to turn professional, we report that it is difficult for music to provide them with their sole means of earning a living.

5.1. New Tools and Practices: Real Work and Working Conditions

If the growing number of emerging musician slashers can be attributed to several trends (ICT development, searching for 'meaning', etc.), it is also associated with uncertainty in the labour market (greater flexibility, loss of earnings, termination of employment, etc.), which is a cause of stress, anxiety and tension for musicians. Being a musician entrepreneur is becoming increasingly complicated, particularly without social capital (Coleman, 1988; Menger, 2002). Therefore, it requires new professionalisation frameworks, more evolutive, throughout life.

Some musicians have to overcome several challenges – competition for scarce resources, difficult working conditions such as low pay, long hours, insecurity and uncertainty by socialising in networks (Beirne et al., 2017). Some of them try to develop organisational forms that can generate work with a high degree of self-management, including managing different projects and timescales, associated with a portfolio of concurrent roles across traditional, digital and online media, managing an unstable income, professional development and identity and leadership (Hennekam & Bennett, 2016; Townley et al., 2009).

The characteristics of these different working conditions can provide the knowledge required to develop more inclusive training practices for accompaniment or sustainable support approaches for professionalisation, by considering the tensions between an increase in self-employment with insecure work, a blurring of the line between work and social life and the necessity to engage collective projects. If some support organisations (such as Trempo) offer a training programme around soft skills based on the 'slasher' mindset, it seems necessary to support their career development on both faces (artistic and entrepreneurial). Musicians can learn the skills that will enable them to thrive in any area of the music ecosystem. This does not mean avoiding stress, but learning to succeed in stressful situations, with training workshops and mentoring programmes to help musicians face theses new career challenges.

5.2. Educating Emerging Musicians: Developing a Career Strategy Based on New Business and Marketing Models

In addition to their artistic skills, musicians need training in business and strategic skills and communication/digital skills to develop their career and need to learn about partnership development, business plans, sales techniques and negotiation, fundraising and endorsement, royalties tracking and copyright management, etc. This can be done through workshops and mentoring programmes, for example, that focus on marketing and communication tools such as mood board creation, branding and storytelling, audience analysis, YouTube and Spotify channel management, community management, smartphone shooting, etc.

5.3. The Influence and Place of Local Ecosystem

It seems necessary to unpack the specific working practices of these musicians, particularly the young artists and 'slashers' to conceive more efficient local support for professionalisation. If institutional and political organisations (particularly, at the city level) want to support the music sector and professional musicians, it seems relevant to address their issues through the framework of entrepreneurship-as-practice. Therefore, they will be able to target more homogenous groups facing common issues (e.g. group of established artists, more professionalised individual musicians in their country, artists at the very beginning of their musical career and artists engaged in diversification). This can facilitate the design of support and training programmes and encourage musicians to engage with the process and content.

At the national level (in France), the legal and tax system seem necessary to be reconsidered.[4] To overcome some weaknesses, we point out – at the city level – the diversity of some collective practices, both loose and networked, where musicians, institutions and formal support organisations try to interact and share knowledge in order to foster new sustainable and inclusive professionalisation paths (such as Trempo). In some instances, we have identified alternative organisational forms for developing new sustainable relationships as a means of political resistance to the dominant culture (e.g. new kinds of events/venues, collaborations or festivals). Therefore, it seems relevant to consider these practices to design support and training programmes that include a broad range of organisations, and particularly stakeholders in the music value chain, such as record labels, universities, training centres and music schools, and local authorities.

5.4. Promoting New Forms of Collaboration Between Musicians and the Music Ecosystem

Collaboration between musicians and the ecosystem must be reformed to give musicians the place they deserve within the music value chain. Collaboration is potentially a critical pathway to change, enabling musicians to move beyond a 'content supplier' role to a 'partner' role. They need to develop the skills and entrepreneurial attitudes to interact with music professionals so that at match-makings, panels, showcases and speed-meetings, emerging musicians will be able to talk on more equal terms with managers, programmers, publishing and recording companies, PR, media, etc.

6. CONCLUSIONS

This research brings a new look of the real work of musicians through the EAP perspective. By questioning and observing what musicians do and say, the entrepreneurship-as-practice perspective helps us to capture both the characteristics of the practice itself and its potential implications for individuals, organisations, policy-making and education in the twenty-first century. It points out that the problem of multiplication or diversification encompasses situations of versatile monoactivity, pluriactivity and polyactivity requiring new analytical frameworks in organisation studies and entrepreneurship fields. It raises complex issues caused by the many new organisational and technological challenges which can support new practices in a musician's creative work, but which also require skills to be development to become more professional. This involves combining work and employment but also includes entrepreneurial work throughout life. We can observe how earning a living by playing music presupposes versatility/flexibility. Pluriactivity or polyactivity are sustainable strategies for musical work, which is on the boundary between entrepreneurship and salaried work.

Looking beyond the creative entrepreneur, reduced or even impoverished to an entrepreneurial function, or as an archetypal start-up figure, this research underlines the interesting theoretical framework and relevance of 'entrepreneurship-as-practice' for understanding and analysing entrepreneurial work in creative industries. We agree with the critical perspective on entrepreneurship (Germain & Jacquemin, 2017) that challenges this opposition between wage earners and entrepreneurship. Moreover, beyond the specific features of French legislation in the music sector, with intermittent status and the presumption of a salary, we report the porosity of universes and the complexity to address the real work of artists. Through the EAP perspective, we can deal with more complex social phenomena and produce 'interesting results' for both practitioners and policy-makers to support creative and cultural entrepreneurship in the twenty-first century.

NOTES

1. The slasher is so-called because it carries out several activities, in reference to the '/' sign separating the enumeration of its various activities; multi-active, the slasher cumulates several salaried jobs, or one salaried job and one or more self-employment jobs, or several self-employment jobs. Bohas A., Fabbri J., Laniray P., de Vaujany F-X., (2018). Hybridations salariat-entrepreneuriat et nouvelles pratiques de travail: des slashers à l'entrepreneuriat- alterné'. *Technologie et innovation, ISTE OpenScience, 18*(1), 1–19.

2. For instance: musical and technical dimension of the profession, political, legislative and social dimension of the live performance (regulations, conventions, contracts ...), knowledge of the actors of the music ecosystem, project methodology to become a project leader and to be an independent entrepreneur, knowledge and use of social networks, new technologies (to record, disseminate, share ...).

3. Trempo has a Slash programme that supports musicians with a variety of programmes from mentoring for songwriters to Entrepreneurship/Business for those in the music business.

4. For a further article, it will be interesting to explore the impact of state through taxation policy and the peculiarity of intermittence. If It seems that in the UK there is more flexibility to arrange one's affairs and work in multiple ways simultaneously, the French system can be seen as more restrictive and punitive, but it can offer some free professionalisation approaches. A next paper comparing how the tax/benefits systems of various nations affect those in the creative industries could be revealed.

REFERENCES

Banks, M. (2006). Moral economy and cultural work. *Sociology*, *40*(3), 455–472.

Banks, M. (2017). *Creative justice: Cultural industries, work and inequality*. Rowman & Littlefield.

Beirne, M., Jennings, M., & Knight, S. (2017). Autonomy and resilience in cultural work: Looking beyond the 'creative industries'. *Journal for Cultural Research*, *21*(2), 204–221.

Boltanski, L., & Chiapello, E. (1999). *Le nouvel esprit du capitalisme*. Gallimard.

Bréchet J.-P., & Schieb-Bienfait N. (2011). L'entrepreneuriat confronté au pluralisme théorique: La Nécessité d'une project-based view. *Revue de l'Entrepreneuriat*, *10*(2), 29–44.

Boyle, D., & Oakley, K. (2018). *Co-operatives in the Creative Industries. Think-piece*. Co-Operatives UK.

Chapain, C., Emin, S., & Schieb-bienfait N. (2018). Cultural and creative entrepreneurship: Key issues of a still emergent research field. *Revue de l'Entrepreneuriat*, *18*(1), 29–37.

Coleman, J. (1988). Social capital in the creation of human capital. *American Journal of Sociology*, *94*, 95–120.

Cooke, P., & Lazzeretti, L. (2018). *The role of art and culture for regional and urban resilience*. Routledge.

Department for Culture Media and Sport (DCMS). (1998). *Creative Industry Task Force Report*. Department for Culture, Media and Sport. www/dcms.gov.uk.

Department for Culture, Media and Sport (DCMS). (2001a). *Creative industries mapping document, Creative Industries Task Force*, UK Department for Culture, Media and Sport. www/dcms.gov.uk.

Department for Culture Media and Sport (DCMS) (2001b). *Green paper: Culture and creativity: The next 10 years*. http://www.culture.gov.uk/reference_library/publications/4634.aspx/

Department for Culture Media and Sport (DCMS). (2006). Developing entrepreneurship for the creative industries. The role of higher and further education. www/dcms.gov.uk

Department for Culture Media and Sport (DCMS). (2007). *The Creative Economy Programme: A summary of Projects commissioned in 2006*. Department for Culture, Media and Sport. www/dcms.gov.uk

Department for Culture Media and Sport (DCMS). (2009). *Creative industries economic estimates statistical bulletin*. Department for Culture, Media and Sport. www/dcms.gov.uk

Department for Culture Media & Sport (DCMS). (2016). *DCMS sectors economic estimates*. https://www.gov.uk/government/uploads/system/uploads/attachment_data/file/544103/DCMS_Sectors_Economic_Estimates_-_August_2016.pdf

Department for Digital, Culture, Media & Sport (DCMS). (2017). *Independent review of the crea-tive industries.* https://assets.publishing.service.gov.uk/government/uploads/system/uploads/attachment_data/file/649980/Independent_Review_of_the_Creative_Industries.pdf
DeFillippi, R. (2015). Managing project-based organisation in creative industries. In C. Jones, M. Lorenzen, & J. Sapsed (Eds.), *The Oxford handbook of creative industries* (pp. 268–284). Oxford University Press.
Ellmeier, A. (2003). Cultural entrepreneurialism: on changing the relationship between the arts, culture and employment. *International Journal of Cultural Policy, 9*(1), 3–16.
Evans, G. (2009). From cultural quarters to creative cluster – Creative spaces in the new city economy. In M. Legnér & D. Ponzini (Eds.), *Cultural quarters and urban transformation: International perspectives.* Klintehamn.
Farrell, M. P. (2001). *Collaborative circles: Friendship dynamics and creative work.* University of Chicago Press.
Florida, R. (2002). *The rise of the creative class, and how it's transforming work, leisure, and everyday life.* Hazard.
Garrett, L. E., Spreitzer, G. M., & Bacevice, P. A. (2017). Co-constructing a sense of community in coworking spaces. *Organization Studies, 38*(6), 821–842.
Gartner, W. B, Stam, A. M. C, Thompson, N., & Verduijn, K. (2016). Entrepreneurship as practice: grounding contemporary practice theory into entrepreneurship studies. *Entrepreneurship & Regional Development.* (Call for Papers, Special Issue in *Entrepreneurship & Regional Development.*)
Germain, O., & Jacquemin. A. (2017). Voies et voix d'approches critiques en entrepreneuriat. *Revue de l'Entrepreneuriat, 16*(1), 7–18.
Greenman, A. (2011). Entrepreneurial activities and occupational boundary work during venture crea-tion and development in the cultural industries. *International Small Business Journal, 30*(2), 115–137.
Hall, P. (2000). Creative cities and economic development. *Urban Studies, 37*, 639–649.
Hanage, R., Scott, J. M., & Davies, M. A. P. (2016). From great expectations to hard times: A longitudi-nal study of creative graduate new ventures. *International Journal of Entrepreneurial Behaviour & Research, 22*(1), 17–38.
Haynes, J., & Marshall, L. (2018). Reluctant entrepreneurs: Musicians and entrepreneurship in the 'new' music industry. *British Journal of Sociology, 69*(2), 459–482.
Hennekam, S., & Bennett, D. (2016). Self-management of work in the creative industries in the Netherlands. *International Journal of Arts Management, 19*(1), 31–41.
Hjorth, D. (2017). Critique nouvelle – An essay on affirmative-performative entrepreneurship research. *Revue de l'Entrepreneuriat, 16*(1), 47–54.
Hjorth, D., & Steyaert, C. (2007). Entrepreneurship as social change. Edward Elgar Publishing. (Movements in Entrepreneurship Series, No. 3).
Landry, C. (2000). *The creative city: A toolkit for urban innovators.* London: Earthscan.
Lange, B. (2011). Professionalization in space: Social-spatial strategies of culturepreneurs in Berlin. *Entrepreneurship and Regional Development, 23*(3–4), 259–279.
Lindgren, M., & Packendorf, J. (2003). A project-based view of entrepreneurship: Towards action-orientation, seriality and collectivity. In C. Steyaert & D. Hjorth (Eds.), *New movements in entrepreneurship* (pp. 86–102). Edward Elgar.
Lindkvist, L., & Hjorth, D. (2015). Organizing cultural projects through legitimising as cultural entre-preneurship. *International Journal of Managing Projects in Business, 8*(4), 696–714.
Lingo, E., & O'Mahony, S. (2010). Nexus work: Brokerage on creative projects. *Administrative Science Quarterly, 55*(1), 47–81.
Lingo, E., & Tepper S. J. (2013). Looking back, looking forward: Arts-based careers and creative work. *Work and Occupations, 40*(4), 337–363.
McRobbie, A. (2002). From Holloway to Hollywood: Happiness at work in the new cultural economy. In P. Du Gay & M. Pryke (Eds.), *Cultural economy* (pp. 97–115). Sage Publications.
Menger, P. M. (1999). Artistic labor markets and careers. *Annual Review of Sociology, 25*, 541–574.
Menger, P. M. (2002). *Portrait de l'artiste en travailleur.* Edition du Seuil.
Menger, P. M. (2009). *Le travail créateur. S'accomplir dans l'incertain* (670 pp.). Gallimard/Seuil.

Morris, J. W. (2014). Artists as entrepreneurs fans as workers. *Popular Music and Society*, *37*(3), 273–290.

Naudin, A. (2018). *Cultural entrepreneurship, The cultural worker's experience of entrepreneurship*. Routledge.

Oakley, K. (2014). Good work? Rethinking cultural entrepreneurship. In C. Bilton & S. Cummings (Eds,), *Handbook of management and creativity* (pp. 145–159). Edward Elgar.

Oakley, K., & O'Brien, D. (2016). Learning to Labour Unequally: Understanding the relationship between cultural production, cultural consumption and inequality. *Social Identities*, *22*(5), 471–486.

O'Connor, J. (2010). *The cultural and creative industries: A literature review* (2nd ed.). Creativity, Culture and Education Series. Creativity, Culture and Education.

Orianne, J.-F. (2010). (dir.) with Brahy, R., Fraiture, S., Megherbi, S., *L'insertion professionnelle des comédiens, étude de cas à la sortie du conservatoire national de Liège*. Presses Universitaires de Liège.

Paradeise, C. (1998). *Les comédiens. Profession et marchés du travail*. PUF.

Rouleau, L. (2013). Strategy-as-practice research at a crossroads. *Management*, *16*(5), 574–592.

Sarasvathy, S. (2001). Causation and effectuation. *Academy of Management Journal*, *28*(2), 243–263.

Schatzki, T. R., Knorr-Cetina, K., & von Savigny, E. (Eds.). (2001). *The practice turn in contemporary theory*. Routledge.

Schieb-Bienfait, N., Saives A.-L., Charles-Pauvers B., & Emin S. (2018). Grouping or grounding? Cultural district and creative cluster management in Nantes-France. *International Journal of Arts Management*, *20*(2), 71–84.

Scott, M. (2012). Cultural entrepreneurs, cultural entrepreneurship: Music producers mobilising and converting Bourdieu's alternative capitals. *Poetics*, *40*(3), 237–255.

Steyaert, C. (2007). Entrepreneuring as a conceptual attractor: A review of process theories in 20 years of entrepreneurship studies. *Entrepreneurship and Regional Development*, *19*(6), 453–477.

Steyaert, C. (2017). Positioning entrepreneurship studies between critique and affirmation, Interview with C. Steyaert by O. Germain & A. Jacquemin. *Revue de l'Entrepreneuriat*, *16*(1), 55–64.

Stjerne, I. S., & Svejenova, S. (2016). Connecting temporary and permanent organizing: Tensions and boundary work in sequential film projects. *Organization Studies*, *37*(12), 1771–1792.

Tarassi, S. (2018). Multi-tasking and making a living from music: Investigating music careers in the independent music scene of Milan. *Cultural Sociology*, *12*(2), 208–223.

Teague, B, Tunstall, R., Champenois, C., & Gartner, W. B. (2021). an introduction to Entrepreneurship as practice. *International Journal of Entrepreneurial Behavior & Research*, *27*(3), 569–578.

Thomson, K. (2013). Roles, revenue, and responsibilities: The changing nature of being a working musician. *Work and Occupations*, *40*(4), 514–525.

Townley, B., Beech, N., & McKinlay, A. (2009). Managing in the creative industries: Managing the motley crew. *Human Relations*, *62*(7), 939–962.

Throsby, D. (2008). The concentric circles model of the cultural industries. *Cultural Trends*, *17*(3), 147–164.

Whittington, R. (2006). Completing the practice turn in strategy research. *Organization Studies*, *27*(5), 613–634.

CHAPTER 11

A CRITICAL APPRAISAL OF CHALLENGES FACING FASHION ENTREPRENEURS IN BAME AND DISADVANTAGED COMMUNITIES

Samuel Osei-Nimo, Emmanuel Aboagye-Nimo and Doreen Adusei

ABSTRACT

Inequality in the creative industries often serves as the starting point for public debates over culture in the UK. Academic literature has long recognised the precarious nature of the fashion industry. This chapter offers a critical review of the relationships of power existing in the support offered to ethnic minorities in disadvantaged communities in the fashion and creative sectors in the UK. In addressing these issues, a Foucauldian perspective is adopted. The chapter focuses on Black, Asian, and minority ethnic (BAME) fashion entrepreneurs' challenges in promoting young designers from disadvantaged communities.

Our findings show that the BAME entrepreneurs are active agents who are essential in identifying and shaping new creative and talented young designers. The chapter contributes to the debate through a critical review of the relationships of power existing in the support offered to ethnic minorities in disadvantaged communities in the fashion and creative sectors in the UK.

Keywords: Fashion entrepreneurship; young designers; power; creatives; diversity; disadvantaged communities; Foucauldian perspective

Creative (and Cultural) Industry Entrepreneurship in the 21st Century
Contemporary Issues in Entrepreneurship Research, Volume 18A, 151–163
Copyright © 2024 by Samuel Osei-Nimo, Emmanuel Aboagye-Nimo and Doreen Adusei
Published under exclusive licence by Emerald Publishing Limited
ISSN: 2040-7246/doi:10.1108/S2040-72462023000018A011

1. INTRODUCTION

The creative and cultural industries have been recognised as economic and cultural growth assets in the UK. The UK's creative industries contributed £115.9 billion to the economy in 2019 (Department of Digital, Culture, Media, and Sport, 2019). This amount represents a 43.6% gain over 2010 and places the industry under 6% of the overall gross domestic product. A longstanding issue that often emerges in creative entrepreneurship discussions and literature is the overlooked contribution of successful fashion entrepreneurs from ethnic minorities and disadvantaged communities (Grillitsch, 2019; Smith et al., 2019). Leadbeater (1999) characterised creative industries such as fashion as being led by cultural entrepreneurs, not professionals, who maximise the potential and ingenuity of others. In their investigation of Black, Asian, and Minority Ethnic (BAME) participation in innovation, Vorley et al. (2019) found that because mainstream support for business-led initiatives is difficult to locate or access, minority groups underutilise it.

This chapter offers a critical review of the current state of the UK fashion industry. It critically explores and reviews the power dynamics at play in the support provided to ethnic minorities in disadvantaged communities in the fashion and creative industries in the UK. Using Foucault's concepts of power and governmentality, we examine and uncover the complexities and power relationships inherent in implementing and disseminating entrepreneurial and innovative initiatives in the UK (Foucault, 1977; McKinlay & Starkey, 1997). Governmentality emphasises a method of thinking about government, defined as the domain in which power resides (Lemke, 2001). It is an attempt to shape human conduct by calculated means in contrast to discipline, which seeks to reform designated groups through detailed supervision (Li, 2007). We have attempted to understand the challenges BAME fashion entrepreneurs face in promoting young designers from disadvantaged communities by asking:

> What innovative ways do BAME fashion entrepreneurs utilise to overcome societal and institutional hurdles when supporting young designers?

To answer the above, we explore the many aspects of an individual's existence including issues of self-empowerment and self-reliance among BAME fashion entrepreneurs, which can be 'problematised' in contemporary British society. We also examine the issues of power that contribute to shaping 'entrepreneurial' processes and the broader fashion industry practices concerning disadvantaged communities. Additionally, we examine the relationship between power and differential social positioning and further analyse the importance of social class in shaping entrepreneurial culture and power in the UK fashion sector. The chapter reveals that BAME entrepreneurs are active agents who play an important role in recognising and shaping new innovative and skilled young designers. Their agency, however, varies substantially depending on how these entrepreneurs access various resources and government backing, which is frequently closely tied to their socio-economic standing.

2. DISCOURSES OF FASHION AND CREATIVE ENTREPRENEURSHIP

The research on creativity has advanced from attention on psychological studies of ostensibly creative individuals to a comprehensive awareness that originality is frequently the result of formal and informal organisational interactions (Berti & Simpson, 2021; Fetrati et al., 2022). Brown et al. (2010) argue that numerous studies of creativity have adopted a mainstream/managerialist perspective and are obsessed with mediating the 'challenges' associated with encouraging creativity in organisations (Ford & Porter, 2008), with little focus on the significance of such discourses in generating power relations. As with various organisational and social debates, Doolin (2002) contends that entrepreneurial discourses are not the only dominant forms of discourses at work in contemporary communities and organisations.

The recent emphasis on how creative industry entrepreneurs and actors located in impoverished and disadvantaged communities have exposed the worsening of existing populations' precarious economic conditions, especially BAME groups, as a result of the creative economy (Banks & O'Connor, 2017). McRobbie et al. (2019) mention that the fashion sector as a locus of creative labour has not successfully drawn critical voices of social mobility in the way other creative sectors have mobilised energies in such directions in recent years. They also stress that the fashion sector has the potential to become a much more egalitarian and diverse sector, and this is an opportune time, given the increased social consciousness that has emerged in recent years.

Brown et al. (2010) note that dialogues on how work is and should be executed in the creative industries are frequently shaped by workers' views of their professional identities and their organisation's conceptually creative identity. Furthermore, Froehlicher et al. (2007) highlight how government policies, whether national or regional, influence creative industries. They argue that the concept of creative industries represents a 'new economy' where growth is expected to be generated; thus, focusing on the industries' economic viability, a new type of 'governmentality emerges. In the UK, the government policy has emphasised efficiency and self-sufficiency as the economic model for creative industries, which has increased labour fragmentation and prominent self-employment features (Hill, 2021).

Political discourses in many mature liberal democracies, such as the UK, have been saturated with references to 'enterprise'. The term 'discourse' refers to a formal way of thinking communicated through language in which reality is classified and represented within specific periods (Foucault, 1977). This is mainly due to the predominance of 'market' institutions in the constitution and reproduction of such societies (du Gay, 2004; Rose, 1999). Under Margaret Thatcher, 'enterprise culture' gained prominence in UK politics (Peters, 2001). This concept represented a shift from the Keynesian welfare state and towards a deliberate attempt at cultural restructuring and engineering based on the neo-liberal model of the entrepreneurial self, symbolised by a change away from a 'culture of dependency' and towards one of 'self-reliance' (Besley & Peters, 2007). The term 'enterprise' refers to both the ideal enterprise organisational structure and a combination of self-reliance, initiative, and the ability to accept responsibility and accountability for one's own actions and those of others (du Gay, 2004). Thus, 'enterprise as a neo-liberal government rationality' refers to defining organisational behaviour in such a way that it results in autonomous, productive, self-regulating, entrepreneurial behaviour on both a collective and individual level (Doolin, 2002, p. 372).

The past two decades have seen a significant rise and dominance of the discourses on the creative economy, creative industry, creative labour, and the creative class in Western scholarship on fashion designers (Mao & Shen, 2020; McRobbie, 2015; McRobbie et al., 2019). For instance, the nature of the fashion sector enables the observation of institutional development towards a creative economy, in which the blue-collar garment and textile businesses have morphed into a white-collar fashion industry (Gurova & Morozova, 2018; Yagoubi & Tremblay, 2015). However, the discourses emerging from the fashion sector over the recent years have presented a conflicting and often fragmented sector where the fashion designer, typically a pillar in the creative economy, is exposed to insecurity and instability rather than being a source of economic prosperity and job creation.

Fashion designers are viewed as contributors to the creative economy, which values creativity as a necessary component of economic growth. Consequently, the 'creative class' as a source of knowledge and invention and the creative clusters as a stimulating laboratory for creativity and entrepreneurs became models for government and urban policies throughout the Western world (Landry, 2008). Gurova and Morozova (2018) describe these models as representing a distinct sort of labour as creative labour, typically characterised by risk-taking and adaptability. This labour is carried out by the new entrepreneurial workers (Neff et al., 2005), who adhere to the concept of the 'new spirit of capitalism'. These workers exemplify a 'neoliberal model of entrepreneurial self' (Peters, 2001, p. 58) in that they are unconcerned about adopting responsibilities traditionally managed by the government and perceive these actions as their own (Neff et al., 2005, p. 313). Nonetheless, entrepreneurial work in the fashion sector is well-known for its lack of state protection, long work hours, lack of consistent cash flow, and stress and anxiety, among other hurdles.

3. CREATIVE LABOUR, FASHION, AND CHALLENGES

The current political and economic discourses on the creative economy place fashion designers in a difficult position to balance their practical realities with the recognition and worth of their creativity. McRobbie et al. (2019) argue that the overriding philosophy of glamour persists, pushing more intractable issues into the background. They add that the UK fashion sector operates somewhat in a bubble, governed by the British Fashion Council (BFC), which serves as the mouthpiece of the sector with the ability to enlist the might and resources of top organisational executives and other influential personalities. As a result, a top-down agenda has emerged that overlooks small-scale entrepreneurs and individuals whose star status has been eclipsed, or those operating on a modest budget. The debate further gets murkier when assessing how ethnic minorities have historically been excluded from or consigned to the creative sector's periphery despite the widespread belief that diversity stimulates innovation. The discussion here heeds the call made by Hesmondhalgh and Saha (2013) to consider issues of power, race, and ethnicity when theorising cultural production; thus, the section unearths the underlying themes that support diversity in the creative industries, particularly the fashion sector.

First, the means of exclusion for ethnic minorities and those in disadvantaged communities is their structural disadvantage in social networks (Zanoni et al., 2017). Since cultural norms are generally taken-for-granted, they are primarily conveyed through socialisation into the dispositions of the privileged majority, to which ethnic minorities and the lower classes have little or no access (Bourdieu, 1993). These networks play a significant role in the fashion sector which is generally organised around temporary projects and collaborations, defined by short-term or freelance contracts and a flexible work structure. Additionally, the opportunity to network and establish collaborative ventures and tap into support plays a critical role in success in the creative sectors (Aage & Belussi, 2008).

Another problem for ethnic minorities fashion entrepreneurs and those based in disadvantaged communities is that the dominant discourse of diversity has gained prominence in the sector over the past two decades, overlooking their challenges and instead celebrating their socio-demographic identities as a source of creativity (Zanoni et al., 2017). Additionally, some studies have contested negative perceptions of disadvantaged communities, arguing that their creativity stems from a group's unique socio-cultural position and capacity to monopolise certain cultural products in urban environments (Basu & Werbner, 2001; Pang, 2003) and can serve to circumvent any challenge.

3.1. Governmentality and Enterprise Culture

Governmentality, a concept developed by Michel Foucault in his Collège de France lectures on the macrophysical practices of government (see Foucault, 1981), was based on the foundations of his previous studies on the 'microphysics' of power and discipline. The concept of governmentality, according to Foucault, sees the state as a logical agent controlling itself and others while asking about the 'type of rationality being used' (Foucault, 1981, p. 226). Doolin (2002) argues that its purpose is to normalise the self-regulating subject, covering not just state-sponsored programmes but also private and public-sector institutions and individual behaviour. Governmentality, in this view, is not the overt extension of control from a central point of power but rather the conduct of conduct – influencing others' behaviour through influencing their autonomous subjectivity. In Foucault's analysis, the government is not restricted to the state but encompasses all power-based relationships (Froehlicker et al., 2007).

Over the past few years, the neo-liberal curtailment of the government's role in the UK has diminished its ability to mediate the market to attain the conventional welfare goals of full employment and educational equality (Peters, 2001).

Neo-liberals were conceptually attempting to re-moralise the link between welfare and employment and make individuals responsible for investing in their own education. However, neo-liberal governments began dismantling arrangements for government support, substituting individualised employment contracts and subjecting workers to the market's vagaries. Some researchers are often sceptical about promoting the enterprise culture, such as the creative sectors, arguing that such measures only provide the means for analysis and the prescription for change (Besley & Peters, 2007; Peters, 2001).

It is also important to note that research on minority entrepreneurship has benefitted immensely from intersectionality; the methodology improved understanding of barriers to resources, networks, and clients resulting from participation in several minority groups (Romero & Valdez, 2016). Romero and Valdez (2016) discovered, via an intersectional viewpoint, that various dimensions of identity and collectivity of a social group impact the ability of associated members to mobilise resources and support that drive entrepreneurialism. For example, Masquelier (2019) argues that even though experiences of precarity vary by class, gender, ethnicity, country, etc., how one perceives the reality of precarity relies on one's social position, which is itself the result of overlapping techniques of power and dominance. Through an intersectionality lens, Vorobeva (2022) argues that entrepreneurship is inextricably tied to power, control, advancement, and prosperity in the dominant narrative and has attracted many minorities seeking a more positive self-image, acquiring legitimacy, bringing good change to their communities, or combating negative stereotypes.

4. THE UK FASHION SECTOR

The UK fashion industry has seen a shift in the past two decades, with retailers adjusting their sourcing decisions to reflect their increased leverage over suppliers. There is a growing concern that as more and more UK fashion retailers choose to source their products off-shore, the employment situation in the market will likely continue to deteriorate.

The government shapes fashion policies from conception to sale. The BFC pressed the UK government to confirm the pandemic's impact on British fashion (BFC, 2021). The COVID-19 crisis destroyed the fashion industry's above-average growth over the last decade (Oxford Economics, 2020). A generation of creative talent is at risk of extinction, jeopardising the UK's position as the creative epicentre of global fashion. Social media and digital technologies have given young designers a low-cost way to enter the market, but a lack of industry data hinders companies' ability to identify trends and opportunities (Bird et al., 2020; Oxford Economics, 2020).

According to Foucault, power in the fashion industry is exercised through surveillance, individualisation, exclusion, and normalisation (Kearins & Hooper, 2002). Power shapes designers' behaviour and conduct, resulting from how the government and industry measures, norms, and practices regulate practices. Fashion industry regulations include supply chain structures, funding for SMEs and designers, and mentorship programmes for young, disadvantaged designers. Miller and Rose (2008) view governing as a problematising activity because the government's regulations have their own political or economic objectives in mind. Therefore, the 'calculations, techniques, apparatuses, documents, and procedures' (Rose & Miller, 1992, p. 175) may not benefit fashion designers.

By implementing fashion norms and standards at the industry's national and local levels, such as funding routes and educational initiatives, conceptions of ethical and unethical designs and methods have become possible, paralleling the broader discourses on creativity and innovation that include so many actors and agencies. These techniques and many other interventions produce the 'self-regulating, calculating individual' (Miller, 2001, p. 381). In this self-disciplining manner, the government and 'experts' have had the ability to influence the conduct of individual fashion designers across the UK.

4.1. Support for Young Designers

Government funding is critical to ensuring fashion's future in the UK. The fashion industry has benefitted from funding from many bodies. These include the European Regional Development Funds, the Mayor of London, and the Department for International Trade. The funding has helped develop businesses and the wider industry, allowing the stakeholders to collaborate on testing new showcasing platforms and supporting emerging talent from disadvantaged communities. Despite this support, numerous fashion enterprises fail due to a lack of funding to support their effort. Fashion entrepreneurs face barriers to financial backing since their business concepts are frequently viewed as high-risk investments with low margins and a hard return on investment, making them less appealing to banks and investors. Government support for creative enterprises remains extremely limited in terms of the number of different support schemes and duration.

Some prominent funding and supporting agencies in the UK, such as BFC and NESTA (National Endowment for Science, Technology and the Arts), support the fashion industry's future growth and success by focusing on education, grant-giving, and business mentoring, further enhancing the UK's position as the best place to study, start, and develop a fashion business. This raises the question of the government's role in this support equation for young designers. Gurova and Morozova (2018) suggest that fashion designers utilise state and community support and organisational activities to address the lack of resources. At a macro level, the government can and most often hold a significant role in the creative industry policy infrastructure development (Hesmondhalgh & Baker, 2008).

Unfortunately, the primary challenge with supporting young designers is their entrepreneurial mindset since they prefer to operate independently rather than seek government support (Peters, 2001). Inherent to budding entrepreneurs is a strong sense of autonomy (Neff et al., 2005) and a culture of self-reliance (Peters, 2001). In the UK, fashion and creative entrepreneurs generally mistrust the government, which appears ineffective in assisting entrepreneurs (Vorley et al., 2019), prompting the BFC and NESTA to call for additional support during the Covid-19 pandemic.

Nonetheless, this does not imply that upcoming fashion designers would refuse governmental support. Currently, the young designers remark that information on government support is not always readily accessible, the methods for selecting grantees are not always straightforward, and the amount of paperwork is so convoluted that it outweighs the amount of money that can be received as support. The government fails when it attempts to join in market activities, at least from the perspective of these fashion and creative entrepreneurs. The support has been limited, with the BFC even establishing a 'Fashion Fund' to support creative fashion businesses and individuals to survive the COVID-19 pandemic in 2020. Even with these opportunities provided by the 'experts' in BFC, the selection criteria were premised on exceptional creativity, although many ethnic minority entrepreneurs regularly cite experiences of bias when attempting to connect with such mainstream agencies (Gbadamosi, 2019; Nwankwo, 2013).

4.2. Disadvantaged Communities, Networks, and Role Models

BAME fashion influencers face the same disadvantage BAME people across all industries face, in that their white equivalents are treated with more value, more opportunities and ultimately, more respect. (Unsah Malik (Social Media Expert) cited in *ELLE UK Magazine*)

Ethnic minorities, women, and certain groups from disadvantaged communities have often been described as the most insecure and volatile groups with regard to precarity (Fantone, 2007). The precarious nature of work has been noted as a developing tendency in labour markets, particularly in cultural sectors such as fashion (Gill & Pratt, 2008). McRobbie (1998) has described the precarious existence of workers throughout the British fashion industry, characterising the industry as one held together by short-term contractors who, due to the demands of juggling two or three jobs simultaneously, find it difficult to plan more than six months. When dealing with precarity at the meso-level, a strong professional community of fashion designers can be highly beneficial, particularly in fashion design and the broader sector. 'Network sociality' is prevalent, implying the importance of social capital, such as access to networks and the necessity of networking as part of one's job duties (Gurova & Morozova, 2019; Wittel, 2001).

Fashion plays a vital role in UK's economy and diversity by employing markedly from the BAME communities, particularly in the sub-sectors of wholesale and manufacturing (CFP, 2005). In addition to innate creativity, factors such as the presence of role models in a young person's life may work as a catalyst in the journey to becoming a fashion designer (Min & Wilson, 2019). Individuals from more wealthy socio-economic origins have been demonstrated to be more successful in their entrepreneurial endeavours based on their ability to first recognise an entrepreneurial opportunity (Anderson & Miller, 2003). Understanding the relevance of personal connections and how they might support their efforts through personal or professional networks is an example of an environmental element that was also found to be connected with greater success (Tremblay, 2012). Therefore, there is a strong argument that young fashion designers, especially those from ethnic minorities and disadvantaged communities, need experience, education, and, more importantly, role models with experience beyond the initial entrepreneurial stages (Min & Wilson, 2019). Socio-cultural elements such as family, networks, or other role models who are also entrepreneurs might help spark the desire in young people from marginalised and disadvantaged communities.

Specialist mentors are the preferred means of support, but available ones are so sought after that they are spread too thinly (CFP, 2005). The CFP highlighted in their research the lack of appreciation and recognition for such benevolent entrepreneurs' experience when developing and uplifting emerging talents in such communities. Nonetheless, it is argued that minority businesses and entrepreneurs can help the government achieve its top post-Covid priority of 'levelling up' deprived areas outside London (Bird et al., 2020). Parker (1992) says that discourses that offer a socially recognisable identity create specific subjectivities and allow actors to speak with different levels of power and authority (du Gay, 2004). The increasing prevalence of ethnicity as a representation of 'subordinate difference' in Western societies requires creatives whose name, appearance, and other visible signs can be associated with diverse ethnic backgrounds to mobilise and incorporate, adapt, address, or resist ethnicity in the construction of their identity, particularly their creative identity (Zanoni et al., 2017). Thus, such discourses constrain and empower unequally the identity work of individuals as well as their capacity to confront hegemonic discourses that reproduce unequal power relations to their detriment via their identities (Alvesson et al., 2008). As Eugene et al. (2020) identified, black entrepreneurs (in this context, including other ethnic minorities) face other hurdles in addition to the lack of mentors or familiar faces in the industry. Social media algorithms are also 'inherently' racist as they have been tailored for white designers and larger corporations. However, new Black creators, creatives, educators, and advocates are able to share their lives and products directly to a ready market, thereby making it easier to circumvent the hurdles that had plagued the industry for so long.

As the fashion market stands, BAME creatives and entrepreneurs have worked to gain direct access to end-users through social media and other means. As shown in Fig. 1, traditional entry into the fashion market has often been riddled with 'elitism' and restrictions associated with gatekeepers. Unfortunately, Black creatives and other non-white creatives struggle to gain recognition when they approach the market through conventional means. *My hope is that, as black people, our raw talent is now at the forefront of the conversation* Ola Alabi (quoted in *GQ Magazine*, 2021). In trying to gain access to end-users, the new breed of creatives has resorted to social media and other direct means to access the market (see below).

5. CONCLUSION

This chapter has looked at how the concept of 'enterprise' in the fashion and creative sectors has emerged as a dominant thinking in Western societies, one that

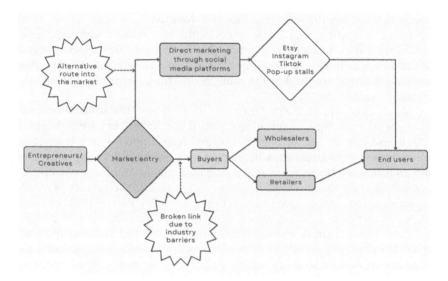

Fig. 1.   BAME Entrepreneurs and the Fashion Industry.

appears to underpin all political and socio-economic policy interventions, including supporting young BAME designers and individuals from disadvantaged communities. We have also discussed how access to social networks and experienced fashion designers who serve as role models can afford new opportunities for young designers from disadvantaged communities and help them address precarity and autonomy issues.

The Federation of Small Businesses (FSB) (2020) argues that creative entrepreneurship can help ethnic minorities achieve social mobility and revitalise economically disadvantaged communities when adequately supported by policy. Moreover, Collins (2020) has challenged researchers and stakeholders to reconsider how their perspectives on race, class, and gender may foster empathy for social change and equality. Collin (2020) argues that asking who the subordinate and dominant groups are in the fashion sector may likely help to address how these hierarchies impact young ethnic minority fashion designers. The crucial point is that policy responses should not impose hierarchical and homogenous structures, as with many current business and entrepreneurial support mechanisms (Nwankwo, 2013). Instead, they should be sufficiently adaptable and attentive to the situations of various ethnic areas, considering the historical settings from which the current conditions of entrepreneurship have emerged.

The lack of access to financial resources has been repeatedly mentioned as a significant barrier for young BAME fashion designers. People from ethnic minority backgrounds in the UK face more significant access-to-finance challenges than any other community subgroup (Vorley et al., 2019). Further research should explore the role of social media and help young designers overcome these challenges. Additional studies would also be needed to explore the potential impact of recent activism and social movements, such as 'Black Lives Matter' and '#MeToo', on the creative sectors, particularly fashion.

REFERENCES

Aage, T., & Belussi, F. (2008). From fashion to design: Creative networks in industrial districts. *Industry and Innovation, 15*, 475–491.

Alvesson, M., Ashcraft, K. L., & Thomas, R. (2008). Identity matters: Reflections on the construction of identity scholarship in organisation studies. *Organisation, 15*(1), 5–28.

Anderson, A. R., & Miller, C. J. (2003). Class matters: Human and social capital in the entrepreneurial process. *The Journal of Socio-Economics, 32*(1), 17–36.

Banks, M., & O'Connor, J. (2017). Inside the whale (and how to get out of there): Moving on from two decades of creative industries research. *European Journal of Cultural Studies, 20*(6), 637–654.

Basu, D., & Werbner, P. (2001). Bootstrap capitalism and the culture industries: A critique of invidious comparisons in the study of ethnic entrepreneurship. *Ethnic and Racial Studies, 24*(2), 236–262.

Berti, M., & Simpson, A. V. (2021). The dark side of organisational paradoxes: The dynamics of disempowerment. *Academy of Management Review, 46*(2), 252–274.

Besley, T., & Peters, M. A. (2007). Enterprise culture and the rise of the entrepreneurial self. *Counterpoints, 303*, 155–174.

BFC. (2021). *British Fashion Council annual report 2020/21*. Retrieved, August 22, 2022, from https://www.britishfashioncouncil.co.uk/uploads/files/1/BFC%20Annual%20Report.pdf

Bird, G., Gorry, H., Roper, S., & Love, J. (2020). *R&D in creative industries survey – 2020*. Department for Digital, Culture, Media and Sport by OMB Research.

Bourdieu, P. (1993). *The field of cultural production*. Columbia University Press.

Brown, A. D., Kornberger, M., Clegg, S. R., & Carter, C. (2010). 'Invisible walls' and 'silent hierarchies': A case study of power relations in an architecture firm. *Human Relations, 63*(4), 525–549.

CFP. (2005). *Fashion sector investment plan*. City Fringe Partnership.

Collins, P. H. (2020). Toward a new vision: Race, class, and gender as categories of analysis and connection. In J. Brueggemann (Ed.), *Inequality in the United States: A reader* (pp. 25–44). Routledge.

Doolin, B. (2002). Enterprise discourse, professional identity and the organisational control of hospital clinicians. *Organisation Studies, 23*(3), 369–390.

du Gay, P. (2004). Against 'Enterprise' (but not against 'enterprise', for that would make no sense). *Organisation, 11*(1), 37–57.

Eugene, W., Jimenez, Y., Muravevskaia, E., Lopez-Ramirez, C. and Gilbert, J. (2020). Moving beyond stuck: A design-based approach to enhancing minority tech startup launches. In *HCI International 2020 – Late Breaking Posters: 22nd International Conference*, HCII 2020, Copenhagen, Denmark, July 19-24, 2020, Proceedings, Part I 22 (pp. 19–26). Springer International Publishing.

Fantone, L. (2007). Precarious changes: Gender and generational politics in contemporary Italy. *Feminist Review, 87*, 5–20.

Federation of Small Businesses (FSB). (2020). *Unlocking opportunity: The value of ethnic minority firms to UK economic activity and enterprise*. Federation of Small Businesses.

Fetrati, M. A., Hansen, D., & Akhavan, P. (2022). How to manage creativity in organisations: Connecting the literature on organisational creativity through bibliometric research. *Technovation, 115*, 102473.

Ford, C., & Porter, R. (2008). Creativity. In S. R. Clegg & J. Bailey (Eds.), *International encyclopedia of organization studies* (pp.308–313). SAGE.

Foucault, M. (1977). *Discipline and punish: The birth of the prison*. Vintage.

Foucault, M. (1981). Omnes et singulatim: Towards a criticism of political reason. In S. McMurrin (Ed.), *The Tanner lectures on human values* (Vol. 2). University of Utah Press.

Froehlicher, T., Guillemin, A., & Apangu, P. (2007). *Creative industries, governmentalities and heterotopias: The case of local government in France*. Université de Liège.

Gbadamosi, A. (2019). Women-entrepreneurship, religiosity, and value-co-creation with ethnic consumers: Revisiting the paradox. *Journal of Strategic Marketing, 27*(4), 303–316.

Gill, R., & Pratt, A. (2008). In the social factory? Immaterial labour, precariousness and cultural work. *Theory, Culture and Society, 25*(7–8), 1–30.

Grillitsch, M. (2019). Following or breaking regional development paths: On the role and capability of the innovative entrepreneur. *Regional Studies, 53*(5), 681–691.

Gurova, O., & Morozova, D. (2018). Creative precarity? Young fashion designers as entrepreneurs in Russia. *Cultural Studies, 32*(5), 704–726.

Hesmondhalgh, D., & Baker, S. (2008). Creative work and emotional labour in the television industry. *Theory, Culture and Society, 25*, 97–118.

Hesmondhalgh, D., & Saha, A. (2013). Race, ethnicity, and cultural production. *Popular Communication: The International Journal of Media and Culture, 11*(3), 179–195.

Hill, I. R. (2021). Spotlight on UK artisan entrepreneurs' situated collaborations: Through the lens of entrepreneurial capitals and their conversion. *International Journal of Entrepreneurial Behavior & Research, 27*(1), 99–121.

Leadbeater, C. (1999). *Living on thin air: The new economy*. Penguin.

Li, T. M. (2007). Governmentality. *Anthropologica, 49*(2), 275–281.

Kearins, K., & Hooper, K. (2002). Genealogical method and analysis. *Accounting, Auditing and Accountability Journal, 15*(5), 733–757.

Landry, C. (2008). *The creative city: A toolkit for urban innovators* (2nd ed.). Earthscan.

Lemke, T. (2001). The birth of bio-politics: Michel Foucault's lectures at the College de France on neo-liberal governmentality. *Economy and Society, 30*(2), 190–207.

Mao, J., & Shen, Y. (2020). Identity as career capital: Enhancing employability in the creative industries and beyond. *Career Development International, 25*(2), 186–203.

Masquelier, C. (2019). Bourdieu, Foucault and the politics of precarity. *Distinktion: Journal of Social Theory, 20*(2), 135–155.

McKinlay, A., & Starkey, K. (Eds.). (1997). *Foucault, management and organisation theory: From panopticon to technologies of self*. SAGE.

McRobbie, A. (1998). *British fashion design: Rag trade or image industry?* Routledge.

McRobbie, A. (2015). *Be creative: Making a living in the new culture industry*. Polity Press.

McRobbie, A., Strutt, D., & Bandinelli, C. (2019). Feminism and the politics of creative labour: Fashion micro-enterprises in London, Berlin and Milan. *Australian Feminist Studies, 34*(100), 131–148.

Miller, P. (2001). Governing by numbers: Why calculative practices matter. *Social Research, 68*(2), 379–396.

Miller, P., & Rose, N. (2008). *Governing the present: Administering economic, social and personal life*. Polity Press.

Min, S., & Wilson, J. (2019). How do fashion designers emerge? An empirical investigation of their entrepreneurial processes. *International Journal of Fashion Design, Technology and Education, 12*(1), 35–45.

Neff, G., Wissinger, E., & Zukin, S. (2005). Entrepreneurial labour among cultural producers: 'Cool' jobs in 'hot' industries. *Social Semiotics, 15*(3), 307–334.

Nwankwo, S. (2013). Entrepreneurship among British Africans: Moving forward by looking backward. *Journal of Enterprising Communities: People and Places in the Global Economy, 7*(2), 136–154.

Oxford Economics. (2020). *The projected economic impact of Covid-19 on the UK creative industries*. Oxford Economics Ltd.

Pang, C. L. (2003). Belgium: From Proletarians to Proteans. In R. Kloosterman & J. Rath (Eds.), *Immigrant entrepreneurs: Venturing abroad in the age of globalization* (pp. 195–211). Berg.

Parker, I. (1992). *Discourse dynamics*. Routledge.

Peters, M. (2001). Education, enterprise culture and the entrepreneurial self: A Foucauldian perspective. *Journal of Educational Enquiry, 2*(2), 58–71.

Romero, M., & Valdez, Z. (2016). Introduction to the special issue: Intersectionality and entrepreneurship. *Ethnic and Racial Studies, 39*(9), 1553–1565.

Rose, N. (1999). *Power of freedom: Reframing political thought*. Cambridge University Press.

Rose, N., & Miller, P. (1992). Political power beyond the State: Problematics of Government. *The British Journal of Sociology, 43*(2), 173–205.

Smith, A. M., Galloway, L., Jackman, L., Danson, M., & Whittam, G. (2019). Poverty, social exclusion and enterprise policy: A study of UK policies' effectiveness over 40 years. *The International Journal of Entrepreneurship and Innovation, 20*(2), 107–118.

Tremblay, D. G. (2012). Creative careers and territorial development: The role of networks and relational proximity in fashion design. *Urban Studies Research, 2012*, 1–9.

Vorley, T., Smith, H. L., Owalla, B., Coogan, T., & Wing, K. (2019). *Supporting diversity and inclusion in innovation: A study identifying the opportunities, challenges and support needs of disabled and ethnic minority innovators*. Innovation Caucus, Innovate UK and Economic and Social Research Council.

Vorobeva, E. (2022). Intersectionality and minority entrepreneurship: At the crossroad of vulnerability and power. In L. P. Dana, N. Khachlouf, A. Maâlaoui, & V. Ratten (Eds.), *Disadvantaged minorities in business. Contributions to management science*. Springer.

Wittel, A. (2001). Towards a network sociality. *Theory, Culture and Society, 18*(6), 51–76.

Yagoubi, A., & Tremblay, D. G. (2015). *Culture, innovation and entrepreneurship: Challenges in the fashion industry*. International Forum on Knowledge Asset Dynamics, 10–12 June.

Zanoni, P., Thoelen, A., & Ybema, S. (2017). Unveiling the subject behind diversity: Exploring the micro-politics of representation in ethnic minority creatives' identity work. *Organisation, 24*(3), 330–354.

CHAPTER 12

CREATIVE INDUSTRIES IN CAMEROON: PROBLEMS AND PROSPECTS

Ernestine Nnam Ning

ABSTRACT

Increasing evidence from high-income countries has revealed the positive impacts of creative entrepreneurship on the local economy, and these have attracted substantial attention in recent years. Creative industries are considered as the seedbeds for innovation; they are highly innovative and productive and are seen as drivers of economic development and social change. Creative industries are distinctive in that they have several transaction networks and income streams. Although creative industries are generating increasing interest in the minds of researchers and policy-makers in developed countries, the institutional and economic settings in Cameroon and other developing nations may not be so conducive to creative industries. The available evidence is insufficient to understand their performance and sustainability, let alone to estimate their contribution to the rest of the economy. This chapter demonstrates how the creative industries could contribute to the economic and social development of a nation. The chapter further explores the current situation of creative industries in Cameroon, with a focus on the artists of popular and folk music, the challenges they are facing, and provides ways forward.

Keywords: Creative industries; popular and folk music; entrepreneurship; problems; prospects; Cameroon

Creative (and Cultural) Industry Entrepreneurship in the 21st Century
Contemporary Issues in Entrepreneurship Research, Volume 18A, 165–177
Copyright © 2024 by Ernestine Nnam Ning
Published under exclusive licence by Emerald Publishing Limited
ISSN: 2040-7246/doi:10.1108/S2040-72462023000018A012

1. INTRODUCTION

Entrepreneurship research has become an established discipline over the past decades with the emerging of cultural and creative entrepreneurship, a relatively young research field within entrepreneurship research (e.g. Hagoort, 2007; Klamer, 2011; Lounsbury & Glynn, 2001). There is a pressing political recognition that creative industries can fuel growth.

United Nations Conference on Trade and Development, UNCTAD (2021) has been publishing Creative Economy Reports. Africa's creative economy can trigger a value chain between artists, entrepreneurs, distributors and support services across multiple sectors to provide modern jobs (Boix-Domenech et al., 2017). Arts and culture are essential in society. It allows people to explore ideas, evoke emotions, produce and influence change as well and rippling positive ideas with their work (Campi et al., 2022). It gives people a chance to be educated and empowered and perceiving world issues indirectly (UNCTAD, 2021). Arts and culture's role has been recognised in poverty reduction and in achieving many of the 17 Sustainable Development Goals (SDGs). Apart from being a poverty alleviation tool, cultural/creative entrepreneurship stamps a national identity even on those who have been dispossessed and disempowered of their political statehood (Taylor & O'Brien, 2017).

Sub-Saharan Africa, Cameroon inclusive is the cradle of creative industries, a rapidly growing sector, with visual arts, crafts, cultural festivals, paintings, sculptures, photography, publishing, music, dance, film, radio, fashion and video games to architecture (Adedeji, 2016; Pedro & Njogu, 2020). These are fundamental aspects that would allow individuals and communities to benefit from the values and the opportunities they will generate. Creativity is the new money, and it is time for Cameroon to reap its benefits, but research is showing that creativity isn't just great to have. It's an essential human skill perhaps even an evolutionary imperative in our technology-driven world (Taylor & O'Brien, 2017). Cameroon has a large cultural diversity and it is often considered a miniature version of Africa. The country holds 250 ethnicities and languages, which involves a lot of dancing rhythms and subsequently various types of traditional music, dance, design and arts (Adao et al., 2019; Sone, 2021; Tagne & Evou, 2020; UNESCO, 2005).

However, Cameroon's presence in the global markets for creative goods and services has been stagnated by its limited supply capacity, lack of intellectual property knowledge, obsolete policies and regulations, as well as under investment in the industry, particularly infrastructure and education (UNESCO, 2021). The importance of creative industries, as an enabler of development, has not been taken into consideration. Now is the time to ensure that creative industries should claim their place at the heart of all sustainable development efforts.

2. CULTURAL/CREATIVE INDUSTRIES AS DRIVER OF DEVELOPMENT

Creative industries have the power of culture to inspire and unite people, the power to create employment and generate better livelihoods and the power to foster transformative change within communities, cities, countries and across societies (Kim & Kim, 2014). It builds a steady path to human development by strengthening the entrepreneurial skills of cultural and creative industry actors, reinforcing the competence of decision-makers and enhancing equal participation of various social groups and individuals in creative activities (Domingo, 2016).

Over the years, the International Fund for Cultural Diversity (IFCD) (2022) has demonstrated that the emergence of a dynamic cultural sector contributes to revitalisation of the local economy, an enabling policy environment as well as positive social changes. The IFCD (2022) projects allow individuals and communities to benefit from the value generated and the opportunities offered by the cultural and creative industries. By fostering participation and inclusion, the IFCD (2022) is contributing to inclusive sustainable development and ensuring that artists, cultural professionals and citizens have the capacity to create, produce, distribute and enjoy a broad range of cultural goods and services, thus contributing to building institutional, organisational and individual capacities, which aim to promote development at national, regional and local levels, *United Nations Educational, Scientific and Cultural Organization* (UNESCO, 2021). This clearly demonstrates that no society can flourish without creativity, culture and the people.

When free expression appears to be on retreat, music has a unique ability to empower silenced voices and brings together diverse people who want to drive change (Chen et al., 2015). Although it promotes economic growth and social inclusion, but creating an inclusive environment is usually complex and requires efforts to first unpack the complexities (Ryan, 2022; Daniel, 2020). Artists (creative entrepreneurs) capture and manage the narratives of the community and speak to humanity in ways that nothing else can (Piergiovanni et al., 2012). Thus music inspires and unites people, creates employment, generates better livelihoods, reduces stress, empowers and fosters transformative change within communities in cities, countries and across societies (UNIDO, 2013), yet the creative sector often struggles to access funding thus missing out on opportunities to explore new projects or take those all-important creative risks.

Music helps to awaken consciences by encouraging reflections and changes challenges issues (Bilton & Cummings, 2014; Edmondson & Weiner, 2013). Most musicians compose music to express their emotions and share their visions, which could be necessary for good decision-making, policy formulation and adjustment in the society or country (Sone, 2021). There is need to reinforce cultural and creative industries, to develop professional artistic and creative skills and to establish effective and better informed policies (IFCD, 2022).

2.1. Related Literature Review

There is no unified definition of creative entrepreneurship as the creative industry concept includes several subsectors that promote development, social justice and cultural exchange and offers the potential for wealth and job creation when accompanied by appropriate policies and strategies (IFCD, 2022). Creative entrepreneurship is the carrying out of a novel combination that results in something new and appreciated in the cultural sphere (Swedberg, 2006). They are usually freelance artists and creative workers who are forced to act as entrepreneurs because of unemployment and changing labour market conditions in the cultural sector (Ellmeier, 2003; Konrad, 2010). Scott (2012) understood creative entrepreneurship as a subjectivity combining three elements. First, these individuals create new cultural products such as songs, crafts, etc. Second, they are oriented towards accessing opportunities. Third, they have to find innovative ways of doing it.

Creative entrepreneurship is the untapped natural or inborn human resources whose potentials are yet to be utilised (Franco & Njogu, 2020). It is an inspirational energy and knowledge that stimulates many individuals to undertake new ventures with a vision of transforming their societies in the future (Domingo, 2017; Baum, et al., 2009). Human beings are generally creative in nature; therefore, no country is short of creativity (Innocenti & Lazzeretti, 2019). When creative talents and creative entrepreneurship are supported and rewarded by institutions, innovation surfaces (Baumol, 2010; IFCD, 2022). This support of creativity explains why certain societies are productively solving their most pressing problems and achieving progress while others are lagging behind in spite of the abundant and rich creative talents they possess (Boix-Domenech & Soler-Marco, 2017). Therefore creative industry is 'an economy where the main wealth which is the cultural product, benefits from an environment that is favourable to its creation and its distribution' (Bilton, & Cummings, 2014). It is an economy where imagination is the raw material and skills the main infrastructure (Lazzeretti et al., 2017). Creative industries play an important role in the economic, social and urban development of a nation and are also a powerful engine for innovation and competitiveness (Nathan et al., 2016; UNCTAD, 2018).

The main objective of this chapter is to understand the challenges faced by musicians of popular and folk music in Cameroon and provide solutions.

2.2. Understanding Folk and Popular Music

2.2.1. Folk Music

Music has always been important for individuals, society and culture for different reasons, and folk music is the most important one in a society and culture (Adeogun, 2018). A person is best identified by the group he/she belongs to and culture is critical to give any group an identity that it needs and longs for (Sylvanus, 2020). Folk music is the art of telling and narrating stories of joys and sorrows which people have been living with, in the simplest way (Nnamani, 2014). It is usually a satire that talks about moral issues in a style that only insiders can understand (Amara et al., 2021). It is a popular form of entertainment in villages that is performed during ceremonies such as funerals, enthronement ceremonies, princely weddings and rituals (Adeogun, 2018) Folk music is unchangeable and is usually passed orally from one generation to the other, thus making it unattractive throughout the years (Nnamani, 2014; Tangem, 2017).

Although folk music is usually associated with a poor reputation because many people think that it is the emblem to an outdated era; however, it is the music of the people (Nnamani, 2014). Its lyrics and rhythms are usually about people and culture (Amara et al., 2021; Idolor, 2020). It keeps the people connected to their past, their culture and heritage (Ndubisi & Kanu, 2022; UNESCO, 1999). Thus keeping the past alive and providing the right direction to the future. Folk music is determined by the instruments that are used to produce it and is inspired by the songs and rhythms created to accompany dancers in their body expression (Moffor, 2021). Among these instruments are tom-toms, drums, jingle calabashes, tambourines, balafons, castanets, guitar, flutes, whistle, pipes and tuning forks, saxophone and vibraphone (Moffor, 2021). These various instruments are played to give rhythm to traditional dances (Mbaegbu, 2015).

However, the current fast-growing technology is producing artificial sounds that are invading the market, and with the evolution of norms in societies and major shifts among populations, traditional music has quickly adjusted to modern standards and should not be relegated to the past (Ndubisi & Kanu, 2022).

2.2.2. Popular Music

Popular music is music that is highly appreciated by a large majority of the populace and this is manifested in the way popular radio and television stations and other disseminating agents play them all the time (Oyugi, 2012). It evolves from folk music and the artists promulgate the social significance of folk songs by following the footsteps of their ancestors in traditional African societies and continue to broadly criticising the themes of the folk music and evaluating the political, economic and social environment of the society in order to promote the interest of the citizens for stability, peace, job employment and other relevant development (Hall, 2015; Sylvanus, 2018).

The chapter postulates that popular and folk music are vibrant and dynamic forms of oral music shaped by social, economic and political forces in the environment (Tangem, 2016). It demonstrates how popular and folk music can open a window of understanding the current political, economic and social climate in Cameroon with a view to drawing implications for positive change. The chapter concludes by recommending that, if the creative industry (folk and popular music) is to be enhanced, then the challenges faced by artists have to be effectively addressed and improved, and Cameroonians on their part should also be ready and willing to undergo a revolutionary change of mind set (Sone, 2019).

2.3. Research Approach

This is an exploratory study with 10 musicians, 5 from popular music and 5 from folk music.

Popular music artists were randomly picked from among the 10 Regions of Cameroon. To have a deeper understanding of a specific culture, folk music artists were specifically selected from Wum, Menchum Division in the North West Region of Cameroon. Folk music was chosen to show that although folk rhythms are being replaced by new fusion of local sounds and imported beats in other parts of the country, folk music in Cameroon still plays a major role on the national cultural scene, and despite the progress in modern technologies, some artists are trying to practice their art with a certain originality (Mbaegbu, 2015). Meanwhile popular music was chosen to examine fundamental issues of national concern and also because it has a high potential to influence a society's perception and sense of direction (Ndubisi & Kanu, 2022).

Interviews were administered with structured and semi-structured questionnaires to have an in-depth understanding of the challenges which these artists are facing in the process of creating and generating social and economic wealth (Yin, 2014). In order to trace some of the folk artists, snowballing effect was used to spot them in major quarters in Wum town such as Kusu, Wakah, Zunghfuh, Naikom and overside, Mahgha, Tselahah and overside, Wendu up and down, and Wanangwen. Folk artists in Wum such as Njang, Kebum, Mbaya and Ufueng (Nyanga dance in pidgin) which means 'beautiful dance' in English were interviewed. Although there are so many types of popular music in Cameroon, the focus was on makoussa and bikusi artists. These are the two most popular among all others. Makoussa originated from the Litoral Region, while bikutsi is from the Central and Western Regions of Cameroon.

Questions were administered based on their motivations to music, their freedom to expression, music development, sources of funding and support. Probes and observation (overt and covert) were used to source for more information. Both the popular and folk artists had similar challenges; for instance, the environment is not enabling and lack of financial support are some of the challenges they are facing. Most of them were school drop-outs, and unemployment pushed them to music as a last resort. Data were collected and analysed based on themes.

3. FINDINGS

3.1. Financial Constraints in the Creative Process

Raising finance was a major challenge faced by these artists with no support from the government. They relied heavily on invitations to ceremonies and musical concerts within and without the country to raise finance. These concerts usually are occasional, and that is the only way the society could give back to the musicians. While some popular artists were invited to occasions within the country to play music, others were occasionally invited by Cameroonians abroad to do same. Folk artists were taking advantage of ceremonies in the villages to survive financially. However, social distancing and lockdown during COVID-19 pandemic made the situation worse as there were no ceremonies nor musical concerts in the villages and cities. Musicians suffered without national and international concerts.

3.1.1. Popular Artist

> I love to play music. I am a good music composer and a singer .... My music thrills the public ... but I do not have financial support from the government .... I can't release new music often as I would like to, because of financial difficulties ....

3.1.2. Folk Artist

> I play folk music in Wum villages for entertainment during ceremonies .... I usually get hired for a little fee, ... on lucky days during ceremonies, some other villagers may also support me financially as I sing, ... what I get from these ceremonies are mostly food, drinks, and recognition in the villages ...etc.

3.1.3. Popular Artist

I often get hired within the country to play music during occasions like weddings, birthday ....
Cameroonians abroad occasionally invite me to entertain them, but that was before covid-19
and all these were very helpful to me .... but covid-19 spoilt everything as we had to observe
social distancing. Live has been so tough since then ....

3.1.4. Folk Artist

My music is highly appreciated only in my village ... but for more than one year I could not play
music because of covid-19 and social distancing .... Although many people died there were no
ceremonies and even till date I don't often get hired because people are still scared of crowd ....
Financially, it is difficult ....

3.2. Piracy: A Major Challenge to Folk and Popular Music

The main obstacle of these creative entrepreneurs (artists) in generating economic benefit is based on the management of the creative process. The musicians do not benefit much from their music as expected. Their main source of
income is from 'live music, not recorded' (Brown, 2016). They are over exploited
and are at the mercy of piracy, counterfeiting, bootlegging of compact discs
and tapes, and other forms of infringement such as unlicensed broadcasting
(Brown, 2016; Nguindip & Ntemen, 2021). Piracy remains a major obstacle
due to weak copy and intellectual property rights as well as poor enforcement
capabilities.

3.2.1. Popular Artist

When I release my CDs, only few copies are usually sold as at the time of release .... I don't
actually breakeven because of duplication ... and I can't help the situation, it is so discouraging,
we need help ....

3.2.2. Folk Artist

I am in the village locality with poor infrastructure and constant power failure .... I don't have
CDs nor have I gone on u-tube ... but people do video and tape my music in ceremonies ....

It was revealed that not all those musicians whose music are on YouTube are
aware that their music has been downloaded from YouTube and other websites
which are unrecognised internationally. Some Bloggers and DJs are possible
exploiters. Some of these Bloggers publish 'blog posts' and create 'blog sites'
and some of them are self-proclaiming marketing guru (internet marketers, who
either own or manage blogs) (Brown, 2016; Nguindip & Ntemen, 2021). Some
of the musicians especially folk artists have no consent that their music is being
exploited by some DJs and Bloggers who just want to keep activating their websites to attract clients and make more money (Shaw, 2012, 2013). Laws governing music are weak or even absent in most African countries and Cameroon
specifically (Benavente & Grazzi, 2017; Ndubisi & Kanu, 2022). No protocol
is followed for releasing music and this renders the music sector economically

drained, leaving some of the artists struggling to make profits for really good music, hence they are exploited.

3.3. Creating an Enabling Environment for Creative Entrepreneurs

This chapter reveals a complex relationship between musicians and the government/politicians. Politics tend to follow on the heels of courageous artists who are helping to expand the society's imagination and seed ideas that grow into social movements for social change (Rodriguez-Pose & Lee, 2020). Artists compose music to express either their positive or negative emotions of the soul while others do so for economic reason and to gain greater recognition (Nyamnjoh, 2005). In most cases, music has endeared as well as jeopardised the lives of the artists with respect to the powers that be (Njogu & Maupeu, 2007). Music expresses the genius of artists but has in some cases been perceived as ridiculing persistent weaknesses of the government to the society.

While some artists compose music to hail and glorify the government by celebrating appointments and birthdays, others do so to denounce and ridicule the government in terms of corruption, bribery, embezzlement, nepotism and favouritism (Sone, 2021). Notwithstanding some have sought to straddle both worlds, serving politicians, while at the same time making economic gain and gaining recognition. Cameroonian artists have different political stances and as the political regime changes, their status and fortunes also change (Nyamnjoh, 2005).

The music of those lavishing praises on their leaders are usually used on TV, news and sports, but music that are perceived to be ridiculing the government are often banned and the musicians punished (Sone, 2021). As a result of this, some musicians have tended to compose music that worship the wishes of powerful politicians to gain favour. However, this does not convey the actual problems of the society to the government for change and societal growth.

Although the government often make pledges to support, cultural entrepreneurs, these pledges are useless unless acted upon. The hopes and dreams of musicians get drowned in the empty promises of the government (Moore, 2017; Ryan, 2022). When these musicians do not see or feel a reasonable path forward, and when financial institutions do not support the cultural sector, they start to disconnect and make up for this lack of support. They take matters into their own hands, making sure that their businesses flourish (Byerly, 2017; Kah, 2015).

3.3.1. Popular Artist

> We had a peaceful protest march for government support in Yaoundé but, we were poorly treated ... some of us were thrown on the floor, brutalized, and beaten, as if we were dangerous criminals ... some are still under threat today ... We can't freely express ourselves ... we have no voice .... we just comply ...

3.3.2. Popular Artist

> Some artists have suffered detention without being charged while others have been jailed and imprisoned because their music is focused on the problems of the society and was perceived to be ridiculing the government ...

3.4. Music as a Means of Employment

The current political unrest has degenerated into economic crisis and unemployment among youths has risen at an alarming rate. Most musicians in Cameroon are youths who are forced into music as their only job option. Thus music is seen as a 'last resort'. This indicates that it is not just an issue of unemployment but also the quality of the job. Only formal 'white collar jobs' are viewed as good jobs in most developing countries and Cameroon in particular, anything short of that is just a means of survival and not a job. This is because the society has no respect for these jobs and they are not well paid. Everyone is aiming for a 'white collar job' which of course may never come (Ning, 2021). Youths' expressions, however, tend to be subject to much criticism and are hardly ever allowed a voice in the established media (UNIDO, 2013).

3.5. Implications of this Chapter

It is imperative to know that for the creative economy to grow, it needs to operate under a functioning system of intellectual property rights. Musicians should establish good marketing strategies even before they launch their music. This would enable them to make some profits. But how could this be possible since most of them don't have marketing knowledge?

Musicians should be listened to as that may help in formulating good policies that will bring lasting solution to potential and existing problems in the communities. Cultural entrepreneurs are at the heart of the cultural and creative industries. They innovate, inspire and entertain, while driving economic and social development. To foster sustainable development through creativity, the government needs to ensure that artists and cultural professionals develop relevant skills, including technical and vocational (Beattie, 1999). Supporting the creative economy, the media, museums, theatres, cinema and music, is vital because it diversifies economic activities (Franco & Njogu, 2020). With these infrastructures, there is the proliferation of ideas and innovation that lead to progressive development to individuals and the society.

There should be an atmosphere where individuals can rise up and speak for themselves and their communities (UIFCD, 2016). In this perspective, the rights of artists and the rights of citizens are exactly the same. The main policy challenge is to create an enabling environment where the exertion of rights is not just respected or tolerated but promoted. When cultural policies create a more favourable environment for artists and cultural entrepreneurs to thrive, new and better opportunities arise. When these artists and entrepreneurs are able to refine their skills or learn new ones, they are more equipped to make the most of these opportunities. There is need to facilitate critical thinking by youth and instil change and transformation in economies and societies at large.

The future depends on how the next generation is trained to be humane. It is difficult to face the world of tomorrow without culture, and unless the 'human element' is valued, there will not be advancement in other areas (Emielu, 2011). Therefore youths' empowerment is an asset for their communities and countries and should be supported. Capacity building in the creative industries requires that young people should be provided with tools to express themselves.

It is important to stress that, as the world is engaged in the implementation of the SDGs, we must bear in mind that development cannot be sustainable if it does not address the aspirations and expressed emotions of individuals in the society, which is another name for their liberty. When people feel they can participate as actors and consumers in the cultural life of their community, be it local, national or global, they are empowered (Bakhshi & McVittie, 2009). Investment in creativity is an investment in a sustainable future. It is only when creativity is allowed to express itself that it can influence people, giving them the opportunity to be creative and encouraging them to share their views and talents. Therefore, while focusing on multiplying investments, it is also crucial to invest in people (UNIDO, 2013). The cultural and creative industries can play a key role in cultivating a more fertile ground because investing in culture and creativity also means paying more attention to everyone in our societies.

Although Cameroon International Music Festival (CIMFEST), through the ResiliArt movement, supports the synergy of Cameroonian Artists to sketch a roadmap for peacebuilding and economic resilience through the power of Culture (UNESCO, 2021), there should also be grass root promotion of artist-friendly policies where artists and creators can both innovate and reap the benefits of their work.

Contributing to the growth of this sector will create a virtuous circle that encourages entrepreneurship and cultural production. The government has a key role in designing, implementing and monitoring robust institutional and regulatory policies that will commercialise and support creative entrepreneurship and artists in particular.

4. CONCLUSIONS

The cultural and creative industries are at the core of sustainable development. They have the capacity to generate inclusive economic growth, while producing social benefits that empower individuals and communities. Culture is an economic sector, which deserves investments as such. There are returns in terms of jobs and growth but the role of culture goes beyond that. With culture comes a conception of development that is sustainable in the sense that it is centred on individuals' capacity for entrepreneurship or freedom to express their aspirations and their projects.

The objective of an integrated, prosperous and peaceful Africa must be fully owned by African youths from the design to the implementation, and the creative industry plays an important role in such a transformation. There is need to promote young talents in the music sector and professionalise young people by offering training courses in vocal technique and the opportunity to record in studio. This will not only strengthen their musical creativity and technical skills, but will also develop musical supply chain from training to support, to creation, all the way to distribution. Thus creating more jobs, promoting diversity of cultural expressions and regional integration because people like listening to music that they can relate to.

The chapter is thus a cry for help that should bring together all those involved in this good cause such as public authorities, cultural communities, artist trade associations and others to take some resolute actions to allow younger generations to claim ownership of traditional music in Cameroon, which is currently declining and making room for some 'unproductive interbreeding' (Noule, 2015). Tangible measures need to be considered if they wish to preserve and develop authentic Cameroonian music, which is inspired by musical wealth. It is important for Cameroon's traditional values to be preserved and developed in order to inspire present and future generations to be more creative and competitive on the international stage.

This study has some limitations of lack of indicators, data and statistics to quantify and qualify the impact of this dynamic on local economies. This is because very little research has been done in this area in this context. However, the findings may be suitable to understand the problems and prospects of creative industry (music) in Cameroon. The study has contributed in extending the literature of creative entrepreneurship. It has revealed the challenges musicians are facing in Cameroon and a way forward. Future research could be on the scalability and sustainability of creative industries with specific interest on 'Folk and Popular music'. There could be further exploration on other aspects of the creative industry, for instance, crafts, textiles and fashion, theatre, film, painting, book publishing, design, etc., and their impact in the society.

Some of the limitations of this study were the lack of indicators, data and statistics to quantify and qualify the impact of this dynamic on local economies. This is because very little research has been done in this area and in this context. Future research could explore other aspects of the creative industry, for instance, crafts, textiles and fashion, and design, etc. and their impact in the society.

REFERENCES

Adao, R., Kolesar, M., & Morales, E. (2019). Shift-share designs: Theory and inference. *The Quarterly Journal of Economics*, *134*(4), 1949–2010.

Adeogun, A. O. (2018). A historical review of the evolution of music education in Nigeria until the end of the twentieth century. *Journal of the Musical Arts in Africa*, *15*(1–2), 1–18.

Amara, A. P., Oripeloye A. H., & Ugochukwu, U. N. (2021). Contextual expositions of Igbo proverbs in selected Mike Ejeagha's folk songs. *Asian Research Journal of Arts & Social Sciences*, *14*(1), 11–18.

Bakhshi, H., & McVittie, E. (2009). Creative supply-chain linkages and innovation: Do the creative industries stimulate business innovation in the wider economy? *Innovation*, *11*(2), 169–189.

Baum, S., O'Connor, K., & Yigitcanlar, T. (2009). The implications of creative industries for regional outcomes. *International Journal of Foresight and Innovation Policy*, *5*(1–3), 44–64.

Baumol, W. J. (2010). *Micro theory of innovative entrepreneurship*. Princeton University Press.

Beattie, R. (1999). *The creative entrepreneur: A study of the entrepreneur's creative processes*. A thesis submitted in partial fulfilment of the requirements of the University of Abertay Dundee for the degree of Doctor of Business Administration.

Benavente, J. M., & Grazzi, M. (2017). *Public policies for creativity and innovation: Promoting the orange economy in Latin America and the Caribbean*. Inter-American Development Bank.

Bilton, C., & Cummings, S. (2014). A framework for creative management and managing creativity. In C. Bilton & S. Cummings (Eds.), *Handbook of management and creativity* (pp. 1–12). Edward Elgar.

Bloom, D. E., & Williamson, J. (1998). Demographic transitions and economic miracles in emerging Asia. *World Bank Economic Review, 12*, 419–455.

Boix-Domenech, R., & Soler-Marco, V. (2017). Creative service industries and regional productivity. *Papers in Regional Science, 96*(2), 261–279.

Brown, S. C. (2016). Where do beliefs about music piracy come from and how are they shared? *International Journal of Cyber Criminology, 10*(1), 21–39.

Byerly, I. (2017). What every revolutionary should know: A musical model of global protest. In J. Friedman (Ed.), *A Routledge history of social protest in popular music* (pp. 229–248). Routledge.

Campi, M., Dueñas, M., & Tommaso C. T. (2022). *Do creative industries enhance employment growth? Regional evidence from Colombia*. Inter-American Development Bank (IDB).

Caves, R. E. (2000). *Creative industries: Contracts between art and commerce (No. 20)*. Harvard University Press.

Chen, M. H., Chang, Y. Y., & Lee, C. Y. (2015). Creative entrepreneurs' guanxi networks and success: Information and resource. *Journal of Business Research, 68*(4), 900–905.

Daniel, R. (2020). The creative process explored: Artists' views and reflections. *Creative Industries Journal, 15*(1), 3–16.

Domingo, P. (2016). *Investing in music report. The value of record companies*. IFPI.

Domingo, P. (2017). *Global music report 2017, Annual state of the industry*. IFPI.

Edmondson, J., & Weiner, R. (2013). Radical protest in rock: Zappa, Lennon, and Garcia. In J. Friedman (Ed.), *A Routledge history of social protest in popular music* (pp. 142–156). Routledge.

Emielu, A. M. (2011). Popular music and youth empowerment in Nigeria. *Journal of Performing Arts, 4*(2), 59–70.

Franco, P. A. I., & Njogu, K. (2020). *Cultural and creative industries supporting activities in Sub-Saharan Africa: Mapping and analysis*.

Hall, R. (2015). Enhancing the popular music ensemble workshop and maximising student potential through the integration of creativity. *International Journal of Music Education, 33*(1).

Hagoort, G. (2007). *Cultural entrepreneurship: On the freedom to create art and the freedom of enterprise, summary version*. Utrecht: Utrecht School of the Arts, Research Group Art and Economics.

Idolor, E. (2020). Repackaging traditional music lyrics to sustain and project. *Journal of Linguistics, 21*(1), 137–150.

IFCD. (2022). UNESCO *diversity of cultural expressions. Investing in creativity and transforming societies*.

Innocenti, N., & Lazzeretti, L. (2019). Do the creative industries support growth and innovation in the wider economy? Industry relatedness and employment growth in Italy. *Industry and Innovation 26*(10), 1152–1173.

Kah, H. K. (2015). Understanding conflicts in Cameroon history through Awilo's song 'contri don Spoil'. *East West Journal of Business and Social Studies, 4*(2), 80–104.

Kim, J.-G., & Kim, E.-J. (2014). Creative industries' internationalization strategies of selected countries and their policy implications. *KIEP, World Economy Update, 4*(26).

Klamer, A. (2011). Cultural entrepreneurship. *The Review of Austrian Economics, 24*, 141–156.

Lazzeretti, L., Innocenti, N., & Capone, F. (2017). The impact of related variety on the creative employment growth. *The Annals of Regional Science, 58*(3), 491–512.

Lounsbury, M., Glynn, M. (2001). Cultural entrepreneurship: Stories, legitimacy, and the acquisition of resources. *Strategic Management Journal, 22*(6–7), 545–564.

Mbaegbu, C. C. (2015). The effective power of music in Africa. *Open Journal of Philosophy, 5*(3), 176–183.

Moffor, E. T. (2021). The dynamics of the xylophones in Cameroon grass fields arts. *EAS Journal of Humanities and Cultural Studies, 3*(2), 86–96.

Moore, A. (2017). Conclusion: A hermeneutics of protest music. In J. Friedman (Ed.), *A Routledge history of social protest in popular music* (pp. 387–399). Routledge.

Nathan, M., Kemeny, T., Pratt, A., & Spenser, G. (2016). *Creative economy employment in the US, Canada and the UK: A comparative analysis*. Nesta.

Ndubisi, E. J. O., & Kanu, I. A. (2022). The value of African music: The past, the present and the future. *Journal of Arts and Humanities, 1*(2), 5–92.

Nguindip, N. C., & Ntemen, T. D. (2021). Assessing and evaluating the complexities surroundings copyright infringement in Cameroon: Rethinking the nomenclature of reforming the regulatory environment in Cameroon. *International Journal of Legal Law and Civil Research, 1*(2), 10–21.

Ning, E. N. (2021). Entrepreneurship and economic development in Africa: A paradox. In D. M. Nziku & J. J. Struthers (Eds.), *Enterprise and economic development in Africa* (pp. 15–37). Emerald Publishing Limited.

Nnamani, S. N. (2014). The role of folk music in traditional African society: The Igbo experience. *Journal of Modern Education Review, 4*(4), 304–310.

Noule, G. M. F. (2015). *Traditional music in Cameroon*. https://www.musicinafrica.net/magazine/traditional-music-cameroon

Pedro, A. I. F., & Njogu, K. (2020). *Cultural and creative industries supporting activities in Sub-Saharan Africa, mapping and analysis.* IFA Edition Culture and Foreign Policy.

Piergiovanni, R., Carree, M., & Santarelli, E. (2012). Creative industries, new business formation, and regional economic growth. *Small Business Economics, 39*(3), 539–560.

Rodriguez-Pose, A., & Lee, N. (2020). Hipsters vs. geeks? Creative workers, STEM and innovation in US cities. *Cities, 100*, 102653.

Shaw, Z. (2012). In defence of free music: A generational ethical road over the industry's corruption and exploitation. *Mediapocalypse.* http://www.mediapocalypse.com/in-defense-of-free-music-a-generational-ethical-high-road-over-the-industrys-corruption-and-exploitation/

Shaw, Z. (2013). Musician exploitation: Who's really responsible? *Mediapocalypse.* http://www.mediapocalypse.com/musician-exploitation-whos-responsible/

Sone, E. M. (2021) Power, powerlessness and radical protest in contemporary Cameroonian Popular Music. *Muziki: Journal of Music Research in Africa* (Forthcoming, December 2021).

Sylvanus, E. P. (2018). Popular music and genre in mainstream Nollywood. *Journal of Popular Music Studies, 30*(3), 99–114.

Sylvanus, E. P. (2020). The relevance of music to African commuting practices: The Nigerian experience. *Contemporary Music Review, 39*(1), 37–58.

Tagne, J. S., & Evou, J. P. (2020). Cultural diversity and performance of Cameroonian companies. In *Cultural factors and performance in 21st century businesses* (pp. 144–163). IGI Global. https://doi.org/10.4018/978-1-7998-3744-2.ch007

Tangem, D. F. (2016). Oral history, collective memory and socio-political criticism: A study of popular culture in Cameroon. *Tydskrif vir Letterkunde, 53*(1), 160–178.

Tangem, D. F. (2017). Beyond art, history and social discourse: A study of folk art as indigenous knowledge system in the grass field of Cameroon. *International Journal of Humanities Social Sciences and Education, 4*(9), 58–74.

Taylor, M. R., & O'Brien, D. (2017). Culture is a meritocracy: Why creative workers attitudes may reinforce social inequality. *Sociological Research Online, 22*(4), 27–47.

UNCTAD. (2018). Creative Economy Outlook Trends in international trade in creative industries.

UNCTAD. (2021). *Creative industry 4.0: Towards a new globalized creative economy.*

UNESCO. (1999). *The value of culture.* Position paper for the forum "Development and Culture," Inter-American Development Bank/UNESCO, Paris, March 11–12; UNCTAD XIII, Doha, Qatar, 2012.

UNESCO. (2005). *Convention on the protection and promotion of the diversity of cultural expressions.*

UNESCO. (2021). ResiliArt Cameroon: *Music and creativity beyond the crises to foster peace.*

UNESCO International Fund for Cultural Diversity (UIFCD). (2016). *Diversity of cultural expressions.*

United Nation Industrial Development Organisation. (2013). *Creative industries for youths unleashing potential and growth.* Vienna International Centre.

Yin, R. (2014). *Case study research design and methods* (5th ed.). Sage Publication.

CHAPTER 13

AN EXAMINATION OF THE RELATIONSHIP BETWEEN CREATIVE IDENTITY AND ENTREPRENEURIAL IDENTITY

Jacqueline Jenkins

ABSTRACT

This chapter critically evaluates the role of creative identity and how this shapes entrepreneurial identity. The main driver for creative practitioners is one of being 'creative', but this is in combination with the factors that support entrepreneurial behaviours, and it provides the narrative for their entrepreneurial identity. The quest to operate successfully as a creative practitioner in the creative industries drives entrepreneurial behaviour. The research examines the relationship between creative identity and entrepreneurial identity and how these two identities intertwine. To respond to this question, the study critically evaluates the concept of creative identity and entrepreneurial identity with fourteen creative practitioners in the UK, working as either chartered architects or freelance photographers. The research employed a qualitative approach and interpretivist ontology. Semi-structured interviews were undertaken with the participants. The key finding that highlights the driver for entrepreneurial identity is the quest to operate successfully as a creative practitioner in the creative industries. This quest is underpinned by the desire to be able to express their creative identity, often referred to as a creative 'voice'. Entrepreneurial identity and entrepreneurial behaviours function as conduits in which creative practitioners channel their primary driver of creative identity. This chapter

Creative (and Cultural) Industry Entrepreneurship in the 21st Century
Contemporary Issues in Entrepreneurship Research, Volume 18A, 179–192
Copyright © 2024 by Jacqueline Jenkins
Published under exclusive licence by Emerald Publishing Limited
ISSN: 2040-7246/doi:10.1108/S2040-72462023000018A013

*contributes to the knowledge about creative practitioners' entrepreneurial iden-
tity and creative identity and how these two identities relate to each other.*

Keywords: Creative identity; practitioners; entrepreneurial identity; UK;
architects; photographers; qualitative

1. INTRODUCTION

Identifying oneself as a 'creative' person is a primary driver for a career within
the creative industries. The concept of being a 'creative' underpins a strong sense
of self identity for many creative entrepreneurs who seek to deploy their artistic
creativity (Glăveanu & Tanggaard, 2014). Their sense of 'creative self' forms part
of their identity and acts as a conduit for their need to produce creative outputs
as a way of expressing their creative identity or creative voice. In essence, they are
responding to the question of, 'Who Am I?', which is embedded within identity
theory (Kreiner et al., 2006).

Social identity arises when a person feels that they share common characteristics with individuals within a group. They develop a sense of belonging, which
provides a self-defining social category (Burke & Stets, 2009) essentially responding to the question, 'Where do I belong?' (Oyserman et al., 2004). This goes some
way to providing an understanding of how notions of the identity of oneself as a
creative person form a sense of social identity as part of a community of creative
people or 'creatives' as a collective noun.

Whilst being a 'creative' form a strong sense of their self-identity for many
creative practitioners, the concept of being an 'entrepreneur' is less prevalent.
Often creative people struggle with notions of being an entrepreneur as these
sit less comfortably with their notion of their self-identity (Werthes et al., 2018).
They are more focused on expressing their creative identity.

Entrepreneurial identity is connected to entrepreneurial processes or activities
(Navis & Glynn, 2011), formed in a dynamic process which requires self-reflec-
tion (Gioia et al., 2013) and changes over time (Kreiner et al., 2006). Barrett and
Vershinina (2017, p. 440) opine,

> entrepreneurs, likely an individual, actively construct their identity through what is and is not
> available to them (i.e., capital) and what is and is not possible or can be done in the context in
> which they operate (i.e., habitus).

In essence, this is a response to the question, 'How can I achieve what I want to
do?'

This chapter examines the relationship between creative identity and entrepreneurial identity for creative practitioners. This relates to notions of creative
identity and being part of a collective of creative people. In order to operate
professionally, creative practitioners need to operate commercially. Subsequently,
their creative output needs to generate economic value (including socio-economic). Operating commercially and generating creative outputs which have an
economic value has an influence on entrepreneurial identity and entrepreneurial

behaviour. The research study explored the manifestations of self-identification in creative industries, with first, a creative, and second, an entrepreneur. Do these two identities intertwine?

The research took a qualitative approach and interpretivist ontology. Semi-structured interviews were conducted with 14 people working in the creative industries in the UK. The research was based in two industries: architecture and photography. Therefore, the research participants were working as either a chartered architect or a freelance photographer. The data was analysed using thematic analysis which provides a flexible yet systematic approach for identifying, analysing, and reporting patterns/themes across a dataset (Braun & Clarke, 2006).

The link between individual creative practitioners' sense of creative identity and entrepreneurial identity can be considered as a typology within which there are four different sub-sections. The author identified these four different sub-sections in their research as *indisputable creative identity, devoted creative identity, altruistic creative identity*, and *embedded creative identity*.

2. LITERATURE REVIEW

The study draws on literature from three separate but overlapping fields. The first one is on the literature that has a critical view on creative entrepreneurship. The second one is on entrepreneurial identity; it also covers creative entrepreneurs. The third one is on identity and how it is related to entrepreneurship.

2.1. Micro-identities

Individuals do not have just one identity, but several micro-identities (Kreiner et al., 2006; Shepherd & Haynie, 2009). These micro-identities include self-identity, social identity, and professional identity. Professional identity includes conceptualisation of personal motivation and values in development of their future career role by the individual (Meijers, 1998, p. 200).

2.2. Creative and Entrepreneurial Identities in the Creative Industries

The vision of a successful career in the creative industries is driven by a range of factors. This includes, but is not limited to, generating an output which has economic or socio-economic value. Therefore, creative practitioners' entrepreneurial behaviour is driven by their desire to express their creative identity via the production of creative outputs in the pursuit of a successful career. Rae stated that:

> the challenge of developing a sustainable business model for a new creative enterprise is at the heart of the learning process and current understanding is both theoretically and practically limited, representing an important area for enquiry. (2012, p. 606)

Even once they have overcome the challenge of transforming their ideas into viable enterprises, creative practitioners can face conflict over balancing their creative identity with the need to exhibit entrepreneurial behaviours. The need to exhibit entrepreneurial behaviours forms the foundation for entrepreneurial identity. However, an individual's entrepreneurial identity and creative identity are not formed in isolation. The multiple nature of identity lends itself to the recognition that identity is formed concerning significant others (Warren, 2004). Entrepreneurial identity is shaped by the industry environment the individual is operating, or seeking to operate, within (Yitshaki & Kropp, 2016). Entrepreneurial identity is shaped by both individuals' networks and the industry environment. Given that context can shape entrepreneurial actions and motivations (McMullen & Shepherd, 2006) and that context is not static but dynamic, it is likely that context will influence entrepreneurial identity. Personal support networks and the context in which they are operating are significant to shaping entrepreneurial identity. It is this sense of belonging to a network and of being part of a creative community which shapes creative practitioners' formation of collective identity.

The formation of creative identity can be triggered by both extrinsic motivations such as money and intrinsic motivations that reflect the inner drive of the creative practitioners such as artistic creation (Frey & Jegen, 2001). It follows that this combination of motivations can be a factor in shaping entrepreneurial behaviours and subsequent entrepreneurial identity. Hartley et al. (2012) suggest that there are innate similarities between artist and entrepreneur; both are agents to introduce change into cultural and economic systems. Both are often highly motivated and risk-tolerant. Both are motivated by complex desires (recognition, status, self-actualisation, and lifestyle as well as material rewards). There is a substantial overlap in personality traits and socio-demographic profiles of artists and entrepreneurs. They are often 'outsiders', highly 'independent', of above-average intelligence and imagination, with a high tolerance for ambiguity, risk-lovers (O Cinneide & Henry, 2007), and with an unusual degree of persistence.

2.3. The Multidimensionality of and Interplay Between Identities

This duality of creative identity and entrepreneurial identity can create tensions between artistic/creative values and economic values (Inversini et al., 2014). This tension means that creative practitioners can be challenged in obtaining a balance between art and commence in their identity (Taylor & Littleton, 2008) when forging their career. This in turn adds to the conflict of navigating a successful career within the creative industries whilst still maintaining notions of creative integrity and values (Werthes et al., 2017). They question how they maintain their artistic integrity and artistic freedoms whilst at the same time monetarising, their creative outputs by operating commercially (Beech et al., 2016; Coulson, 2012; Umney & Kretsos, 2014). Bilton et al.'s (2021) state that creatives are motivated by the need to balance intrinsic and extrinsic rewards by applying the right amount of 'fire' to the creative process. Creative practitioners' identity is therefore intertwined with entrepreneurial activities and outcomes (Bhansing et al., 2020).

For many creative practitioners, their future career aspirations are driven by their desire to produce outcomes which enable them to express their creative identity. It is this desire to be able to express creativity which drives entrepreneurial behaviours and provides the stimulus for entrepreneurial performance (Patten, 2016). Their entrepreneurial identity is developed as an enabler for their core creative identity. Entrepreneurial identity and entrepreneurial behaviours are conduits in which to channel their primary driver of creative identity. Moreover, their success in expressing their creative identity in the form of producing creative outputs and those outputs having a value, either economic or socio-economic, is intrinsically linked to their entrepreneurial behaviours (Poorsoltan, 2012). It is this concept which forms the basis for the research study.

3. METHODS

The study is situated within the domain of creative industries. A high proportion of creative practitioners hold higher education degree-level qualifications (Davies, 2013). Additionally, a high proportion of creative practitioners work freelance (Hartley et al., 2012). To better understand the construct of being a 'creative', the study explores the interplay between creative identity and entrepreneurial identity to discover motivational push/pull factors and concepts of 'creative identity'.

To investigate the links between creative identity and entrepreneurial identity, the study used qualitative research methods. Qualitative research allows for deeper understanding of behaviour in real-world dynamic settings (Eisenhardt, 1989). The methodological framework took an interpretivist position as this position holds the view that social reality is a subjective construction based upon interpretation and interaction (Quinlan, 2011).

This study forms part of a larger study. The study focused on two UK creative industries: architecture and photography. The study participants were practitioners working as either chartered architects or photographers, mostly freelance/self-employed (see Table 1 for details). This enabled the study to review the research question and objectives from multiple standpoints and perspectives with the objective of fully understanding the factors that shape entrepreneurial identity. This ensured a robust dataset that could be triangulated and analysed to explore emerging themes and patterns from the data.

4. OVERVIEW OF THE RESPONDENTS

The study inclusion criteria of being either self-employed or running their own business for at least one year was selected, as this is the point at which businesses either fail or continue to operate (Cohen, 2011). Following ethical guidelines, the individual identities of the participants in the research remain anonymous and pseudonyms have been applied in the reporting of the findings.

4.1. Data Collection Methods

In-depth, semi-structured interviews were conducted with all 14 participants. The interviews lasted between 50 and 120 minutes, and they were recorded electronically and fully transcribed. This technique is considered the primary investigation method in qualitative research as it allows in-depth details to be revealed from the study participant's perspective (Ebneyamini et al., 2018).

Table 1. Brief Biography of Research Participants.

Creative Industry	Location (UK Region)	Brief Bio	Pseudonym
Photography	East Midlands	1–4 Years freelance. One year in other roles before setting up practice	Amy
Photography	East Midlands	5–10 Years freelance. Over 10 years in other roles prior to working as a freelance photographer	Beatrice
Photography	East Midlands	15–20 Years freelance. Over five years in other roles prior to working as a freelance photographer	Claire
Architecture	East Midlands	Over 25 Years in practice. Not freelance	Amanda
Architecture	East Midlands	Over 10 Years in practice. Not freelance	Bertie
Photography	West Midlands	5–10 Years freelance. Over 20 years in other roles prior to working as a freelance photographer	Deborah
Architecture	East Midlands	1–4 Years freelance; 5–10 years in practice before going freelance	Clive
Architecture	North West	5–10 Years freelance; 15–20 years in practice before going freelance	Donna
Photography	South West	1–4 Years freelance following graduation	Elsa
Photography	South West	15–20 Years freelance. Worked in another creative industry freelance. Over 20 years to date before photography	Derek
Photography	West Midlands	5–10 Years freelance following graduation	Edmund
Architecture	East Midlands	15–20 Years freelance; 1–4 years in practice before going freelance	Elspeth
Architecture	West Midlands	5–10 Years freelance; 20–25 years in practice before going freelance	Frank
Architecture	East Midlands	2–4 Years freelance; 25–30 years in practice before going freelance	Gerald

The deployment of the qualitative semi-structured interviews was considered appropriate to collect complex career and life narratives. Participants were asked questions about their motivations to pursue a creative career and the decision to start their own business. Factors that influenced entrepreneurial identity formation were explored. This approach was particularly useful for collecting in-depth information and life stories (Denzin & Lincoln, 2011; Silverman, 2014, 2017) about their motivations, professional values and career/business choices.

4.2. Data Analysis

Thematic analysis was used to process the knowledge created by the interactions between researcher and participant. The six-stage thematic analysis process devised by Braun and Clarke (2006) was applied in the study. Noting that these stages are not simply linear, moving from one stage to the next but instead are an iterative process, where one moves back and forth as required throughout the phases. The dataset was analysed using a combination of theoretical, experiential, and thematical analysis methods (Braun & Clarke, 2013). Coding was performed using QSR International's NVivo Version 11 software to conduct qualitative analysis and build a theoretical framework as well as writing notes of memories of the interview experience. This method enabled close examination of the transcripts for thematic patterns, while NVivo provided a means of storing, retrieving, categorising, and encoding the text (Gibbs et al., 2002).

5. FINDINGS

The formation of one's creative identity often starts in childhood, with individuals enjoying and gaining recognition for creative activities such as drawing, painting, and model-making. Erikson (1968) proposed that childhood is the time when the sense of identity is based on 'I am what I learn to make work' (Erikson, 1968, p. 127). For the participants, this continued throughout their childhood years and was a determinant factor in their choice of degree subject and subsequent career choice. The concept of creative identity is more than their professional identity, it was formed very early on in their lives. They were very clear about the concept of being a creative as a descriptor of themselves. This concept of being 'a creative' was formed within their sense of self-identity. The sense of creative self was described as being very strong and very much part of who they were as a person. The concept of an entrepreneurial identity was not as strong as creative practitioners were upon expressing their creative identity.

5.1. Factors Shaping Creative Identity and Entrepreneurial Identity

The main motivational factor for the participants within this study, as either an architect or photographer, was the need for a career that gave a creative output. These themes have been drawn from the data to determine what the drivers are that help to form concepts of the creative self. The research has drawn upon the inferences of the creative self and notions of creative identity.

However, for the practitioner participants, this sense of creative self only had significance and meaning if it was embedded within a role that enabled their sense of creative self to be expressed, usually by producing a creative output or expression. For this creative output or creative expression to have personal creative value and meaning, it also needed to have a monetary value.

It was this combination of creative output with an economic value equals creative identity, which gave the participants a real sense of themselves as a 'creative'.

Fig. 1 illustrates that there are two elements combined in the identity of being creative. The data suggests that each element needs to be in harmony for the individual to have a sense of their creative self.

5.2. Creative Identity

The concept of creative identity alone was meaningless without the expression of being creative and generating a creative output. The creative output needed to have value, whether this was economic, social, or environmental value, or a combination of these. It was only when the individual had formed a balance of

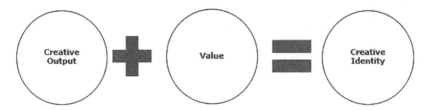

Fig. 1.   Creative Output Which Has a Value (Either Economic or Socio-economic)
Equals Creative Identity. *Source:* Author's own.

these factors; creative identity equals creative output which has economic/socio-
economic value, that this provided them with their sense of being a 'creative'.

Participants align their creative identity with a desire to have a role that provides both a creative output and expresses the concept of 'not wanting to do a real
job'. Effectively, doing a role that they really enjoy and love (Blair, 2001; Taylor,
2011) forms the driver for entrepreneurial behaviour. This combines their sense of
creative identity with aspects of entrepreneurial formation.

5.3. Entrepreneurial Identity

To pursue a creative role the participants developed entrepreneurial formation
by enterprise behaviours, attributes, and competencies leading to the creation of
something that had both cultural and economic value. The aversion to doing a
'real job' had nothing to do with work avoidance; instead, it was underpinned by
their desire to be creative. This desire to be creative manifested into enterprise
behaviours, attributes, and competencies and therefore was identified as a factor
that supported entrepreneurial formation.

> I always knew I wanted to do something creative, and it was kind of an entrepreneurial thing
> that interested me first. I figured out that I loved photography and it meant that I didn't have to
> go out to WORK [emphasis]. Edmund

As the above extract highlights, there is a dialogue between the desire to be
creative by working either as an architect or photographer and being an entrepreneur. This dialogue forms the participants' rationale for choosing their career in
the creative industries and articulating their entrepreneurial outcomes.

5.4. The Relationship Between Creative and Entrepreneurial Identities

The construct of multiple identities is complex and multifaceted but then so are
human beings. Creative practitioners can cohere career identities, combining both
the creative and entrepreneurial elements in a synergetic manner (Schediwy et al.,
2018). It is all about the motivations behind the desire to construct multiple identities. One of the primary theories on the development of motivations has been
to classify them into 'push' and 'pull' factors (McClelland et al., 2005; Schjoedt
& Shaver, 2007; Segal et al., 2005). Push factors are characterised by personal or
external factors and often have negative connotations. Pull factors are those that
draw people to start a business such as seeking out an opportunity. In general pull

factors tend to be more prevalent than push factors (Dawson & Henley, 2012). There are factors around an individual's characteristics and behaviours that support entrepreneurial formation such as the strong desire of 'not wanting to do a real job' and a 'difficult start in employment' which trigger a strong drive to do something else. These could be categorised as push factors. On the other side, there is a higher prevalence of pull factors such as 'having a career that they enjoy'.

Whilst being a 'creative' forms a strong sense of their self-identity for many creative practitioners, the concept of being an 'entrepreneur' is less evident. For creative practitioners the construct of their entrepreneurial identity is across a spectrum. Creative practitioners' expressed views ranging from positive to negative in relation to themselves as an 'entrepreneur'. There are three main categories identified; those participants that 'absolutely' identify themselves as entrepreneurial, those that 'reluctantly' identify themselves as entrepreneurial, and those that would 'inconceivably' identify themselves as entrepreneurial, see Fig. 2

Across this spectrum, there were participants who clearly and positively identified themselves as being an entrepreneur. They recognised this label as their self-identity in terms of their behaviours towards their career and how they approached and ran their businesses.

5.5. Combined Creative and Entrepreneurial Identities Typology

The study findings indicate that producing work which has commercial value seems to serve as a validation of creative identity. Therefore, creative identity and entrepreneurial identity are intertwined whether the concept of entrepreneurial identity sits comfortably or not. Noting that the concept of entrepreneurial identity is across a spectrum, the concept of creative identity is not homogeneous and universal either. Self-identity is complex and multifaceted. Given that individuals integrate many micro-identities, the combination of creative identity and entrepreneurial identity intertwines to operate commercially and provides validation of themselves as creative professionals.

The author identified the construct of combined creative and entrepreneurial typology with four different sub-sections in their research. They are *indisputable creative identity, devoted creative identity, altruistic creative identity*, and *embedded creative identity.*

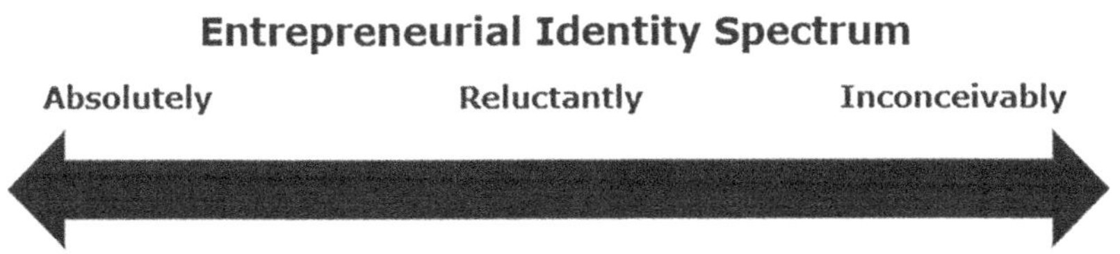

Fig. 2. The Entrepreneurial Identity Spectrum. *Source:* Author's own.

5.6. Indisputable Creative Identity

This term has been applied when participants define their sense of creative self as 'not sure what else they would do'. This defines their sense of creative self or creative identity to be the thing they do because they could not imagine doing anything else. Therefore, it becomes their identity through the planned absence and detachment of any other identity. It should be emphasised that this 'indisputable creative identity' does not support the narrative that they had a sense of being not sure what else they would do, in terms of who they are, or other career options. Moreover, the narrative describes the concept of their creative identity as being so all-consuming they could not imagine being anything other than a 'creative'.

> It's part of my identity .... If you took it away, I'm not sure what you'd replace it with really. — Frank

Therefore, their sense of being creative is indisputable as no other alternatives could be envisaged.

5.7. Devoted Creative Identity

This term has been applied when participants define their sense of their creative self-using terms of romantic endearment such as love; 'I love being an architect'. This concept of doing a role that they love has been explored in literature (Taylor, 2011) and is an archetypal definition of the concept of creative identity. This evolves into further issues discussed in other studies about the downsides of this driver in terms of doing what you love – for little or no pay (Pratt & Jeffcutt, 2009).

5.8. Altruistic Creative Identity

This term has been applied when participants defined their sense of creative self with regards to their creative outputs as 'being a tool for good'. They utilise their creative identity as a driver for positive change. They seek to produce creative outputs that have socio-economic value. These outputs have the potential to make a positive impact on society such as documentary photography or designing a school building.

> That school I was mentioning, was in the second poorest ward in [name of place]. It was a really, really, deprived area. You could feel the effect it had, I think any school would have, with a nice design it felt a bit special. I really believe that love and care in well-designed architecture can send that message out. — Gerald

Their primary driver for creative identity is altruism and the sense of being in a role that enables them to work for the greater good of society. This motivational driver is very similar to those of social entrepreneurs who are driven by factors beyond just financial, but also social and environmental (Roundy, 2017).

5.9. Embedded Creative Identity

This term has been applied when the participants define their sense of creative self as being an innate part of their persona. This differs from 'devoted creative identity' in that they do not always describe this in such a positive way using terms of romantic endearment such as love. Put more simply, this is how they see themselves and who they are in terms of their constructed personal sense of self.

> Yes. I think architects are a very particular type of person. My husband is not an architect ....
> I used to have a lot of parties... it was probably mainly architects at the parties, everyone was
> very creative, the way they dressed, the way they talked, the things they were interested in, and
> as I say my husband would come in and bring some of his friends and the marked difference is
> very startling. — Elspeth

The above extract discusses Elspeth's perception of the differences between herself and her architecture friends and her husband and his friends who are not architects. Here Elspeth is trying to define how she and her friends are 'creatives' and how this is embedded within their internal expressions such as what they are interested in and in their external expressions such as the way they dress as an understanding of their (and her) sense of creative self, which is inherent in terms of who they are. So, this term of creative identity is entrenched in the sense of their social identity – we are creatives. Furthermore, it is entrenched in a sense of belonging to a wider collective and sharing a sense of space and cohesiveness.

6. DISCUSSION AND CONTRIBUTION

This chapter discussed the significance of the concept of being a creative as a contributor to an individual's identity. The concept of creative identity generally sits comfortably with creative practitioners. Indeed, they often recognise this within themselves. The construct of social identity is formed as individuals feel they share a sense of belonging with other creative people. The study found that the concept of creative identity alone is meaningless without the expression of being creative and generating a creative output. The creative output needs to have value, whether this was economic, socio-economic, or environmental or a combination of these.

Whilst the concept of creative identity sits comfortably with creative practitioners, the concept of an entrepreneurial identity does not always fit so comfortably (Werthes et al., 2018). The study moves on from this point to identify that the research participants had different notions of the concept of themselves as an entrepreneur. The concept of being an entrepreneur or exhibiting entrepreneurial behaviours was varied and complex. Some of the participants were very comfortable with using the term to describe themselves, and others were more reluctant to admit to this aspect of themselves and the need to behave in entrepreneurial ways to commercialise their creativity. The study found the concept of being an entrepreneur ranged across a spectrum from absolutely an entrepreneur, reluctantly an entrepreneur, to the concept of being an entrepreneur as inconceivable. This duality of creative identity and entrepreneurial identity can create tensions between artistic/creative values and economic values (Inversini et al., 2014). The study found that whilst these tensions exist, nevertheless the commercialisation of creative outputs validates creative identity and professional identity.

To operate commercially creative practitioners, they need to be able to generate an income from their creative outputs. It is this need to operate commercially and generate an income that provides the impetus for entrepreneurial behaviours. Therefore, the concept of creative practitioners' professional identity is intertwined with entrepreneurial activities and outcomes (Bhansing et al., 2020).

Individuals do not have just one identity, but several micro-identities (Kreiner et al., 2006; Shepherd & Haynie, 2009). The study identified that the construct of entrepreneurial identity ranges across a spectrum. The study recognised that individuals are complex and multifaceted and therefore creative identity is not homogenous and universal. The author identified the combined creative and entrepreneurial identities typology with four different sub-sections in their research. They are *indisputable creative identity, devoted creative identity, altruistic creative identity*, and *embedded creative identity*.

This study noted the significance of a creative identity for individuals wishing to pursue a career within the creative industries, which has implications for creative discipline education practice. Furthermore, combining the different elements of creative and entrepreneurial identities enables creative practitioners to work commercially, which has implications for creative practice and theory.

7. CONCLUSIONS

The limitations of this study include the sample size of 14 creative practitioners and also the timeframe in that participants were only interviewed once. Finally, the participants were based in just two industries.

Further research on this topic could be expanded to take into account of the significance of context and other factors that shape individuals' sense of identity. These factors could include characteristics which are likely to influence perceptions of self and their creative identity such as the role of gender, ethnicity, and sexual orientation. In addition, a longitudinal study could include interviewing participants more frequently over a longer time period to explore how these perceptions of creative identity and entrepreneurial identity change, if at all.

This study provided key insights into the significance of the role of creative identity and entrepreneurial identity, and how these combine to enable creative practitioners to work commercially, by producing work which has a commercial value and validates their creative identity.

REFERENCES

Barrett, R., & Vershinina, N. (2017). Intersectionality of ethnic and entrepreneurial identities: A study of post-war Polish entrepreneurs in an English city. *Journal of Small Business Management*, *55*(3), 430–443.

Beech, N., Gilmore, C., Hibbert, P., & Ybema, S. (2016). Identity-in-the-work and musicians' struggles: The production of self-questioning identity work. *Work, Employment and Society*, *30*(3), 506–522.

Bhansing, P. V., Wijngaarden, Y., & Hitters, E. (2020). Identity work in the context of co-located creative entrepreneurs: How place influences professional identity. *International Journal of Arts Management*, *22*(2), 7–23.

Bilton, C., Eikhof, D. R., & Gilmore, C. (2021). Balancing Act: Motivation and creative work in the lived experience of writers and musicians. *International Journal of Cultural Policy*, *27*(6), 738–752.

Blair, H. (2001). "You're Only as Good as Your Last Job": The labour process and labour market in the British Film Industry. *Work, Employment and Society*, *15*(1), 149–169.

Braun, V., & Clarke, V. (2006). Using thematic analysis in psychology. *Qualitative Research in Psychology*, *3*(2), 77–101.

Braun, V., & Clarke, V. (2013) *Successful qualitative research: A practical guide for beginners*. London: SAGE.

Burke, P. J., & Stets, J. E. (2009). *Identity theory*. Oxford University Press.

Cohen, N. (2011). Data mask level of UK business failures. *FT.com*. https://ntu.idm.oclc.org/login?url=https://www.proquest.com/trade-journals/data-mask-level-uk-business-failures/docview/877891418/se-2?accountid=14693

Coulson, S. (2012). Collaborating in a competitive World: Musicians' working lives and understandings of entrepreneurship. *Work, Employment & Society*, *26*(2), 246–261.

Davies, R. (2013). *Introducing the creative industries: From theory to practice*. Sage Publications.

Dawson, C., & Henley, A. (2012). "Push" versus "pull" entrepreneurship: An ambiguous distinction? *International Journal of Entrepreneurial Behaviour & Research*, *18*(6), 697–719.

Denzin, N. K., & Lincoln, Y. S. (2011). *The Sage handbook of qualitative research*. Sage.

Ebneyamini, S., & Sadeghi Moghadam, M. R. (2018). Toward developing a framework for conducting case study research. *International Journal of Qualitative Methods*, *17*(1), 1–11.

Eisenhardt, K. M. (1989). Building theories from case study research. *The Academy of Management Review*, *14*(4), 532–550.

Erikson, E. H. (1968). Identity: Youth and crisis. *Journal of Extension*, *6*(4).

Frey, B. S., & Jegen, R. (2001). Motivation crowding theory. *Journal of Economic Surveys*, *15*(5), 589–611.

Gibbs, G. R., Friese, S., & Mangabeira, W. C. (2002). The use of new technology in qualitative research. Introduction to Issue 3(2) of FQS, Forum Qualitative Sozialforschung/Forum. *Qualitative Social Research*, *3*(2).

Gioia, D. A., Patvardhan, S. D., Hamilton, A. L., & Corley, K. G. (2013). Organizational identity formation and change. *The Academy of Management Annals*, *7*(1), 123–193.

Gläveanu, V. P., & Tanggaard, L. (2014). Creativity, identity, and representation: Towards a sociocultural theory of creative identity. *New Ideas in Psychology*, *34*(1), 12–21.

Hartley, J., Potts, J., Flew, T., Cunningham, S., Keane, M., & Banks, J. (2012) *Key concepts in creative industries*. Sage.

Inversini, M., Manzoni, B., & Salvemini, S. (2014). The making of a successful creative individual business model. *International Journal of Arts Management*, *16*(2), 55–63.

Kreiner, G. E., Hollensbe, E. C., & Sheep, M. L. (2006). Where is the 'me' among the 'we'? Identity work and the search for optimal balance. *Academy of Management Journal*, *49*(5), 1031–1057.

McClelland, E., Swail, J., Bell, J., & Ibbotson, P. (2005). Following the pathway of female entrepreneurs. *International Journal of Entrepreneurial Behaviour & Research*, *11*(2), 84–107.

McMullen, J. S., & Shepherd, D. A. (2006). Entrepreneurial action and the role of uncertainty in the theory of the entrepreneur. *Academy of Management Review*, *31*(1), 132–152.

Meijers, F. (1998). The development of a career identity. *International Journal for the Advancement of Counselling*, *20*(3), 191–207.

Navis, C., & Glynn, M. A. (2011). Legitimate distinctiveness and the entrepreneurial identity: Influence on investor judgments of new venture plausibility. *Academy of Management Review*, *36*(3), 479–499.

O Cinneide, B., & Henry, C. (2007). Entrepreneurship features of creative industries. In C. Henry (Ed.), *Entrepreneurship in the creative industries: International perspective* (pp. 72–86). Edward Elgar Publishing.

Oyserman, D. (2004). Self-concept and identity. In M. B. Brewer & M. Hewstone (Eds.), *Self and social identity* (pp. 5–24). Blackwell Publishing Ltd.

Patten, T. (2016). Creative? … Entrepreneur? – Understanding the creative industries entrepreneur. *Artivate: A Journal of Entrepreneurship in the Arts*, *5*(2), 23–42.

Poorsoltan, K. (2012). Artists as entrepreneurs. *International Journal of Entrepreneurship*, *16*(1), 77–94.

Pratt, A., & Jeffcutt, P. E. (2009). *Creativity, innovation and the cultural economy*. Taylor & Francis Group.

Quinlan, C. (2011). *Business research methods*. Cengage Learning.

Rae, D. (2012). Action learning in new creative ventures. *International Journal of Entrepreneurial Behaviour & Research, 18*(5), 603–623.

Roundy, P. T. (2017). Social entrepreneurship and entrepreneurial ecosystems. *International Journal of Social Economics, 44*(9), 1252–1267.

Schediwy, L., Bhansing, P. V., & Loots, E. (2018). Young musicians' career identities: Do bohemian and entrepreneurial career identities compete or cohere? *Creative Industries Journal, 11*(2), 174–196.

Schjoedt, L., & Shaver, K. (2007). Deciding on an entrepreneurial career: A test of the pull and push hypotheses using the panel study of entrepreneurial dynamics data. *Entrepreneurship, 31*(5), 733–752.

Segal, G., Borgia, D., & Schoenfeld, J. (2005). The motivation to become an entrepreneur. *International Journal of Entrepreneurial Behaviour & Research, 11*(1), 42–57.

Shepherd, D., & Haynie, J. M. (2009). Birds of a feather don't always flock together: Identity management in entrepreneurship. *Journal of Business Venturing, 24*(4), 316–337.

Silverman, D. (2014). *Interpreting qualitative data*. SAGE.

Silverman, D. (2017). *Doing qualitative research*. SAGE.

Taylor, S. (2011). Negotiating oppositions and uncertainties: Gendered conflicts in creative identity work. *Feminism & Psychology, 21*(3), 354–371.

Taylor, S., & Littleton, K. (2008). Art work or money: Conflicts in the construction of a creative identity. *Sociological Review, 56*(2), 275–292.

Umney, C., & Kretsos, L. (2014). Creative labour and collective interaction: The working lives of young jazz musicians in London. *Work, Employment & Society, 28*(4), 571–588.

Warren, L. (2004). Negotiating entrepreneurial identity: Communities of practice and changing discourses. *International Journal of Entrepreneurship and Innovation, 5*(1), 25–35.

Werthes, D., Mauer, R., & Brettel, M. (2018). Cultural and creative entrepreneurs: Understanding the role of entrepreneurial identity. *International Journal of Entrepreneurial Behavior & Research, 24*(1), 290–314.

Yitshaki, R., & Kropp, F. (2016). Entrepreneurial passions and identities in different contexts: A comparison between high-tech and social entrepreneurs. *Entrepreneurship & Regional Development, 28*(3–4), 206–233.

INDEX

music as means of employment,
173
piracy, 171–172
related literature review, 167–168
research approach, 169–170
understanding folk and popular
music, 168–169
Cameroon International Music
Festival (CIMFEST), 174
Cameroonian artists, 172
Centers for Disease Control and
Prevention (CDC), 76
Central board of film certification
(CBFC), 122
Chinmay Organisation for Rural
Development (CORD), 93,
96–97, 100
Annual Report, 99–100
Pandemic Programme
Interventions, 101
Chinmaya Rural Primary Health
Care and Training Centre
(CRPHC & TC), 97
Cluster theories, 23
Co-creation of aesthetic value, 33, 35
Collaboration between musicians and
music ecosystem, promoting
new forms of, 146
Communication
from CIC, 114–115
tools, 145
Communitarians, 22, 84
Community artists, 5, 12
Community development, 5
Community engagement and
contribution, 5
Community of practice, 70
Community-based inclusion and
rehabilitation programme,
100
Community-Based Livelihood-Farm
and Allied Sector
(CBL-FAS), 100
Concentric Circles model for CCIs, 10
Conceptualisation, 53

Continuous thinking process, 94
Conversion process, 109
Cooperation, 84–85
Core-periphery spill-over model, 25
COVID–19, 101
business models, 78–79, 84
challenges faced by creative
entrepreneurs during
outbreak of, 98–99
COVID-19-induced lockdown
periods, 6
creative entrepreneurship and,
95–96
crisis, 156
customer needs and product
development, 82–83
disease, 98
entrepreneurial mindsets, 81–82
findings, 80–81
innovative and hybrid business
models, 82
literature review, 77
marketing approaches, 79–80,
84–85
mask-makers as emerging creative
entrepreneurs
during, 77
methods, 80
motivations and mindsets, 77–78,
83–84
pandemic, 76–77, 83, 113, 170
Craft entrepreneurship, 12
Creation, 48–49
Creative activities practiced by SHGs,
99
CBL-FAS, 100
Chinmaya Shanta, 100–101
community-based inclusion and
rehabilitation programme,
100
E-Sanjeevani App, 99
seven Js, 101
Swadhyaya classrooms, 100
vegetable and dairy production,
100

Printed and bound by CPI Group (UK) Ltd, Croydon, CR0 4YY

18/12/2023

08210386-0001